PERIOD DETAILS

Wallpapers used on the endpapers and on pages 1, 3, 4 & 5 are from The Temple Newsam Collection from Zoffany.

JUDITH AND MARTIN MILLER

PERIOD DETAILS

MITCHELL BEAZLEY

PERIOD DETAILS
A SOURCEBOOK FOR HOUSE RESTORATION
JUDITH AND MARTIN MILLER
Chief Contributor **Margaret Crowther**
Consultant in America **Fayal Greene**
Kitchens chapter **Robin Murrell**

Edited and designed by Mitchell Beazley International Ltd,
Artists House, 14-15 Manette Street, London W1V 5LB.

Project Manager and Senior Executive Art Editor
Jacqui Small
Executive Editor **Robert Saxton**
Assistant Art Editor **Prue Bucknall**
Production **Philip Collyer**

BRITISH LIBRARY CATALOGUING IN PUBLICATION DATA
Miller, Judith H.
  Period details : a sourcebook for house restoration.
  1. Dwellings —— Conservation and restoration
  I. Title II. Miller, Martin, *1946-*
  728.3′028′8   NA7125
  ISBN 0-85533-650-1

The publishers have made every effort to ensure that all
instructions given in this book are accurate and safe, but they
cannot accept liability for any resulting injury, damage or loss
to either person or property whether direct or consequential
and howsoever arising.
The authors and publishers will be grateful for any
information which will assist them in keeping future editions
up to date.

Typeset by *Bookworm Typesetting, Manchester*
Colour reproduction by *Novacolour Ltd, Birmingham*
Printed in Portugal by *Printer Portuguesa, Indústria Gráfica, Lda.*

Cover photograph by Fritz von der Schulenburg

Code letters in picture captions refer to the photographic
sources listed on page 191.

CONTENTS

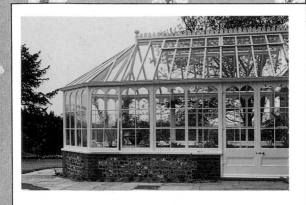

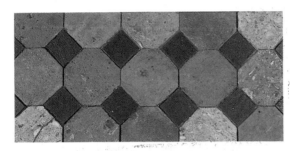

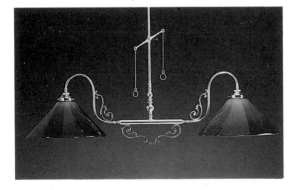

FOREWORD BY JUDITH MILLER 6

INTRODUCTION 8

DOORS 26	WINDOWS 54
FLOORS 66	WALLS 74
CEILINGS 96	STAIRS 106
FIREPLACES 114	BATHROOMS 138
KITCHENS 146	LIGHTING 154

EXTERIORS 160

CONSERVATORIES 166

GLOSSARY 168	BIBLIOGRAPHY 169

DIRECTORY 170

ACKNOWLEDGMENTS 191	INDEX 192

The past decade has seen a remarkable and accelerating interest in period houses – in the idea of living in a home with traditional character. Property advertisements with their emphasis on "authentically restored" – rather than "completely modernized" – show that estate agents are more alive to this fundamental change of taste than are many architects and interior designers.

In Britain, the post-war impulse to replace the old with the new destroyed many good period houses, especially in the inner cities, and replaced them with characterless blocks of flats. But we are fortunate still to have about 6 million buildings built before 1920. This book deals with the restoration of a very wide range of such buildings from 16th-century farm cottages to Georgian terraces and Victorian mews. We made a decision to concentrate not on the grand houses which are well documented in other books but on the kind of old houses that are on the market.

As our principal aim is to convey a sense of what looks right in terms of period style, the book is highly visual, with nearly a thousand photographs dealing with everything from skirting boards to panelling, from door knobs to kitchens.

Successful restoration begins with understanding your house as a total entity. To do this, you have to read, to look and to listen. There are excellent books on old houses, many wonderful museums and individual experts in various periods who can help with dating and explaining how houses were used – an important aspect of understanding the house. Was the original drawing room in your house on the first floor? Was the kitchen in the basement? Where were the original fireplaces? Which was the master bedroom?

All questions to be answered before rushing to the nearest salvage yard. It is also important to educate your eye. Buy magazines; build up files of images; ask to see your neighbour's cornicing; approach a local historical society for visual reference. All of this will build up an idea of what is right historically but also what is pleasing to you. You, after all, have to live in the house. You have to like it.

With tradition goes responsibility. Luckily, people now realize we have as much duty to preserve and restore a terrace of houses built in 1870 as we do to maintain a Queen Anne manor house. Both contribute to the heritage of our country. On a more personal note, creating a period feel, finding out what should be in a house, what colour the walls would have been, is, quite simply, fun. It can, of course, also be profitable, as shown by the steadily rising values of well-restored houses. One of the most important things to realize is that houses evolve over the centuries. Sometimes the purist can be wrong. The Georgians sometimes adapted Elizabethan houses and the much-maligned Victorians often created interesting additions to Adam-inspired houses (as at Newby Hall). Such developments and variations, additions and oddities, can give the house the acceptable fallibility of an old friend.

Not many of us want to live in a museum. We want our house to reflect our life style. It is important that it should look as though it has been lived in by successive generations. One of our own restorations, which is featured in this book, is Chilston Park at Lenham in Kent. It is basically an Elizabethan house built round a central courtyard. It was thought old-fashioned in the 1720s when the then owner had it re-facaded with a classical Georgian facade but interestingly reused the old bricks. Many other improvements were made through the years and in 1880 the owners introduced a grand staircase hall which filled in the central courtyard. Though a purist would abhor the result, the house has a pleasing feel with its combination of wonderful details from both the Georgian and Victorian periods. This is why I prefer restoration to strict period replacement where possible. Old plaster and woodwork have slight imperfections, and too perfect a finish can be cold, even inhuman. Our affection for an old house should involve a respect for its past. It is important to understand the way it has evolved and to accept the authenticity of this evolution even if it means that the house is not an example of one particular period.

We hope this book goes some way to showing the diversity and delight of period details. The joy of owning an old house and restoring it can become a positive obsession. We have ourselves converted houses as diverse as a 15th-century manor house in Kent which has a 19th-century Pugin-designed concert hall attached, a mid 17th-century stone house in West Sussex, a 19th-century farm labourer's cottage in the Scottish borders, an Arts and Crafts country house in Kent and an Art Deco flat in London. All had their distinctive attractions and we learned a great deal from each one. A period house does not have to be large or grand to be interesting but it does need to have a sense of overall cohesion. If you know how to see and understand their essential character, houses themselves dictate their individual styles. The joy of seeing one's own research reflected in the overall detail of a house is reward enough for all the hard work of restoration.

Judith Miller

INTRODUCTION

When we think of the domestic architecture of the past, we think first and foremost of grand country houses and town mansions – buildings that are rightly famous thanks to their distinguished history and in many cases to their association with a particular architect, such as Inigo Jones or Robert Adam. Of course, few of us can afford to live in homes of such grandeur and esteem. Even if our houses have a long history, they were mostly built not as conscious works of art but principally as homes, in which any one of a thousand daily routines may take place.

Nevertheless, most smaller period houses owe something to the taste of their age, and in this the great architects and patrons were the innovators. Fashions gradually filtered down the social scale. Classical ornamentation and Neo-Gothic detailing – to take just two examples – enjoyed their various waves of popularity not only in the homes of the fashionably rich but also in thousands of proud but unpretentious dwellings built for the prosperous middle classes. The middling professional man, building a home for his family, wished to convey something of his standing in the community by aping what was smart in aristocratic circles. A display of wealth was a good advertisement for his business. But at the same time a careful economy would be observed: display was all very well, in moderation. These feelings, or something like them, have been prevalent for centuries. Despite financial restraints there remains today a great reserve of fine period homes, well constructed, simply and appropriately ornamented, in which it was – and still is – a pleasure to live.

If modest houses reflect the buildings put up by the great, they usually do so after a time-lag, and often in curious ways. Style begins either with a new solution to a practical problem or, more usually from 1550 to the end of the 19th century, with a fashion. The staying power of a fashion generally depends on how compatible it is with practical requirements. This is why classical features, based on the architecture of the ancient Greeks or Romans, appear over such a long period: they were so well adapted to so many different buildings. A practical equation which could be applied to anything from a palace to a potting shed, classical design remains a constant. However, this consistency should not be exaggerated. As constants go, it is a very variable one. Classicism has meant many different things to different generations, departing far from the original intentions in Greece or Rome.

In the absence of documentary evidence, dating a house depends on careful detective work based on materials, layout and architectural and stylistic features. Sometimes the house will incorporate a date-stone, but this should be treated with suspicion. It may denote a date of repair or refurbishment, or even commemorate a marriage. Occasionally, such date-stones have been imported from another building altogether.

Architectural style is more reliable as a dating guide, but you should always bear in mind that the pace of change varied in different regions. Generally, fashions started in the towns and spread out slowly to the countryside. However, the grander rural homes usually flaunted the latest fashions some time before smaller rural houses caught up with the trends. The picture is complicated further by regional variations. If the dating of an old house proves difficult, your local history society will usually help.

Many period homes have evolved by a process of gradual "improvement" and accretion. Modern extensions are generally thought to be unfortunate unless they are built in a style that makes some concessions to history. However, an early house that has been modified over the centuries so that it manifests a wide range of historic styles, different but compatible, may be regarded as no less "authentic" than a house that remains as it was originally conceived. This is largely a matter of personal taste. Some people prefer the charm of the piecemeal. Others like their homes to be homogeneous. Even the recent trend towards "facadism" – preserving or restoring the facade while leaving the remainder of the building out of period – is not without its supporters.

Period features will sometimes be found during the course of refurbishment – perhaps a door or window opening that comes to light after you have removed plaster from a wall. In such cases, you might consider halting the work in progress and changing your plans to incorporate the newly discovered feature.

Decoration, furnishings and interior layout cannot easily be separated in period homes. Each aspect of an interior emerged in association with all other aspects of the house – all of which need to be taken into account when refurbishing in period style. For example, it is not enough to ensure that you have the furniture of the appropriate period. Plasterwork, doorcases, chimneypieces and doors are equally important as indexes of style, and the taste of a period can be obliterated from a room simply by a mistake in the choice of one or more of these elements. On the other hand, certain compromises are inevitable.

Few people would want to sacrifice every modern convenience for the sake of total historic authenticity. However passionately you feel about your period home, there is no reason to go back to unhealthy sanitation, inconvenient cooking facilities, primitive bathrooms or icy-cold draughts. Fortunately, up-to-date fittings are often available either in traditional styles or in low-key modern styles that will not clash with a historic interior. This need for sensible compromise is highlighted most clearly in the case of working buildings that have been converted for living in. Barns, schoolhouses, toll houses, chapels, churches, windmills and railway buildings that have been adapted as homes have all required radical alteration, with decisions taken at every turn as to what to change and what to leave intact. Similar compromises have to be made by those of us who live in large houses that have been divided up into separate units, with the addition of new internal walls. In such circumstances the attempt to create a period feel has to be judged with

2

1 This modest but very fine example of early 19thC architecture is in Islington, north London. In its symmetry, and its ornamental detailing on the fanlight and lower windows, it exhibits the characteristic features of the era.

2 Detail is all-important in period homes: the fireback is no less interesting or significant than the front door. This particular example is a modern reproduction of a 16thC original.

page 7: An example of true conservation in Roslyn, Long Island, New York, this house built in 1836 has been painstakingly restored with absolute attention to detail both outside and inside.

especial care: authentic features such as mouldings, friezes and fireplaces may be out of proportion in rooms that have been reduced in size.

Until the 17th century most houses in Britain were made of wood. It was the holocaust of the Great Fire of London in 1666, more than any other influence, that encouraged the use of non-flammable materials. However, wood remained cheap, easily accessible, and economic to work. Carpenters could build more quickly than stone masons; and in wooded areas without suitable building stone, wood was in any case the obvious choice. The timber-framed house thus remained a familiar feature of domestic architecture.

In Britain the typical all-timber or infill house of around 1200 had a central hall rising through two stories, flanked by parlour and solar on one side and servants' quarters on the other. The parlour was the sitting room for the master of the house; the solar was the family's private bedroom.

The timber-frame house developed from that functionally simple structure, the barn. As in a cathedral, the principle was to provide a framework that through its members carries the weight of the roof to the ground. The walls of these houses are infill only; they bear no direct load. At its simplest, the system consists of two wooden members forming together a gable frame, which is linked by a ridge beam to another, similar frame. Together the frames support the skin of roof and wall. This type of house, in some regions known as the "cruck" house, existed by 1300.

By the middle of the 14th century the disposition of rooms and people in the house was well established. The centre of the structure, the heart of community life, was the hall. Here all ate together, whether it was the lord of the manor and his servants or the yeoman farmer and his farmhands. The staff quarters lay to one side of the hall, and on the other side a single room at

ground and first-floor level gave privacy to the master and mistress. The fireplace, its smoke rising to a hole in the hall roof, was a symbol of the communal, cheek-by-jowl way of living. Interestingly, the open fire persisted in ordinary dwelling places long after the technology of chimneys and fireplaces had been introduced. Loyalty to the open fire as a gathering point in life preserved it in Britain into the 15th century, serving to illustrate an important aspect of the way in which houses developed over the centuries. Technological advances, at least initially, are not always potent enough to overcome the emotional and psychological needs answered by an earlier arrangement. Thus, in an age of central heating, the hearth – even if it throws out no heat – serves an important function as a focal point and symbol of family warmth. And indeed, the pleasure of living in a period home surrounded by period details is similarly based on evocations of traditionalism, community and historical continuity.

The frame house was not without possibilities for decoration. Within the main rectangle of the wooden frame, uprights of wood might be placed close together, between which would be set the infill of wattle and daub or plaster – or brick in the 15th century. This sort of essentially decorative infill (known as "close stud-work") is typical of the south and eastern regions of England. The quantity of wood used was an index of the town's prosperity. Brick too, replacing the plaster, was a sign of wealth, which could be indicated additionally by carving on the wooden frame.

The structural evolution of the house from shelter to home was reflected in the parallel evolution of interior furnishings and fittings. Floors that had previously been laid with mud or rushes were now paved with stone, tiles or brick. The comfort of a wealthy

15th-century home was further improved by replacing the central hearth by a wall fireplace which provided an effective means of warming the solar. In towns, where land was at a premium, the fireplaces and chimneys were arranged in such a way that the maximum number of people would receive heat efficiently – a feature that looks forward to the modern expectations we have of a house and how it should work.

Painted designs on interior walls were a popular type of decoration. In the houses of the great, from the 14th century on, tapestries were used as wallcoverings – usually over just the upper part of walls. The lower half would sometimes be wainscoted with overlapping vertical timbers, a style which developed into the characteristic linenfold panelling of the Tudor period – ribbed woodwork giving the impression of pleated cloth. Heraldic tapestries, hung on pegs, frequently decorated the wall behind the high table. Owners of more modest dwellings contented themselves with painted linen hangings.

Stone, of course, had been used for castles, palaces and cathedrals in Britain throughout the 14th and 15th centuries. It resisted fire, as well as assault. However, it was expensive to work, even in areas where stone was plentiful – such as the Cotswolds. There were some stone houses in England as early as the 13th century, but only in the late 15th century did stone come into general use, largely as an expression of national prosperity at that period. The overall planning of a stone house was not very different from that of a frame house – except when the building served a defensive role. However, stone offered greater scope for design. Projecting structures known as "oriels" are sometimes found nestling in the angle between the main hall and a private wing. Later the term "oriel" came to be applied to a projecting window, which developed with the passage of time into the bay window.

1 An infill of wattle-and-daub was common in timber-frame houses. The traditional thin laths of mud and plaster can be either painted or left natural. Brick infill was more common in grander houses.

2 The Van Nostrand Starkins house in Roslyn, Long Island, shows the functional quality of building of the late 17thC.

3 A 19thC reconstruction porch added to a 15thC house. The timber framing is in this case purely ornamental.

4 This 15thC weaver's house is a good example of timber framing. It is not surprising that many such houses have undergone alteration over the years. Here, the introduction of oriel windows, copied from stones houses of the period, has augmented the basic dwelling.

CG

5-7 *Timber-framed construction was a popular method of building well into the 17thC, and brick with timber infill was again used in the 19th and 20thC. These pictures of a 17thC house belie the fact that much of the building is Edwardian.*

8, 9 *These garden features from the same house sustain the nostalgic mood outdoors.*

10 *Smallhythe Place in Kent, now owned by The National Trust and opened as the Ellen Terry Museum, is an early 16thC half-timbered house, with the typical overhanging (jettied) upper storey.*

In this early period houses tended to grow haphazardly, rather than following a fixed and conscious design. But with the turn of the 16th century we find new ideas and design forces penetrating Britain from France and Italy. This was the first wave of influence from the great European Renaissance, whose heartland was Italy. During the early 15th century, centred on Florence, there was a tremendous revival of interest in the art, literature and design of the ancient Romans, and this had an important effect on the work of Italian architects – initially just in public architecture but later in the grander sorts of houses. Classical columns, pilasters (shallow columns applied to wall surfaces) and rounded arches were incorporated in buildings notable for their symmetry and harmonious proportion. The columns, and the distinctive decorative entablatures which they supported, were categorized according to the ancient system of classical "Orders", depending on the precise decorative arrangement. Columns could be solid-looking Doric, fluted Ionic or delicate Corinthian, with its acanthus-leaved capital. Composite combined Ionic volutes (scrolls) with Corinthian acanthus leaves.

Tudor England, in its anti-papal isolation, was initially not well-placed to be influenced by Renaissance architecture. By the early 16th century a few aristocratic houses had acquired Italianate flourishes, but in a superficial manner only, without radically affecting native English styles. However, the impact of Renaissance architecture was precipitated by the appearance in 1563 of the first English architectural treatise, John Shute's *The First and Chief Groundes of Architecture*, inspired by an architectural study tour of Italy. Before long, the classical Orders which Shute describes were being used as decoration, and as badges of high fashion, on the facades of English country houses such as Longleat in Wiltshire (1546–80) and Burghley House in Northamptonshire.

The significance of these developments for the future of architecture in Britain and America cannot be overestimated. Every column, architrave and frieze on the simplest terraced house of the 18th or 19th centuries has come to be there, indirectly, as a result of the Renaissance passion to recover the glory of Rome in its heyday.

By the mid-16th century many small manor houses were being built entirely of brick, rather than of timber with a brick infill. The wonder of the age was Hampton Court Palace, expensively built in brick and enriched with terracotta ornament and towering chimneystacks, and setting a fashion which persisted through the century. Even in relatively modest houses a complex skyline of spiralling chimneypots may be found, loudly proclaiming the owner's taste and discernment. Tudor brickwork, together with a complex silhouette of stacks and gables and a garden full of topiary, were to become a powerful archetype, an "ideal home", copied in the earlier 20th century not only in new country houses but also in the unlikely setting of suburbia.

The first decades of the 17th century saw a more thorough-going classicism emerge. This was the achievement of one man, Inigo Jones (1573–1652), who was the first architect to bring back to England the purer forms of classical architecture which designers like Robert Smythson had handled half-comprehendingly a generation before.

1, 2, 3 The influence of classical architecture from the 16thC onwards cannot be overemphasized. These examples of the proud use of classical features are a magnificent classical porch of a Carolean house in Kent (1) and a Port Washington (New York) house of 1735.

Jones was entirely at home in the world of classical allusions, and unlike most of his fellow designers actually went to Italy. There he encountered the work of Andrea Palladio. The greatest Italian architect of the 16th century, Palladio had revived and revised the architectural theory of the Roman writer Vitruvius, whose *Five Books of Architecture* describes various building types which Palladio adapted – notably the villa. The Roman villa was a spreading country house with attendant farm buildings. Palladio turned it into a classical pavilion – compact, elegant and well-suited to life in the country estates of the Veneto, the area around Venice where Palladio chiefly worked. It was these buildings which Inigo Jones saw and copied on his return to England – with the help of Palladio's own publication, *The Four Books of Architecture*.

In London, the Queen's House, Greenwich, built as a small-scale retreat for Queen Anne of Denmark, is the single pre-eminent domestic building which we know for certain that Jones designed. Incorporating many innovative features derived from Italy, this is the first classical English villa, ancestor of so many other villas, large and small, designed for daily life. The ground floor is rusticated – finished with cut stone resembling monumental blocks. Each window is marked by a dropped keystone, which lends weight and individuality to the composition. The upper storey is contrastingly lighter, its smooth wall surface broken by windows beneath which there are blind balustrades – that is, balustrades applied to the wall. These prepare the eye for the central loggia taken from Palladio's designs and intended originally for warmer southern climates. The groundplan is simple, effective and adapted to the purposes of the house. The whole is a very modern building in many ways: perhaps the first English house in which a 20th-century spectator can sense the contact between his own world and that of the original occupants.

4 Despite the infiltration of classical influence, many English houses retained a particularly English style. There is nothing Italianate about this stone manor house built in 1640 and substantially enlarged in the mid 19thC. S&P

5 Melton Constable Hall in Norfolk, designed by Sir Christopher Wren and built between 1644 and 1670, shows an impressive English interpretation of classical styles, with its great central pediment echoed by the pedimented doorway, and its hipped roof. The house is reminiscent of the work of Sir Roger Pratt, a follower of Inigo Jones. S&P

6 This house near Hampton Court Palace illustrates the continuing appeal of classicism in the late 19thC, when pilasters, balconies and classical swags were added.

7 The delight in the classical facade was to last in England well into the 18thC. Chilston Park, Kent, was built in the 16thC with a central three-storey porch-turret and a central courtyard. In 1728 the owners refaced the house in refined classical taste.

6

5

7

1

first floor indicated the main living level – the *piano nobile*, raised above the noise and dirt of the street and inaccessible to thieves or enemies. This idea too was derived from Italian practice – in 16th-century Italy the ground floor of a house or palace was heavily defended against the street, with small dark windows.

Covent Garden points forward to modern city design. From the late 17th to the early 20th century grand private houses, and their more modest urban neighbours, conform to the same basic principles of planning, the grand facade suggesting a single splendid building but concealing behind it practical housing for the upper or middle classes.

This innovative concept of housing took root gradually. For some time houses continued to be built in brick, and followed designs closer to those prevalent in Holland than those in Italy. Culturally, England and Holland had much in common in the 17th century. Both were Protestant mercantile countries, opposed to the Catholic might of Spain and the Holy Roman Empire. Trade links were close. Later in the century there was to be rivalry ending in open war. Before this crisis, however, there was considerable enthusiasm in England for the Dutch style of building – the redbrick steep-gabled style favoured by the burghers of Amsterdam and Antwerp. Via England, the Dutch style also travelled to colonial America where it emerged in a modified form.

The successor upon whom Jones's mantle fell was Sir Roger Pratt, a gentleman dilettante architect who built some of the most graceful and lovely houses of the 17th century. Notable among his achievements was the great house of Coleshill in Oxfordshire (now destroyed), where he successfully adapted Palladian designs to the

3

4 Regional variations should always be taken into account by anyone restoring a period house. This English street of the Georgian age is characterized by knapped flintwork, some of which hides earlier timber-framed dwellings.

5,6 These beautifully restored houses in Roslyn, Long Island, New York, were built in the mid-1830s but owe much to the previous century. The interest in vernacular architecture is an interesting trend in conservation today.

Many 18th- and 19th-century houses are arranged around a square – an aspect of city planning that originated in the 17th century. In this too Inigo Jones was involved. The first fully worked out and planned piazza in Britain is that of Covent Garden, for which Jones designed the church, St Paul's. This square reveals a new approach to urban living. It follows the principles of Italian city design by allowing light and air to reach individual houses. Designed to look like a series of grand palaces set around the central space, it in fact provided behind its great facades a number of houses of more modest scale. The tall windows on the

1 In small English country towns such as Mayfield, Sussex, houses and cottages from the 15th to the 19thC present a delightfully varied picture. Many early houses have been refacaded – particularly with weatherboarding in the mid-18thC.

2 This William and Mary red brick house is actually timber-framed. This is unusual at this date: the explanation is that the owner was a timber merchant.

3 Another timber-framed house – a 17thC example, hung with tiles.

2

4

British climate and way of life. Here he used for the first time the double-pile plan, in which two series of rooms run in parallel through the house, linked by a transverse corridor. This system had the distinct advantage of supplying each room with fine windows and therefore good lighting. A similar house, built twenty years later, is Belton in Lincolnshire, where the plan is H-shaped. Both these houses are grand, but they served, well into the 18th century, as models for many smaller and simpler buildings. The steep roof lined with dormer windows, the regular facade around a simple centrepiece, the use of classical detailing in a facade unenriched by columns – all were elements easily adaptable to modest gentlemen's houses.

The archetypal English house at the close of the 17th century (exemplified by Fenton House, Hampstead) is built of brick dressed with stone – that is, stone was used for the doorcase and other architectural details. The windows were quite tall and narrow, with a lean elegant line encouraged by the innovation of the sash window. The roof was high-pitched – perhaps with a wooden balustrade replacing the stone balustrade of grander homes. Of course, this pattern was not followed rigidly. More sophisticated houses (such as Mompesson House in the Cathedral Close at Salisbury) might have a richly carved broken pediment and coat of arms above the door, with stonework and other fine details on the facade adding a sense of density and brilliance to the house. Elegant gate piers and railings might also play their part, strengthening the effect of gracious formality. Such houses, belonging to doctors, lawyers, men of property and gentlemen, were to be found in both city and country. In a townhouse of this period, however grand or simple the facade, the general disposition of rooms and the style of life within them would tend to conform to a certain pattern. The standard format for the single-fronted row house was developed in the early 18th century and held sway in modified form until the early 20th. It featured a front door and hallway at one side and two rooms, one behind the other, at the other side. This kind of house, which ranged over three or four floors with a basement, became known as the "universal plan". Variations on the theme ranged from the simple to the relatively grand.

In double-fronted houses the prevalent plan was based on a square block divided into four rooms, arranged two deep in pairs either side of a central hall or reception area. Front and back rooms were linked by interconnecting doors. The hall led directly to the staircase, which would often be flanked by columns or pilasters to emphasize its importance. Stairs became increasingly gracious, but were still in wood, except in the grander houses, where wrought-iron balustrades in swirling patterns might be found.

5

6

In complete contrast to such practical developments in the planning of townhouses, the early years of the 18th century also saw the fashion for Baroque design at its height. The importance of this theatrical style for the average house is limited. The hallmarks of Baroque are grandeur of scale and a rich strangeness of effect – characteristics that appear mainly in the grand country mansions of the era. However, without an understanding of the Baroque style at its most extreme the curious design elements that appear in quite ordinary houses – boldly modelled garlands, volutes, mouldings and scroll work – can hardly be explained.

The Baroque style takes the formal elements of classical architecture and lends them scale, dynamic movement and singularity. When the style is transposed to England, drama is still the leading impression. It can be found in the detailing of domestic interiors, and in fine deepcut plasterwork and elaborate woodcarving – even in quite small houses. This was the era of Grinling Gibbons, the master woodcarver, whose rich naturalistic carvings set a style that was emulated in numerous houses until naturalism was in due course superseded by the more formal decorations of the Palladian style.

1

1 It is sometimes believed that all building in England in the early 18thC was influenced by the Palladian style, but this is far from the truth. This is a fairly typical early 18thC red brick house of the kind found in villages and towns all over southern England.

2 This classical English doorway exhibits an open-bed entablature with associated pilasters. Such features were influenced by the designs of Kent, Burlington and Campbell and other 18thC innovators, which filtered down from grand houses to more modest homes.

The varieties of taste in smaller houses can seem confusing, because several styles often seem to be asserting themselves at once. The classicism introduced by Inigo Jones was still percolating down to provincial houses when the brief tide of Baroque washed over the architectural scene. Neither had ceased to influence the average country house or small town square when Palladianism began its powerful rule.

The "Queen Anne" house was popular enough not to be easily displaced by the Palladian style. The most distinctive aspects of a typical Queen Anne house of around 1720 were its happy and agreeable proportions and its suitability for daily life. Often there would be an instinctive balance in the placing of windows and doors. The staircase, broad and shallow, would have a fine balustrade. The parlour on the ground floor might be lined with good panelling, but there would be nothing ostentatious in its decoration.

2

Palladianism introduced a new and dominant note in English, and American, architecture. Chief among the prime movers in this new rule of taste was the young Lord Burlington. Inspired by a book by the designer Colen Campbell, *Vitruvius Britannicus*, Burlington travelled to Italy and there absorbed the same lessons that Inigo Jones had learned a hundred years before – the same lessons, but with subtly different effects. He took with him William Kent, a brilliant designer who was to be his main ally in introducing Palladian taste in England. Their idea was to resuscitate the classicism begun by Inigo Jones, but following a new set of rules by which all builders and architects should be guided. Burlington's plan was ambitious: the transformation of the face of English architecture. This dream was very nearly realized, for in one form or another the format adopted by Campbell, Burlington and Kent was to influence the building of all grand houses, and many modest ones, for sixty years.

Among the most interesting of all Palladian building are the villas built by Campbell and Burlington in imitation of Palladio's Villa Rotonda at Vicenza, with its central domed space and portico on each of the four facades. The original is a folly, essentially a banqueting house, and suitable only for a warm climate. Campbell's Mereworth Castle followed this model closely, adapting the plan as much as possible (but with only limited success) to the needs of a small country house. Burlington's own exercise on the same theme, the Chiswick Villa, was designed as an addition to the

3

7

8

4

5

9

family house on his estate west of London, and there was thus no no need for the plan to take account of daily life: the building is purely for show. It was not until forty years later, in8, that a house based on the Villa Rotonda was successfully designed for comfort and daily living–Thomas Jefferson's Monticello in Virginia.

One of the great virtues of Palladian design was the simple and pleasing relation of room to room in the the overall plan, and this too had a major impact: planning becomes particularly important when working in a limited space. Individual elements of Palladianism were also taken over. For example, the Palladian portico, although perhaps serving a more practical purpose in the hot south than in northern zones, was widely copied as an imposing style of entranceway. Another characteristic feature is the "Palladian window" – an arched central opening flanked by two rectangles, with columns in between.

6

3 This somewhat later house, in the Queen Anne style, shows fine Georgian proportions and symmetry with a good classical portico. The combination of glorious brickwork with stone corners and other details help to give the building its impact.

4, 5 Simple Georgian cottages such as these tell us as much about the 18thC as do the grand manor houses and stately homes. Restoration of such buildings will benefit from thorough research into their origins. CG

6 This shallow internal arch in a reconstructed 1760 house in New York shows subdued classical influence, especially in its keystone. This is a fine example of Colonial architecture.

7, 8 The Palladian pediment is sometimes seen in combination with a small circular window and often with dentils – small square or rectangular blocks evenly spaced in ornamental series.

9 A detailed view of stone dentils on a brick townhouse of the 18thC.

The development of classical proportions in the 18th century shows a marked tendency towards increasing slenderness and attenuation. Height and refinement were the keynotes, perhaps expressed (as in Bath's Royal Crescent) by giant Orders of columns rising through all floors. Even the window bars became more and more slim as the century progressed. The Wood family's designs at Bath reflect a new archaeological spirit of accuracy, based on careful study of ancient Roman originals. For many people the characteristic style of the 18th century is "the Adam style" – especially in room decoration. The design ideas introduced by Robert and James Adam in the late 1750s and through the 60s and 70s were new and sophisticated variations on the traditional classical motifs. The secret of the Adam style was the cumulative effect of many finely wrought elements. The genius behind the style was the way in which so

1-4 These interiors (in No. 1, Royal Crescent, Bath, designed by the Wood family) show a delicacy and liveliness indebted to the designs of Robert Adam, whose work became influential from the middle of the 18thC. Adam treated classical motifs with an unprecedented lightness and simplicity, and subordinated every detail – including the bell-pushes – to an overall conception. RC, SC

much variety was subordinated to a greater plan. Furniture, carpets, curtains, door handles – all fitted in harmoniously with the grand scheme. This was the definitive statement of Roman opulence toward which English architecture had been tending for fifty years.

Running counter to the classical influence, an entirely new strain in building styles emerged after the mid-18th century, looking back to the Middle Ages. This was the taste for Gothick – the final K is used of the 18th-century style to differentiate it from the medieval architecture it aped and from the Victorian revival which would succeed it. The vogue for pointed Gothick arches and other mock-medieval features, in

5, 6, 7 The crescent – a curving row of homes – was an architectural form devised by John Wood the Younger at Bath in 1761-65. Note the giant columns which unify the facade.

5

6

7

9

8,9 These two fireplaces from a Georgian house in Bristol show the late 18thC fondness for exquisite decorative details. Such fireplaces were always intended to be painted white to add to the overall effect of airy grace.

both houses and garden buildings, grew through the 1750s and 60s

The Adam brothers and their followers increasingly worked in houses which were remodelled or rebuilt in the newly fashionable castellated romantic style. The interiors themselves remain classical but within a Gothick shell. The overall profile of the house could be fashionably Picturesque. Such exercises need not, however, be Gothick or castellated: they could equally well be Italian in style, and in the latter years of the 18th century and in the early 19th century this was a frequent choice. Just as important for houses of moderate scale was the revival of Greek architecture (led by James Wyatt), which was extremely fashionable in the 1780s and 90s.

8

Externally, the Georgian house, whether large or small, had a plain dignity and elegance, owed in part to the balance between a handsome door and generously proportioned sash windows, symmetrically arranged. The sense of proportion and order, immediately recognizable on the facade, was also reflected within. In the grander homes, the plain dignified exteriors encompassed interiors that were highly ornamental, full of exquisite detailing, yet controlled by good proportion. A reception room was treated as an architectural composition in its own right, with classically inspired features echoing each other to create an integrated effect. For example, a moulded architrave over the door might complement a pediment above a fireplace. Doric pilasters in a doorcase might be echoed in the uprights of the wall panelling, which in turn might reflect the ceiling pattern. Ornamentation could include swags, scrolls, fruit and flower festoons, gryphons and arabesques, or urns and vases – or relief work in strict geometrical patterns. More modest Georgian houses are not architecturally articulated inside, ornament being confined in most cases to skirting boards, dado rails and doorcases.

Georgian townhouses are characterized by unity, balance and elegance, not only when viewed as a whole but also in individual details such as doors, windows and ironwork.

A distinctive feature of early 19th-century houses is the use, on exteriors, of stucco – a type of hard, fine plaster that was coated onto brickwork to counterfeit stone. In the long run, stucco turned out to be an uneconomical finish requiring constant upkeep, without which it deteriorated rapidly. Many owners of period homes will have discovered this to their cost. Frequently stucco is found in combination with the cast-iron verandas, balconies and porches that we associate with the typical Regency house. Cast iron was used for mass-produced fanlights. These could have an impressive filigree delicacy, although the best Regency cast iron is extremely austere.

Among the experiments unleashed by the Picturesque movement, with its fondness for eccentric versions of other times and other places, was the mock country cottage, complete with thatched roof. The Regency idea of a cottage was highly fanciful, bearing little relation to the realities of rural life. However, this cosy ideal, the *cottage ornée* (ornamental cottage), initiates on a modest scale a whole century of romantically revived styles of housing.

The Victorians adapted past styles to their own purposes instead of following them strictly. Middle-class homes were often overcharged with furnishings, creating an atmosphere of exaggerated comfort and affluence, but ornament was frequently restrained, although rich. Externally, a richer Italianate treatment succeeded the Neo-classicism of 1800–1835. However, the stuccoed terrace was still part of a restrained, albeit splendid, unit. The architectural vocabulary was extended: Gothic and "Tudor" detailing could be used as alternatives to classical.

The terrace gradually became less smart, except in certain exclusive areas such as London's Belgravia, Bayswater or Holland Park. The fashionable thing for the aspiring middle classes was to have a detached "villa" in the newly expanded suburbs – or, alternatively, a semi-detached house. The scale of life that could be lived in a semi-detached home was relatively modest. Living-in servants of necessity would be kept to a minimum, although there would be servant accommodation in the attic. The privacy of individual plots, with gardens front and back, reflects a new desire for independence from one's neighbour – a trend that remained prevalent into the 20th century.

The plan of the semi-detached house does not admit of much variation. Clearly, the reception rooms have to abut onto the party wall or there is wasteful repetition of flues and chimney stacks. In the absence of a basement, the kitchen must lie behind the house to preserve the proprieties of the master-servant relationship. Bedrooms and owners' bathrooms were on the first floor. In the typical 1870s house, an attic storey served whatever staff purposes were necessary.

1-5 These grand English townhouses capture the mood of the late Regency/early Victorian period. Highly influential at this time were Sir John Nash's Regent's Park Terraces in London and contemporary developments at Bath. Stucco was favoured on facades, while balconies and canopies added touches of individuality.

6, 7 This New York house built in 1864 has one of the earliest mansard roofs in America. Note the decoratively exuberant brackets and cornices.

8

9

10

11

12

8-12 *The Victorian terrace gave plenty of scope for design variations. The diversity of styles drew on centuries of local, national and international traditions. Such eclecticism adds greatly to the visual interest of our towns and cities.*

13 *These San Francisco houses of around 1880 are typical in their diversity of decoration. The well-maintained paintwork is an all-important aspect of their period charm.*

13

Purpose-built blocks of flats were a feature of the late Victorian period. However, apartment blocks never found in England the favour they enjoyed in France and America – probably for the same reasons that the garden suburb remained the English ideal.

Most Victorians lived in very simple terraces if they occupied a house at all. From the "universal plan" developers created a row house with two reception rooms, kitchen and scullery, four bedrooms, bathroom and attic. The detail varies but the plan does not. The facade has a two-storey bay, its mullions tricked out with a very debased form of Gothic decoration – for example, formalized flowers. The keystone of the arch of the porch often had a grotesque head for ornament. Above the front door, a single window marked the small bedroom.

In some metropolitan areas, gentility and raffish unrespectability fought endless battles over speculative housing. The ever-expanding terraces might fall into multiple occupation almost before they were finished. It is a mistake to think that the decay of the Victorian terrace and its division into flats is a purely 20th-century phenomenon.

In England, Victorian houses make up a small group of standardized types. Variations upon these types were possible, but rare. It is therefore rewarding to turn to parallel developments in 19th-century America. For example, in San Francisco in the 1880s there was a rich diversity of experiments on the basic single-fronted format. This developed as a detached house, but the surprise is in the carpentry. For the debased ornament so repetitively applied in the London type, California substitutes the inventiveness of the individual carpenter. The painted clapboard and the exuberant detail indicate how individual a simple building may become.

While such developments were taking place in towns, the vernacular tradition continued largely unchanged, except where fashion in the form of a landowner and his metropolitan architect had descended upon a village. The important factors in vernacular building have always been practical innovations. For the average farm worker the sash window had more appeal than the Greek Revival simply because it was more useful.

In the Victorian age aspects of this sensible, vernacular tradition were reclaimed for fashion by architects and critics. For example, windows might be placed where they are needed in rooms rather to present a pattern from outside. By taking elements from the vernacular, architects such as A.W.N. Pugin (chief promoter of the Gothic Revival) were able to create a pseudo-vernacular house, irregular for practical reasons rather than simply because irregularity was all the rage.

From the 1870s onwards the Arts and Crafts Movement led a reaction away from the mediocrity of mass-produced Victorian design. The guru of the movement was William Morris, who argued for dignified simplicity and honesty of materials. Morris's ideas were shared by the major Arts and Crafts architects Philip Webb and Richard Norman Shaw. But despite their commitment to better standards for all, Webb and Shaw were most often employed to provide fine large houses for a small wealthy sector of the middle classes. Both were inspired in part by the age in which English architecture had produced the most habitable house: the 17th century. The historic elements – for example, the combination of warm red brick and white woodwork – were transfused by a freshness and originality in the detailing. Windows might be elongated to admit more light, in the process creating a sense of airy delicacy. This was architecture well adapted to reduction for use in a suburb. It did not rely on scale for effect. Shaw provided a number of influential models for domestic architecture – both detached and semi-detached – over the years. They are forerunners of much that we expect in the modern suburban house. The half-timbering of houses such as Cragside in Northumbria initiated a taste that leads directly to the 20th-century popularity of "stockbroker" Tudor.

The characteristic swirling forms of Art Nouveau, which first appeared after 1890, made a modest impact on British furniture, tiles and light fittings, and to a lesser extent on decorative windows and wooden

panelling. Equally admired today is the Art Deco style of the 1920s and 30s, whose plain lines (sometimes combined with geometric ornament) accorded well with mass-production techniques and the need for economy. Art Deco-inspired homes sprouted sporadically in suburbia, alongside an entrenched loyalty to the false timbers that evoked the Golden Age of English architecture. The obstacle to a more widespread acceptance of modernism in domestic architecture was simply that it was associated with factories and office blocks. As in the 19th-century, dwellers in the suburbs wanted their homes to be homely, and stylistically as far removed as possible from any associations with work.

1, 2 The interior of Leighton House, London, may seem eccentric, but it encapsulates all the self-confidence of the late 19thC, as well as reflecting the taste for travel and collecting. The 15thC tiles are Persian. The whole feel of this room is quite unEnglish. Such opulent strangeness seldom fails to delight visitors.   1.11

3, 4, 5 In the late Victorian/ early Edwardian era, houses that may seem rather anonymous to the unaccustomed eye reveal interesting decorative flourishes. Any historic style might be borrowed, from classical pillars and porticos (5) to brick gables of the English Renaissance and mock-Tudor oriel windows (3). Tragically, such buildings are often given unsympathetic extensions (4).

6

7

8

6, 7, 8 *This house dating from 1890 is in a Neo-Renaissance style. The hipped tile roof and projecting bays with gabled pediments are typical of large country houses of this period. Some such houses were designed to be light and airy inside, as here; others have a deliberately dark and cloistered feel. The marble fireplaces and other interior details would fit easily into a house of about 100 years earlier.* S&P

Monarch chronology

DATES	MONARCHS	PERIOD
1558-1603	Elizabeth I	Elizabethan
1603-1625	James I	Jacobean
1625-1649	Charles I	Carolean
1649-1660	Commonwealth	Cromwellian
1660-1685	Charles II	Restoration
1685-1689	James II	Restoration
1689-1694	William & Mary	William & Mary
1694-1702	William III	William III
1702-1714	Anne	Queen Anne
1714-1727	George I	Early Georgian
1727-1760	George II	Georgian
1760-1812	George III	Late Georgian
1812-1820	George III	Regency
1820-1830	George IV	Late Regency
1830-1837	William IV	William IV
1837-1860	Victoria	Early Victorian
1860-1901	Victoria	Late Victorian
1901-1910	Edwardian VII	Edwardian

Doors

The front door is usually the most eye-catching feature of the house, and altering or replacing it without due forethought is all too often disastrous. The mock Georgian door with built-in fanlight is painfully unauthentic, and will look wrong everywhere. Interior doors also need to be looked at carefully in relation to the style of their surroundings. Cheap modern doors in a baldly utilitarian style will look totally out of place if the rest of the interior has well-judged period details. A solid plank door, however well-made, will be intrusive in an elegant townhouse. And an 18th-century-style door, despite its good proportions (or because of them), will look ill at ease in a setting of homely rusticity.

Other common pitfalls include using knobs and knockers of the wrong type (such as wrought iron on painted panelled doors) and the insensitive insertion of glass. On no account should bull's eyes be inserted. Such lapses can spoil not only the door but the house itself.

1 An original wrought-iron spur knocker for a six-panel front door. BH

2 This original 1680s door was enlarged in the 18thC. The hinges are old replacements which fit exactly the marks found on the door. This attention to detail makes all the difference when authentic restoration is the aim. VNS

3 A reproduction of a mid-16thC Gothic arched door and frame. This is an elaborate example for the period, with deep chamfered framing and small panels. SI

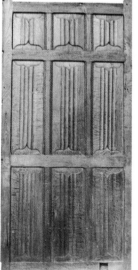

4 A classical Italianate front door and porch on a London terrace house of 1868-74. It is important to research suitable colours for different periods. Here the white-painted stucco dressings and two shades of green on the door are authentic, but the steps are no longer whitened every day by a maid! LSH

5 The brass door furniture of the late-Victorian era was highly refined in comparison with 16thC wrought-iron examples. The contrast is graphically illustrated in the four examples below. Both wrought-iron pieces are modern reproductions. LSH, SI

6 A genuine early-mid 16thC door with linenfold panels. These doors can be tracked down, but not easily. Frequently they do not fit the space intended. It would be a tragedy to cut down such a piece, so you should always take dimensions into account before buying. AH

7 The six-panel door came into vogue at the end of the 17thC. This is a late 19thC example.

8

8 *A massive oak door of the type standard in England from the 15thC until it was overtaken by the framed door with inset panels in the 17thC. It's worth remembering that oak was not always dark. When these houses were built, the oak was a glorious honey colour. Reproduction oak doors are "aged" to suit modern tastes. Imagine a 15thC house with bleached floor boards, honey-coloured beams, doors and skirting boards.*

9 *An oak plank door hung on sturdy iron hinges of the strap and pin type. Note the enormous strap or iron arm which stretches across two-thirds of the door – this drops into a pin set into the door post. The leaded side lights bordering the door and matching the windows are typical of the 15th and 16thC.*

10 *An interior view of the same door, showing the original fittings.*

THE OAK STUDDED DOOR

In Tudor England doors were built to last. Amply wide, they were almost invariably of oak. The simplest were rows of planks, laid vertically, edge to edge, joined and strengthened by oak pegs or iron nails driven through to similar planks (the ledges), usually four in number, set across the back. For simpler houses this type of door continued to be made, in softwood versions, well into the 20th century in Europe and America. Sometimes there were diagonally set braces between the horizontals.

This type of door is known as the batten door. Variations on the theme include doors with narrower boards, or tongued and grooved, or with moulding on the face, or joined like overlapping clapboard; also doors whose ledges are let into the thickness of the wood. Broader planks might be grooved to make them look narrower. Double-thick doors had edge-to-edge

9

10

planks across their width at the back. On external doors the vertical joins were usually protected from the weather by thin strips of oak.

In timber-framed buildings inside and outside doors were mostly square-headed, but when set in stone they were often low-arched, like the windows of the period Square-headed doors might be set against an arched head under the lintel or moulded to give the appearance of an arch.

Linenfold moulding was developed and refined in England during the Tudor period and applied to doors as well as panelling. On both sides of the Atlantic it later became a hallmark of the mock-Tudor style.

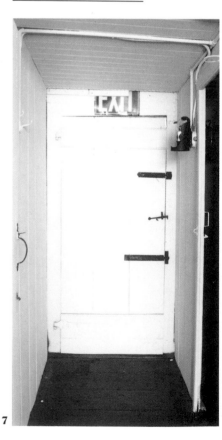

1 Iron butterfly hinges like these have frequently been replaced.

2 Handmade ironwork lends a more authentic "feel" to a reproduction.

3 A plain oak door (right) consisting of vertical planks with oak pegs or iron nails driven into horizontal ledges on the back. On external doors the smooth "right" side faced outward, while on internal doors it faced into the room.

4 A 17thC Spanish or Portuguese door with fielded panels.

5 An early panelled door. Rather crude panelled doors were produced in the 16thC but the style really came into its own in the 17thC.

6 An original door with double bead moulding — note the carving on the door posts.

7 *These basic three-plank doors were used from the early 17thC well into the 18th.* BH

8 *This three plank door in the same New York house is divided and has slightly more intricate wrought ironwork hinges and locks. Note the differing shape and size of the handmade hinges — uniformity was not called for: function was more important than form.* BH

9 *Double entrance doors to a late 19thC house with leaded side lights have as their inspiration the plank doors of the 15thC and 16thC.*

10 *The exterior of this restored New York house of 1680 shows the original placement of the doors. The tall upstairs door is for loading as the staircase was too narrow.* VNS

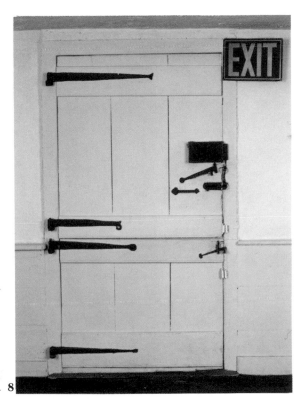

1 *The porchway and plank door of a house dating from the 16thC. The much later stained-glass panels harmonize and, perhaps because of the rather amateurish cutting of the "windows", lend their own charm to the house.*

2,3 *These oak plank doors were introduced into a 17thC house in the early years of the 20thC. The importance of using properly aged wood, traditional methods and wrought-iron work cannot be overemphasized.*

4 *This wrought-iron boot scraper is an early 20thC copy of a 17thC design.*

DOOR CASES

The early, simple method of hanging a door was to attach it to timber posts that formed part of the structure of the building. But later, doors came to be hung on doorposts set against the wall. The join between the post and the face of the wall was concealed by an architrave, which made a surround or case for the door. During the later 17th century, such surrounds were given increasingly decorative treatment in the grander houses. They were ornamented with classically inspired swags and medallions and headed with bold pediments. Inside the house, pediments were often broken: that is, they terminated in an open curve instead of a completed triangle, thus creating a lighter effect. Some pediments incorporated panels designed to contain pictures.

The treatment of door surrounds reflected that of mantelpieces (or chimneypieces as they were then called). Similarly, the style of moulding or carving on the doors themselves was echoed in the panel work on the walls.

5 *An 18thC door typically enhanced by decorative architraves and door surrounds. The addition of panelling elegantly solved the problem of unusually thick walls.*

6,7,8 *These early 19thC architraves show the classic Greek Revival style in both ornate and simple forms.* OMH

9 *By the late 19thC stepped moulding was the most popular form of architrave: sometimes simple and narrow, other times elaborate and deep.*

10 *This chestnut and walnut door with fielded panels is in a New York house dating from 1875. The details of the door and architrave are echoed by the chair rail and panelling.*

6

7

8

5

9

10

PANELLED DOORS

Doors constructed as two panels set within a frame began to appear in the great English houses late in the 16th century, and soon became the norm, taking over from the solid plank door. Until late in the 17th century panelled doors were elaborately moulded and more and more exuberantly carved, painted and gilded to satisfy increasingly Baroque taste.

At the beginning of the 17th century the two-panel form remained the most common, with the heavy panels fielded – that is, raised in profile. Panels were given applied moulding in geometric patterns, and the broad door cases were treated to match. By mid-century, as classical proportions began to govern the design, six, eight or ten panels were inset; and by 1700 the six-panelled door was settling in for its long period of popularity. This was the favourite front door of the entire Georgian period and of the classical style in America. Interior doors had six, four or sometimes only two panels. The panelled door ceased to belong only in the houses of the wealthiest, and was repeated in less expensive wood, often with remarkable craftsmanship, for over a hundred years across the social scale.

In the smallest 18th-century townhouses, where a six-panel front door would be out of proportion, four panels were more usual. Both inside and out, the hand-sawn, increasingly slim panels were set into a rebate into the frame, with applied moulding around their edge. This moulding was absent in humbler houses and on the backs of cupboard doors.

At the beginning of the 18th century, door panels were raised or fielded. However, on external doors, the lower two panels were often flush with the frame. This helped rainwater to run off – as did the outward-curving rails at the bottom of the door. By the end of the century sunk door panels are more frequently found.

1 This light oak reproduction linenfold door blends perfectly with an early house. The simplicity of the wrought-iron hinges and door catch maintains the period character.

2 These 17thC oak double doors were introduced into a 15thC house in Kent in the 1950s. It is important to remember that all is not always what it seems. Early houses have often had many adaptations through the centuries.

3 An interesting mid-17thC divided door showing the influence of both English and Dutch vernacular architecture on a New York house built in 1661.   BH

4 By the middle of the 17thC, oak panelled doors had six, eight or ten panels. These doors were frequently used as replacements for the earlier plank doors, particularly internally.

5 *Eight-panelled solid mahogany doors were much favoured by the first half of the 18thC and often replaced earlier examples.* CP

6 *This double or split door is made to resemble a panelled one by a simple frame around a board and batten body. The plank edges are beaded, a typical form of primitive ornamentation.* VNS

7 *From the late 17thC on, the six-panel door became the most popular form, particularly for front doors, and this was to be the most fashionable during the whole Georgian period.*

8 *This early 19thC four-panelled door in its original door frame remained standard in both Britain and America throughout the 19thC. The white paint work is totally authentic.*

9 *Today you will often find pine doors stripped of generations of paint – a simple treatment which works successfully in many cases. However, the original owners would probably be horrified to see so humble a wood being given such importance.*

5

6

8

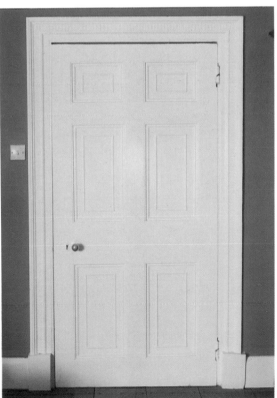

7

9

1

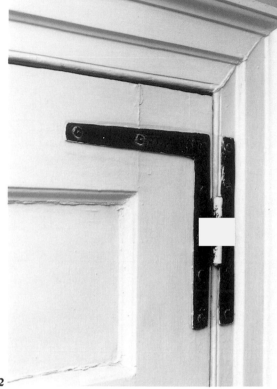

2

3

4

1 *A classic six-panel Georgian door from the late 1760s. The paint on this door simulates the slightly streaked effect produced by the thinner paints used in the 18thC. You can achieve this by dragging a faintly tinted coat of scumble glaze over a surface coat of oil-based paint.* RC

2 *These sturdy iron hinges work as well today as they did in the late 18thC.* MJ

3 *The rectangular fanlight over this six-panel internal door with simple door frame and architrave reflects the understated proportion of late 18thC and early 19thC design. Such features tended to be used in secondary positions or in lesser houses.* MJ

4 *The same door has plain but sturdy brass door furniture with a well-concealed lock on the underside.* MJ

5 *The front porch and doorway of a classic Greek Revival house built in New York c.1835.*

6 *Behind a later louvre door is a mahogany one of 1835 with its original brass fittings. These doors cope well with most weather conditions, apart from strong sunlight, and need virtually no maintenance.*

1 *The porch, double doors and fanlight were most important in changing the facade, in 1728, of an earlier house. The early Georgians had no qualms about bringing an old fashioned house right up to date – with pleasing harmonious results.* CP

2,3,4,5 *By the end of the 18thC the front door of the house had developed into a solid multi-panelled door, and the variations were endless. The Georgians were particularly keen on the semi-circular fanlights which predominate in city terraces. These were originally divided by wooden bars and tended to be of simple design, but as the century progressed classical influences and the use of cast iron allowed intricate designs.*

6,7,8 Both late 18thC and early 19thC houses gave greater prominence to the front door, by use of pillars, brick arches or white painted stone. If a house is in a terrace it is important to view the street as a whole. It is also sensible to get advice on door furniture from a brass specialist.

9,10 In the 19thC front doors continued to mirror the changing faces of architecture. The square fanlight which had appeared in the 18thC gained popularity.

11 This wonderful example of a Victorian Gothic Revival door and fanlight is in a square in North London.

12 An attractive Edwardian door has replacement etched glass in its panels, side windows and rectangular light above despite the arched opening.   LDC

The colour of front doors

One of the most important decisions to be made is what colour to paint the front door. Experts, museums and societies often disagree. Therefore, all that can be suggested is what the authors have found works in practice. On Georgian houses:- white, black, dark green, dark blue, burgundy. On Victorian houses:- brighter colours are acceptable, as is a two-toned effect. If the house is in a terrace consider the whole ensemble, avoiding jarring colours. Brickwork should also be considered. For example, red doors can often compete with the brick colour if the shades are mismatched. You should remember that the colour of the front door is something we inflict on the outside world more than on ourselves: great care should therefore be taken.

FANLIGHTS

From about 1700 the glass fanlight over the front door was developed as an elegant solution to the problem of letting light into the hall and passageway. With glazing bars first of wood, and later of lead or wrought iron, the fanlight window offered scope for endless pattern variations. The influence of the Adam brothers encouraged increasing use of cast iron for delicate patterning. By the end of the century fanlights were being mass produced in a wide range of increasingly informal designs. Loops and spider's webs took over from fans and scallops, and elaborate heart and honeysuckle motifs were popular in the early 1800s.

No one nowadays would want to remove one of these lovely features. However, many were unfeelingly ripped out earlier in the present century. Fortunately, it is possible to find craft workers who will provide new fanlights following designs contemporary with the house.

1 This classical Georgian six-panelled front door has an equally classical fanlight. Such features should, of course, be restored and retained. They are functional, adding to the light in the hallway, and delightful, adding to the overall splendour of the façade.

2 The proportion and feel of this hallway owe much to the American Empire style in this New York house built in 1765 and refurbished, after the owners' trip to France, in 1826. The fanlight and side panels, which are original to the house, are copies of early Colonial glass. MJ

3 This house is a reconstruction of the best colonial architecture from Maine to Charleston, South Carolina. It was built in 1929-30 by the architect Richard Henry Dana as a replica of a 1760 house. Some elements are original, salvaged from old houses being demolished, many more are copies — but perfect and sensitively made. This entrance door of stone is in the formal pedimented Greek Revival style. HH

4 The divided front door (sometimes called a Dutch door) from the inside. The sophisticated panelling reflects that of the chair rail in the hall. By the mid-18thC in this quality of house far more attention was being paid to detail; ornamentation was taking over from pure functional design. HH

5 *This fanlight from an 1830s house in New York shows all the exuberance of the period. The front door was an important statement of wealth and position. Such a fanlight and associated decoration were intended to portray an owner of gentility. Restoration of such a detail requires a skilled craftsman, and even repainting should be done with great care.* OMH

6,7,8,9 *These typical 18thC fanlights were still popular in the 19thC. The intricacy of design was at its height in the mid-18thC and tended, in modest homes, to become less delicate as the century progressed. Standard shapes, such as circles, loops and spiderwebs, were mass produced and used in terraces in cities and towns in both Britain and America.*

10,11 *Many Victorian houses had simple square fanlights, which should be retained, especially when they mirror other houses of the same design.*

Hoods

When not placed within an entrance porch or under a projecting upper storey, outside doors were initially set beneath a moulded projecting lintel which helped to keep off the rain. Alternatively, stone houses had drip mouldings across the tops of doors. In the 1650s decoratively carved wooden hoods began to appear at the head of the door case to afford protection from the weather and add a superb ornamental flourish to the flat front of the house. Supported visually by carved brackets (though often with further concealed support), these hoods are still frequently found, as an unaltered feature, in houses dating from this time onward. Until the 1720s, English examples were often carved in a florid Baroque manner. However, the vigour of the curving acanthus leaves, cherubs and lions' heads, fruits and flowers, was curbed by the influence of stricter Palladian classicism, and hoods went out of fashion.

The brackets and hoods were made of well-seasoned softwood, which was quite deeply carved. Successive applications of white paint has often blurred the details, in which case the old paint should be carefully stripped or burnt off and fresh white paint applied. In shape, hoods of the later period might be arching, coved or modelled to suggest shells. The smaller townhouses had simple, flat, moulded projections which nevertheless had elaborate scrolled brackets. In 19th-century terraced houses hoods often provided a touch of individuality to enliven a relatively plain exterior, as shown by the examples opposite (9).

1

2

3

4

1 *This interesting thatched house in the Bushey Park Estate in London has an equally eccentric porch. Porches frequently mirrored the style of the house and the Victorians, in particular, liked to add interest to a plain facade.*

2,3 *Pillars were frequently employed to give a classical feel to the entrance. These are common features in the 18thC but were also used by the Victorians as a classical revival.*

4 *In this example the functional use of the porch – to give shelter from inclement weather – finds a natural expression.*

5 *A successful modern porch added to a 16thC farmhouse using old timbers and a classic vernacular design.*

6 *The influence of chinoiserie is to be found in the design of porches and furniture at the end of the 18thC and beginning of the 19thC. The pagoda-style top is typical of the Regency period.*

7,8 *Porches were often thought inappropriate, and by the late 18thC the style had reverted to the hood.*

9 *This late Victorian terrace is an example of hoods used purely as decorative features. That such detail was added to quite plain doors shows the Victorians' concern to beautify.*

ENTABLATURES

From the mid-1700s a classical door surround was preferred, with columns or pilasters on each side of the door and a horizontal entablature over the top, with or without a triangular or segmental (curved) pediment. This type of surround, christened the tabernacle frame, was much loved by the Adam brothers. Both inside and out the tabernacle frame persisted throughout the rest of the century, first with Roman orders, then Greek, and with console brackets later replacing the columns.

Above interior doors, broken pediments were often used in the style first adopted some hundred years before. However, towards the end of the 19th century, pediments had fallen out of favour. Inside the home, the areas above the doors now had stucco panels – in parallel with the increasing use of stucco on exteriors.

1

2

1 This door and frame of the early 19thC exhibit all the style of the Egyptian Revival popular at the time. The sphinxes and tall pillars are actually the entrance to the house. The front door is in a small external hallway.

2 This spectacular Georgian door and surround epitomize the classical influences of the later part of the 18thC. Such doors were usually painted white. As with internal cornices, the decoration at the head of the columns can be greatly improved by careful cleaning and repainting.

3 *This wonderful broken pediment above classical columns develops a style popular in architecture and furniture from the mid-18thC on. The beautifully proportioned front door reflects the Georgian love of symmetry.*

4,5 *On less grand houses, entablatures were often much simpler but still had the effect of increasing the elaboration of the door. This was also the case in later Georgian houses. If your entablature is in a bad state of repair or has been removed, a specialist carpentry firm can copy a similar design.*

6, 7 *In the late 18thC the classical columns could be either freestanding or incorporated into the door frame. These columns developed into a mainly decorative feature rather than a structural one. White painted stucco was a common treatment for a door surround. Pilasters were also favoured, as in picture 7.*

CHANGES IN STYLE

With the arrival of Gothic, Greek and Picturesque influences in the early 19th century, there was less stylistic conformity. Decorative details varied immensely according to individual taste. However, certain broad trends can be identified.

A feature of the period was the door with two vertical panels side by side, sometimes narrowing toward the top like doric columns. Sometimes a door would be ornamented with a rectangular frieze and a central circular motif or a reeded lower half. The surround was more and more played down. Front doors became less significant decoratively, the principal decorative element being the fanlight. Treatments ranged from the classic radiating bars like the spokes of a wheel to loops and swirls and spiderwebs. In humbler houses, right until the early 20th century, plainer rectangular fanlights were to be seen in abundance.

Mahogany almost completely replaced oak for doors in grand houses, although for greater economy there was considerable use of Baltic fir, well seasoned and of good quality. More ordinary houses had doors of "dry yellow" deal or American pine. For front doors in stone surrounds, white was the preferred colour, but black, dark green or brown was also considered suitable.

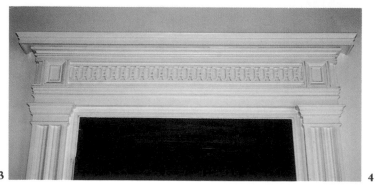

1 *A Federal-style entrance built in 1832 with coffered stone sides and columns. Note that the outer fanlight is heavier than the inner one and the doors echo but do not duplicate each other. This is one of only two surviving examples of the hundreds of similar houses built in New York in the first half of the 19thC.* OMH

2 *The outer door and fan seen through the inner doorway. The regular panelling owes more to the Greek Revival than the Federal style.* OMH

3 *The parlour door frame. On more unusual door frames like this, you may have to take moulds to copy the detail.* OMH

4 *The classic division of a 19thC American house – pocket doors in a double Greek Revival doorway between twin parlours.* OMH

5,6,7 *Three examples of Greek Revival door frames from a New York Neo-classical stone mansion built between 1837 and 1846. The first with understated elegance; the second and third, with their wonderful carving, demonstrating the true opulence of the period.* BP

8 *A six-panel door in the upstairs' reception room has a simple classical frame.* BP

9 *Another Greek Revival door frame from the same house, similar to the one in picture 6, but with a different motif.* BP

10 *The frame of these large mahogany pocket doors is moulded as Corinthian columns.* BP

5   6   7

8   9   10

THE LATER 19TH CENTURY

The narrow Georgian terraced house demanded a narrow entranceway, and a front door proportioned accordingly. However, when the villa was introduced to towns, its wider entrance hall allowed a more generous entrance area, which permitted the introduction of side windows beside a wider front door, often set within a porch. This set the style for Victorian houses.

By the time of the building boom in the middle of the 19th century, mechanization had taken over from hand labour. Hand-sawn door panels had been around five-eighths of an inch thick. The later machine sawn panels were thicker, making the doors sturdier (and also more fireproof). The rules of 18th-century proportion had required the height of a door to be twice (or a little more than twice) its width. Now, though they were still panelled, doors were more various in their ratio of dimensions.

Basement storeys, where they existed, were not so deep as before. The raised ground-floor storey replaced the Georgian *piano nobile*, and the front door set into it was reached by a longer flight of steps.

The Gothic style that was favoured for public architecture also affected domestic buildings profoundly. In doors and window surrounds, coloured brick or carved stone were used – or a stone substitute of moulded papier mâché or powdered wood, frequently painted. Woodwork was grained artificially to look like oak.

With the mushrooming of suburbs from the mid-century onwards, and the spread of simpler terraced houses, the door position was variable. The rhythm of door/window, door/window down the street gave way to window/door, door/window, window/door. To provide privacy, a wooden partition might be added between the two neighbouring doors. Flats were being built to look like terraced houses, with double doors, one for downstairs and one for upstairs.

By the end of the century even the smaller houses had tiled paths leading to the stone steps and front door.

1 *This original doorway to the west wing of a 1735 Port Washington house has simple pilasters and sidelights.* SWH

2 *By 1845, when the east wing porch was added, the taste was for something a little more ornate. The classical Doric columns and the porte-cochère are typical Victorian details.* SWH

3 *Etched glass panels like these are a feature of houses throughout the Victorian period. Fortunately, there are craftsmen who can reproduce the traditional designs.* LSH

4 *These narrower front doors were common in Georgian terraced houses. The square fanlight is typical of the early 19thC.*

5

6

5 *Heavily ornamented brass door furniture vies for attention with the decorative paint treatment. Note the vase motif on the finger plates echoing that on the panel (although in different style).* LSH

6 *Another view of the same door showing more of the painted panels. This house is a unique example of its type. The owner was the chief political cartoonist of Punch and the interior has been kept the same since his death in 1910.* LSH

7 *This heavily moulded architrave repeats the design of the single door panel. The whole is given greater importance by the classical pediment and sombre, marble-like effect of black gloss paint.*

7

8

9

8 *A wide internal door and frame of the late 19thC with a series of formalized carved decorations emphasizing the proportions. 18thC proportion required doors to have a height of a little over twice their width. By 1870, however, many were higher or, as here, wider.* LH

9 *The motto incised over this dining room door salutes the guests and wishes them "good luck". The gilded scroll design repeats that around the door frame.* LH

sheltered within a porch (often with a curved or pointed arch) supported on thin columns. Sometimes now quite brightly painted, doors were four-panelled, with a rectangular light (high window) above. Stained glass became more and more popular, the familiar narrow blue or red framing panels with white stars at their corners later giving way to a more Arts and Crafts treatment, with subtle colours in leaded lights or the curvilinear Art Nouveau patterns which took over at the end of the century.

It is perfectly possible to have leaded panes restored and re-inserted in a front door, or to have a new panel made in the original style. However, such a panel does offer easy entry to burglars and should be backed with toughened burglar-proof translucent plastic .

1 A heavy, patterned velvet curtain trimmed with a deep fringe and thick cord drapes a painted door. Before restoring a Victorian house to this degree of authenticity, it is as well to consider whether you could live in such a claustrophobic atmosphere. It is possible to be true to the character of a house and still live in the 20thC. LSH

2 Another glorious example of Victorian self-confidence! The painted upper panels of the door pick up the motif of the walls, the lower panels are ornamented with coats of arms and the brass door furniture is highly elaborate. The door is swamped, and the whole area given new proportions and greater importance by the heavily trimmed curtains and a matching massive pelmet filling the space between cornice and picture rail. LSH

1

2

3

4

5

3 *This American house built in 1875 has its original chestnut doors with period etched-glass panels which open to reveal a pierced iron grille.*

4 *This late 19thC back door has as its central feature a stained-glass panel which mirrors the designs used throughout the house.* ISH

5,6,7 *It is possible to buy restored doors or new doors made in the style of the late 19thC or early 20th C. Example 5 is a good example of 19thC taste, while 6 and 7 are in the Edwardian style.* LDC

8 *As the 19thC came to a close Art Nouveau patterns became more and more popular for stained glass, as for other forms of decoration.*

6

7

8

DOOR FURNITURE

Until about 1700 latches, hinges and door handles
were usually of wrought iron, and although simple in
their conception they could be beautifuly ornamented.
The simplest hinges, used on batten doors, are those of
the strap and pin type, with a long strap attached to the
door dropping on to a sturdy pin fixed to the door post.

The H hinge was also frequently used on batten
doors. This has two "legs" which interlock by means of
a bar across the middle: one leg is screwed to the door
and the other to the post. The legs were given fancy,
double S-shaped sides, the terminals of which were
often embellished with cockspurs in true Gothic
mannner.

Early external doors had no handles, being closed
only at night and barred with wood on the inside. The
simplest latches then became common: the iron latch,
catch and guide were operated by a large wrought-iron
ring on the plain side of the door. These fittings, or
simple versions of them all remain in keeping with
cottage doors.

Brass rim locks were introduced in the late 1660s.
The knob and working parts were set into a metal box
mounted on the door, and the latch closed into a metal
catch mounted on the door frame. These devices were
much more finely ornamented and were fitted to fine
panelled doors. Elegant little brass handles were
introduced instead of knobs for internal doors, and if
there is a key hole it should be accompanied by
elaborate escutcheons. Finger panels protected the door
from finger marks and provided further scope for
decoration. The basic design stayed in fashion, in
porcelain, pressed metal and finally bakelite, until the
1940s.

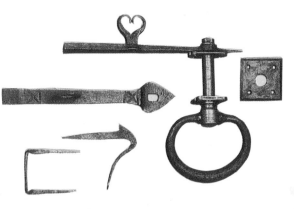

1 *A side door of a mid 18thC New York house showing the iron hardware.*

2 *Thorough research into old types of hardware found in the house gave the actual designs for these replacements. The doors are put together with clenched nails – soft wrought iron nails that are almost impossible to loosen. Contrary to popular belief, board and batten doors were always nailed.* VNS

3 *It is essential to use wrought-iron hinges to give an authentic feel to early doors. SI*

4 *By the 17thC internal door latches had become more decorative and more ingenious than formerly, and made use of brass as well as iron.*

5 *A strap-and-pin hinge on a lightweight plank door.*

6 *These authentic reproductions are readily available from such firms as Stuart Interiors.*

7 *The original iron hinge on an internal stripped and polished pine door.* HH

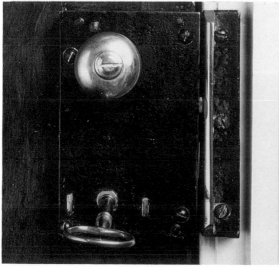

By the beginning of the 18th century door knockers were widely used on front doors. These were made of iron and lent themselves to all sorts of designs, usually based on animal heads. To complement these knockers, plain, bold doorknobs, also of iron, were set at waist height. Later brass knobs and knockers were more showy, but remained modest compared with 19th-century equivalents.

Brass was much less used before the 19th century than we seem to think now. Cast iron was by far the favourite material for door furniture in the Regency period. Ostentatious use of brass became commonplace later in the 19th century, when bells with pulls replaced knockers, until the introduction of porcelain pushes for electric bells.

Art Nouveau lent itself particularly well to door furniture. Its sinuous patterns can be found on large finger plates and bold letter boxes.

8 *It is possible to find excellent reproduction brass door furniture. These examples are perfect for doors from the early 19thC on.* Be

9 *This large solid early 19thC iron hinge supports triple doors. It should be noted that such hinges are brittle and can snap if attacked with a chisel or hammer. They were frequently covered with the stain used for the wood and were meant to blend with their surroundings rather than dominate.*

10 *Substantial brass hinges like this were used on both solid and glazed mahogany doors.* CP

11 *This beautifully-made late 19thC brass door catch is both functional and attractive.* LSH

12 *The original door lock and key of an early 19thC house. These should always be repaired and restored if possible.*

13 *Brass had become the main material for fittings in most houses of stature by the beginning of the 19thC.* CP

1 *A late 19thC example of useful information conveyed by means of a revolving brass plaque.* LSH

2,3 *Two examples of brass door furniture of the late 18thC.* RC

4 *This plain brass reproduction door furniture is perfectly suitable for doors of the late 18th and 19thC.* Be

5 *This wonderful late 19thC brass letter box is original although reproductions abound.*

6 *The choice of reproduction door furniture to suit a late 18th/early 19thC door is vast. The more ornate tends to suit a later house.* Br, Be

7 *As well as brass door furniture, the Victorians used china. These modern examples are available in many paint finishes.* Be

8, 9, 10, 11, 12, 13, 14 *Original brass Victorian door furniture is well worth seeking out as it has the added patina of wear, although there are good reproductions copied from old designs. All these examples are originals.*

15 *A lock imported from England to New York in the 1830s; the knob is 1890s.*

16 *You can see how successive generations have renewed the door furniture here from the marks on the wood. The house was built in 1765 but this polished wooden door knob was made in the 1890s.* MJ

17 *This 19thC brass and glass door knob has a matching keyhole and escutcheon.*

18,19 *This original polished brass door furniture gives an elegant look to late 18th/early 19thC mahogany doors.*

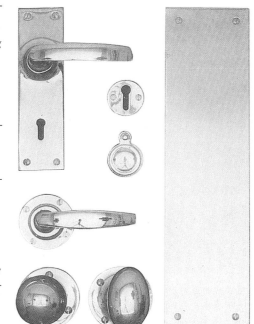

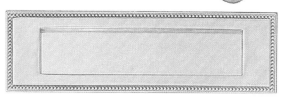

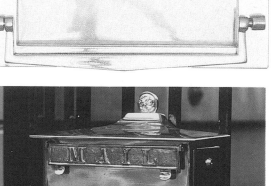

8

9

10

11

12

13

14

15

16

17

18

19

Britain had its own glass industry from the 13th century but it was very rare for windows to be glazed until Tudor times. Even then it was only the nobility and wealthy new classes who could afford to use glass.

Windows were "wind-holes" or "wind-eyes" – necessary to let out the smoke and let in light and air. They were unglazed and tiny, and this tradition continued in smaller houses and in remoter areas well into the 16th century and beyond. A few houses from the Elizabethan period even survived into the 20th century with their windows still unglazed.

Where buildings were of stone, vertical stone posts, or mullions, helped to support the lintel of the window opening. They also served to deter intruders; and timber mullions were fitted in timber-framed houses for the same purpose, even though they were not structurally necessary.

1 Vertical mullions were fitted into the windows of timber-framed houses as well as in stone ones, even though they were not structurally necessary. Setting the square mullions diagonally into the frame admitted more light than square-set posts.

2 The delicate glazing bars between the solid timber mullions would have been added at a much later date.

3, 4 The gable of a 16thC timber-framed house which has square leaded quarries. These are not original but 19thC replacements which harmonize with the building.

5 Diamond-shaped quarries are quite correct for a 15th or 16thC house. Never replace such windows with double-glazed imitation leaded lights, which give a most unsuitable flat look.

3

5

Mullions, whether stone or wood, were usually square in section and set diagonally into the frame, splay fashion, admitting more light than square-set posts. Splayed reveals might be provided around the openings, both outside and in, to let in more light.

Before the introduction of glass, other materials were used – for example, oiled or waxed paper or linen cloth stretched across a lattice frame. Better still was parchment, also on a lattice frame and often decorated with figurative patterns or coats of arms before being brushed with oil. The frames (known as *fenestrals*), made of wicker or fine strips of oak, were still used in remoter places well into the 17th

century, and later still in the poorest houses, where sheepskin or sacking would take the place of parchment. Their criss-cross pattern was echoed in the lead strips (*cames*) which held in place the small diamonds (*quarries*) of glass in the first glazed windows.

DEVELOPMENT OF MULLIONS AND TRANSOMS

The simple mullions of smaller Tudor houses were used to decorative effect in grander dwellings. Taller windows were made, with their lights (the divisions created by the mullions) divided horizontally by transoms. These windows were elegantly proportioned, usually with the dividing line of the transoms being halfway up the window plus the width of the transom.

In houses of timber construction the transoms and mullions were carved as if they were stone, and wood lent itself to a blossoming of ornamental work. The tallest windows would be topped with tracery, usually set within the shallow late medieval depressed arch or the Tudor arch. Such windows often had glazing in their upper parts and a complex arrangement of shutters and fenestrals opening below.

THE CASEMENT WINDOW

The early glass was blown. The ends of the bubbles were cut off and the cylindrical bubble itself was flattened before being cut out into "quarries", to be fitted into a lattice work of lead "cames". At first quarries were diamond or lozenge shaped but roundels of stained glass bearing coats of arms were made by European craftsmen for English houses. There was soon a multitude of quarry shapes, all of them small, because of the limitations of the lead "cames". And while grand new houses were being built with what must have looked like walls of glass, the smaller houses were having casements fitted into their existing window openings. Stone jambs and mullions were hung with iron casements while timber-framed houses had casements made of wood. The whole casement, rather than the pieces of glass within it, was known as the window pane.

By the 17th century, glass was quite readily available. Designs for quarry shapes had proliferated

6 A substantial late 19thC family house has a huge bay in the drawing room with five windows of four panes. This was the late Victorians idea of a Tudor "cottage"!

7 This six-paned arched window is a later addition to a timber-framed house. It is worth pointing out that, even in the interest of historical accuracy, it is not always possible to replace an external feature if the house is a listed building.

8 Casement windows became popular in the 16thC. By the 17thC, glass was readily available and larger, rectangular quarries began to be seen. The bull's eye was a feature of Crown or spun glass. Often this section was remelted, although it might be used in the windows of poorer homes. When its use is as regular as here one would assume it to be a later placement.

6

7

8

1

2

in glass manufacture, and the industry in Britain moved to Lancashire and Newcastle, where sand was plentiful and coal could be used. Larger rectangular quarries of various proportions began to appear, and in the latter part of the century casement windows consisting of wooden mullions and transoms set in a wooden frame were able to hold larger pieces of glass.

Crown or spun glass, blown and spun out into a flat disc, was introduced during this period. The best parts of the disc were used in the wooden frames which were replacing the recently installed leaded lights. Those parts of the discs not suitable for use in replacement windows were usually remelted. However, these "bull's eyes" might be used in the casement windows of the poorer homes – although they were certainly never used in houses of quality.

Despite the fact that windows continued to be subject to renovation over the years, much 17th- and 18th-century spun glass has survived. It is glossy, often marked by tiny air bubbles and recognizable by the fine curving lines of the spinning and its slightly curved surface. As a clue to the age of the house, early glass deserves respect and care when old houses are being restored.

3,4 These 19thC windows in a 17thC house blend well with the early surroundings. Old stained glass was used for the decorative roundels, probably taken from an old church. Our predecessors frequently reused old features and materials.

5 In this 19thC extension to the same house, leaded lights and oak frames were used to blend the extension perfectly with the 17thC core. From the facade it is difficult to distinguish the modern wing.

3

1 This window in a 16thC house has diamond-shaped quarries. As well as the usual lead cames there are lead bracing bars and decorative catches, both fairly typical on a house of this age.

2 A decorative window catch in the same house. In areas such as this (south-east England) where many houses have leaded lights, it is relatively easy to find a glazier to undertake restoration work. The lead used today is softer and holds the glass more firmly.

4

5

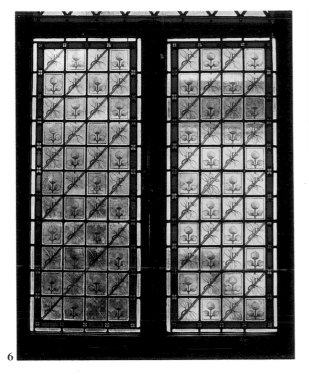

6

7

9

12

10

13

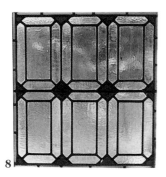

8

11

6 *This stained and painted 19thC glass is in the medieval mood. Notice the return to lead cames and square quarries.* I.SII

7 *More 19thC glass – delicate tracery makes a background for a central monogram in jewel colours; the whole window is bordered with a design of formalized flowers.* I.SII

8 *A small 19thC stained glass window.*

9 *This early stained glass window is a 17thC addition to a 15thC house. Glass like this was reproduced in the late 19thC as part of the Arts and Crafts Movement.*

10 *A beautiful Arts and Crafts roundel, with lilies.* W&W

11 *Another example of the medieval theme in 19thC decorative glass.* G&G

12 *The designs on these brass catches pick up the motifs from nature on the windows.* I.SII

13 *An inset painted glass panel of Ariel from the side window of a Victorian bay. It shows the influence of the Arts and Crafts Movement in England.* I.SII

SASH WINDOWS

Toward the end of the 17th century, sash windows were introduced and began to displace casement windows. The English may have heard about them from the Dutch, but the French regarded them as characteristically English; whatever their origin, they were certainly a feature of British and North American dwellings until well into the 20th century. Well suited to classically inspired architecture, the sash was to appear in every main street and town development throughout the Georgian period.

In the simplest and earliest sashes the panes were propped in position on pegs while open or held in place by a pivoted iron quadrant which fitted into notches in the beading strip. The upper pane was often fixed, in the Dutch manner. The earliest weighted sash windows had solid wood frames flush with the wall, with grooves for the weights. Soon these constructions were replaced by boxed frames in which the pulleys were set and the weights hung – a system which was hardly to change over a period of two hundred years.

The weighted sash was not universal. In some areas casement windows were superseded by sideways-sliding sashes. These too were built into the 20th century. Despite their name, "Yorkshire windows", they are in fact found in numerous English counties. The sliding sash was suitable for smaller windows and could be used in smaller houses and upper storeys where rooms were low.

THE 18TH CENTURY

Until the early 18th century in England, the most popular wood for window frames was oak or other locally available hardwood. Glazing bars were very broad (roughly two inches (5cm) across) and never painted. Although oak continued to be the principal

1

2

3

4

wood for important work, occasionally imported mahogany was substituted. By the 1720s cheaper Baltic fir had been introduced.

The softwoods fir and pine acquired immense popularity. As neither of these woods weather as well as oak, exposed woodwork required a protective coat of paint. White lead paint, primed with red lead, was universally used until the Victorian period. These softwoods were also common on the East coast of America, where painted windows were the norm from an early date.

From 1709, window frames in London had to retreat to a minimum of four inches (10cm) behind the outer surface of the wall to reduce the risk of fire. This created a reveal in the exterior brickwork which was usually plastered and painted white. Elsewhere, houses

5 *It was customary for Georgian houses to have grand reception rooms of noble proportions at first-floor level – the* piano nobile. *This one has large floor-to-ceiling sash windows, with three pairs of panelled shutters.*

6 *Tall windows are a feature of Georgian architecture which give a sense of spaciousness. This window on a half-landing has panelled shutters housed in the deep reveal with panelling repeated around the arch.* GH

still had their window frames flush with the wall or only slightly set in. London houses after 1709 have flat gauged brick arches above the reveals instead of a timber lintel, although white pine lintels were still to be found inside. The new recessed windows were usually furnished with shutters inside the house. These folded back above the window board into splayed or recessed reveals and were fastened with pivoted iron locking bars. Although glazing bars were becoming thinner and thinner in towns, they remained relatively thick in country regions. In grand houses wide oak bars would be carved inside to match the carved mouldings of the panelled shutters.

By 1820 most glazing bars had been reduced in width to half an inch (1cm) or less, and twelve-pane windows (known as six-over-six windows in America) had become standard. In another wave of window replacement, earlier sashes were removed and twelve-pane windows fitted. The rule of classicism, made fashionable by the Palladians early in the 18th century, was applied to buildings of all sizes in Britain and North America.

GEORGIAN VARIATIONS

During the 18th century the treatment of window surrounds and frames varied widely. Plain windows were commonly embellished with misunderstood classical details taken from the many "copy books" which served as textbooks to the British building trade at this time.

The Venetian or Palladian window, with three sections, the side ones narrower than the round-arched central one, had been used by Inigo Jones early in the 17th century. A century later, when classical architectural features were commonplace, this style of window was in evidence even in quite modest houses. In various proportions and with different decorative details, the Palladian window enhanced many a facade at (usually) first-floor level for two thirds of the century. More simply, rectangular windows were divided into three with fixed side lights and a central sash.

The bay or bow typical of Georgian or Regency terraced houses in many towns was very popular from the middle of the 18th century. The word "oriel", once applied indiscriminately to any projecting window, now denoted a window supported by brackets and

1 *Twelve-over-twelve sash windows are characteristic of virtually any house of the period in the East Coast of America. The gargoyle carvings in this example appear over the front windows only.* VC

2 *A dining room window of the 1830s. By 1850 most woodwork was painted white.* OMH

3 *This imposing bay of a house dating from 1875 is flanked by pilasters and defined by the cornicing and ceiling details. The bay is composed of five sash windows, each with just two panes. The ready availability by this time of large sheets of plate glass made it possible to dispense with glazing bars.*

1

2

3

projecting from an upper floor, as distinct from the built-in angled bay or curved bow which often extended almost the entire height of the external wall. Bays were practical, especially in towns, as they admitted more light and cunningly extended the front room without increasing the width of the house. In the 1770s, elliptical and canted bays became popular, stopping complaints about buildings advancing into the street.

At the same time, in British town houses, the *piano nobile*, providing rooms of greater height at first-floor level, was being developed. Georgian architects began to focus their creativity on this storey, by adding entablatures above the windows and pilaster strips which ran between them vertically to the cornice, and by increasing the height of the windows themselves. Some grand American houses, particularly in the South, emulated this fashion.

By the end of the 18th century, even modest builder-designed terraced houses in Britain had a *piano nobile* of increased height, sometimes with small projecting balconies, and often with windows decreasing in proportion.

Windows of this period were more likely to have square than arched heads and tended to be set closer to the face of the wall. Attic rooms were lit by dormer windows which could be square-, round- or segmental-headed. Crowned with their own little roofs, they projected in varying degrees from the house roof and were concealed behind the parapet if one existed.

4 *A finely detailed brass opener from the sashes shown in picture 3.*

5 *A built-in seat is a pleasant feature of this 18thC window.* CP

4

5

9

9 This detail of stripped-back glazing bars shows the Georgian mitre. When replacing such bars it is essential to duplicate this design. Many mass-produced examples have flattened bars.

THE 19TH CENTURY

Plate glass was first introduced in 1773, cast and ground to remove flaws. However, it was not widely used until after 1838 when polished sheet glass became commercially available. Already Gothic influences had begun to make their mark on classical facades. The new age was prepared to sacrifice proportion altogether in pursuit of maximum light and air. Glazing bars could be dispensed with now that large sheets of glass were available.

In the mid-1800s, many older multi-paned windows were replaced with six- and soon four-paned windows. In houses that were reglazed at this time, windows on upper floors were often left undisturbed and many can now be found with four-paned sashes at ground level, Georgian twelve-paned sashes above, and even Stuart casements on the top floor. In America, however, the entire house was often reglazed

THE 20TH CENTURY

By the turn of the century, in England and America, houses were being built with large sash windows, each half consisting of one huge pane. Shutters which could be closed from inside to keep out the light were now more or less abandoned and replaced by exterior blinds. Despite a growing demand for old-fashioned cosiness, the plate glass sash survived, developing into the modern "picture window". A frequent compromise is the sash in which the lower part is one sheet of glass, with smaller panes in the upper part.

There was also a medievalist strain – dating back to William Morris in the second half of the 19th century – which manifested itself in the reintroduction of casements and leaded lights. Mock lattices of applied lead strips appeared in the 1930s and are now common features in "pseudo-Tudor" houses and flats, despite the horror with which they were once viewed and their glaring inappropriateness in older buildings. Equally popular are the metal-framed, smaller-paned windows of the mid-20th century, which today have a period look of their own.

7

8

6, 7 Two examples of shutters from Regency villas, one showing the original brown varnish, the other painted white. It is a matter of personal taste whether to paint or revarnish; however there is no doubt that shutters should be restored and used. They are a form of double glazing and provide extra security.

8 This view shows the shutters in picture 7 open and folded back. Even with curtains these are useful additions. The windows, in an early 19thC house, have the interesting addition of small side panes.

SHUTTERS

Window openings could be shuttered to give substantial protection from intruders and the elements. In Britain, shutters were almost always on the inside, which is why the European-style external shutters unwisely added nowadays look so out of keeping in houses following British styles. Shutters were made strongly of wooden boards, sometimes hinged and folding and sometimes sliding horizontally or up and down, and fastened with wooden bars or iron fastenings. Those which opened horizontally were often housed in the reveals of the inside walls. Shutters and their hinges were usually constructed in a similar way to the doors of the house, and the two developed together.

1 The late 19thC fascination with Oriental styles shows here – red and gold wallpaper, rich green curtains trimmed with gold, shining brass curtain pole. The painting of the woodwork, including the shutters, adds to the sombre grandeur.

Although the window area is large it has the same heavy "feel" as the rest of the room. The tall concertina shutters were a common security feature. Each shutter is made up of four tall narrow sections; these fold into a small wall niche.   I.H

2 The artist who had this London house built in 1877 travelled extensively and was fascinated by Eastern art, and the decoration of this room reflects this taste. The bay is almost a half circle with floor-to-ceiling sash windows taking up most of it. The circular form is defined by the ceiling decoration and emphasized by the unusual curved brass curtain pole. The shutters work on a brass pulley system and are housed in reveals in the wall.   I.H

3, 4 The panelling below this window in an 18thC room matches that on the two pairs of shutters. The back of the shutter is typically plain while the front has intricate moulding.

5 The unusual cutout over the bed in this room in an American house was probably intended to hold fabric. It dates from 1720, when the room was added to an earlier house, and still has its original studs and shingle lath.   VNS

6 Two pairs of bi-fold shutters are still in good working order in this 18thC house in New York. The radiator "box" is panelled to match.   VC

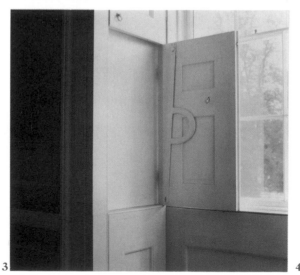

5

6

7

8

9

10

11

12

7 This small 18thC window in a New York house has a pair of triple-fold shutters. In this upstairs room the normal six-by-six panels have been adapted to three panes over six. MJ

8 Houses evolve over the centuries and thus may show a variety of window styles. Early 19thC shutters blend well with 17thC features on this New York house. BH

9 Triple-fold shutters in this dining room of a New York mansion built in 1765 are panelled only on the section which is seen when they are housed in the reveal. The colour of the woodwork is correct for the Federal Period and exactly the same paint formula was used; hence the streaked effect. The wallpaper is a reproduction of one of the era. MJ

10 The narrow proportions of this 1860s floor-to-ceiling sash window in a New York house are changed dramatically when the adjustable shutters are open – the width is doubled. WW

11 This house was built in 1929-30 – a replica of a mid-18thC one; the aim of the architect was to represent the best of colonial architecture between Maine and Charleston, South Carolina. For instance, this Palladian window in the ballroom was copied from a New England mansion. HH

12 The New York mansion featured in picture 9 also shows the influence of later tastes. The hall was designed in American Empire style c.1800 and you will notice that the tall narrow windows with their plain bi-fold shutters are a foil for the rather flamboyant decoration. MJ

1,2 *It is important to have the correct accessories. The silvered glass and pewter tieback and the Empire style brass knob are both suitable for the curtain treatments in this 1830s house.* BP

3 *These parlour windows have Victorian curtains and rods from 1867; the mirror too is Victorian. To gain the full effect it is important to study the whole "look": curtains in particular can give a Georgian or Victorian feel.* OMH

4 *The "Volunteer" chintz by Tissunique Ltd hanging in the Brown Study at Castletown House, Celbridge, County Kildare. It is an exact reproduction of an 18thC Irish chintz showing the review of the Irish Volunteers, Phoenix Park, Dublin, in 1782.* T

1

2

4

5

5 *A fairly elaborate example of the Greek Revival style, this window has a carved pediment over the top and Corinthian columns on either side. The draperies are a copy of originals of 1826.* BP

6 *This is an excellent example of curtaining a Victorian bay. The machine made lace inner curtains are absolutely in period.* LSH

7, 8, 9 *It is important to drape period windows in an appropriate style. Many firms produce copies of historic designs which blend well with a period room. These are some oustanding examples.*

O & L, C & F, O & L.

Sash windows

The lower rail of sash windows may have rotted if rainwater has been trapped around it. It can be professionally repaired by "scarfing" in new wood after the rotten wood has been cut out. The new wood should be well primed before you repaint the frame.

It is a fairly simple job to replace a broken sash cord yourself. However, if the glass is heavy, two people working together will cope better. Upstairs windows should not be tackled by the inexperienced.

1 *Remove the guard beads.* **2** *With the lower sash raised, cut through the unbroken cords at the pulleys.* **3** *Remove the lower window.* **4** *Take off the parting beads.* **5** *Push up the upper window and cut through the unbroken cords.* **6** *Remove the upper window.* **7** *Take out the cover of the weight boxes in the boxed frame (at bottom of sides). (To make this easier, remove old paint with chemical paint stripper.)* **8** *Note how the old cords are tied to the weights. Replace them with new cords cut to the same length: thread the cords through the pulleys and allow to drop down the hollow inside of the frame. Tie to the weights at the bottom. Fix the other ends of the cords to the grooves in the sides of the sash, by nailing.* **9** *Replace the weight box covers and reassemble the window by following instructions 1-6 in reverse order.*

The basement or ground floor is one of the most vulnerable parts of the house. Although most materials used for floors are hardwearing, they may still have suffered from damp and rot. Many have been concreted or adulterated by stick-on tiles; more have to be lifted to insert a damp-proof course. Irrespective of the type of floor or the cause of its deterioration, careful consideration should be given to replacement. A simple regime of maintenance should then make your floor last for centuries yet.

TIMBER FLOORS

These were first used for upper rooms as lofty houses were divided by the insertion of a ceiling. Sometimes they even served as ceiling, floor and joists in one; alternate boards were extra thick, giving them the strength of joists, and the thinner boards in between rested in angular grooves cut along the length of the thicker ones. The underside of the floor was limewashed to make a light ceiling downstairs.

Although oak is by tradition the finest building timber, elm has often been preferred for floorboards since their earliest use, and with good reason. Old elm floors, in cottages as well as larger houses, have developed a beautiful colour and sheen and have a hardness and grain which even oak cannot match.

Early boards were of course sawn by hand, and this was done with a carefree disregard for standardization. As a result the generous boards of older floors, all at least a foot (30cm) wide, are often of different widths and depths, with the supporting joists packed out as necessary to make the boards lie evenly.

As early as the 17th century, imported firs (referred to as deal when imported in ready-cut planks) came into use as a cheap and ready alternative to solid oak or elm. Red fir was reckoned to be almost

1 These yew floorboards are new replacements in a late 18thC house. It is well worth considering bleached boards when replacing a floor, particularly in a basement or kitchen area. RC

2 A floor with 16thC wooden floorboards. These were covered with oil cloth in the later 19thC and hence do not have the deep colour of wood floors polished in the Victorian taste.

3 17thC boards with wooden dowels are more regular and even than those of a century earlier. It is a pity to cover period boards but leaving them exposed causes problems in itself: the floors are frequently uneven, and stiletto heels inflict permanent damage.

4 There is some hesitancy about leaving boards bleached when combining them with period mahogany furniture. However, No. 1 Royal Crescent in Bath shows that this can produce very pleasing results. RC

5 The deep, glorious colour of these oak boards is totally unoriginal. An American visitor to England in 1772 commented that the floors were "washed and rubbed almost daily" and "have a whitish appearance". This pallor did not appeal to the Victorians, who polished the boards.

6 It is possible to buy salvaged floorboards. This early 19thC French oak flooring has good colour and patination. LAS

7 *By the late 19thC floorboards were really intended to be covered – our fashion for leaving them naked, as here, would have shocked the Victorians. A favourite method of covering such floors was Persian or scatter rugs. These have to be treated with care on polished floors.*

7

equal in quality to oak and less subject to woodworm than white fir. At least an inch (2.5cm) thick, the hardwood or good fir boards of the time gave worms a lot to tunnel through, and so have often survived in good condition despite attack.

In Stuart England the nobility had their floors inlaid with woods in different colours, a treatment known as parquetage. By the early 18th century, wooden block floors were being introduced into all the best houses of the gentry, but at the same time deal boards had become the norm for most floors.

Floorboards which had not usually been fixed, and like casements and locks could be removed if the house was vacated, were now fixed to the joists and the boards themselves began to be narrower. Perhaps partly because of the increasing development of a basement level, ground floors, which had rarely been boarded at the beginning of the 17th century, were now of wood.

8 *Parquetage had been used in the grandest houses from the Stuart period; it lost popularity but was reintroduced in the 19thC. The Victorian use of parquet flooring gave an interesting new look to wooden floors; it often replaced the plain oak boards and was covered in places by Persian carpets.*

9 *To polish wooden floors, use a dry polish and polisher – a cloth impregnated with paraffin and malt vinegar gets rid of dust whilst leaving the boards shiny.*

10 *In this late 19thC American house, the boards are totally regular due to mass production. If the colour of the boards offends or the dust becomes unbearable they can be sealed. Try a test area first – seals seep into the boards and too often give a very yellow colour.*

11 *For the purist these Victorian pine floorboards give an authentic look to a 19thC floor.* LAS

8

10

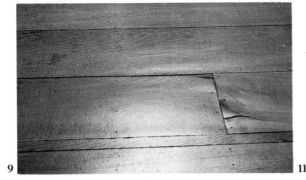

9

11

DECORATION AND COVERINGS

Until the 17th century, wooden floors were strewn with rushes for warmth and to keep down the dust. Sometimes instead of boards, lathes or rushes were laid to make the floor itself and smoothly coated with lime or gypsum plaster. Mats of rush or straw became more usual in the 16th century either on their own or as underlay for rare imported carpets. In the 17th century carpets began to be introduced more widely, especially in London; but they were generally used as hangings or table covers and it was not until at least a hundred years later that they would become at all common for floors.

Throughout the 18th century, floor coverings other than rush, straw or grass mats were still unusual, but paler, knotted deal boards were painted to darken them and hide their imperfections (in Bath, a mixture of soot and beer was used for the purpose). Later in the century, although the smart new houses were often carpeted, even when their floors were of good quality deal or Dutch oak, other fashions were developing. Floor colouring and patterning and the use of patterned, oiled floor cloths were much more common than carpets going into the 19th century.

To make plaster floors suitable for elegant houses pigments were added to plaster of Paris, and different parts of the country had long had local ways of colouring and patterning solid floors. Painted floors were an extension of this tradition and became very popular. With the application of stencilled patterns as well as plain coloured floors, the simple technique developed in North America into a fine craft which is enjoying a revival today.

In England patterned cloths were used to hide the imperfections of a deal floor. When placed under the table they made cleaning easier, and their geometric patterns in strong colours provided a decorative alternative to simple woven mats before cheap home-manufactured carpets became available.

THE 19TH CENTURY

More carpets were to be found in the 19th century, but floor painting survived in plain-painted and glazed floors, and in the borders round the carpet, which were often painted in the same colour as the rest of the room's woodwork. Oil cloths were also still used, on their own or to provide a surround to a central carpet; these were floral patterned, with designs more and more like Turkish carpets, or any other covetable carpet pattern. They developed a *trompe l'oeil* quality for, like the linoleum flooring and modern vinyls of which they were ancestors, they were patterned to look like natural materials – stone, marble or wood, knots and all. Then, as now, these cloths were despised by persons of "good taste".

By the middle of the 19th century carpets were common in the main rooms of even small houses, and linoleum replaced oil cloths at the end of the century. Floor boards, still about an inch (2.5cm) thick, were only about four inches wide (10cm) in better houses, though up to nine inches (23cm) wide in poorer quality dwellings. Tongued and grooved boards, which had been introduced in the 1820s, were increasingly machine-prepared and hence of even width. The timber used was well seasoned and will not usually have shrunk.

1 *Floor cloths were a practical 19thC solution to floor covering, especially in entrance halls. Either home-made or commercially manufactured, they were usually of canvas covered with many layers of paint and varnish, and were the forerunners of modern linoleum. This example, with a marbled pattern and a border adapted from a carpentry design, is an exact copy, painted onto linoleum, of a design that might have been used originally in this New York mansion of 1840.* BP

2 *This floor covering from this mid-19thC house in Lancaster, Pennsylvania, is laid throughout first-floor front and rear halls. It is stencilled in a geometric pattern to imitate tiles. The backing is made of cork, the surface is oil cloth. This was an extremely popular method of floor covering in both Britain and America at this time.* JBF

3,4 *This late 19thC linoleum border interestingly mimics the key pattern dado.* LSH

5 *This bleached beech tongue-and-groove flooring is a good modern solution to the challenge of replacing a period floor.*

6, 7, 8 *In parallel with the current interest in polished floorboards, stencilled floors are now very popular, and can be found in many colours and designs.* LG

9 *This staircase is carpeted in "Higford", a design based on an early 19thC pattern and seen here in its original colouring, in an American house.* C & F

6

7

8

9

PROBLEMS AND SOLUTIONS

Timber had become standard for ground floors during the 19th century, though it was not until 1860 that such floors were required by law to have an air gap beneath them. From 1900, air bricks were also provided in order to keep the air circulating, but neglect together with dislike of draughts have meant that this ventilation has often been stopped and the timber floors may well now be rotten as a result. To prevent deterioration of floor boards at ground level it is important to restore good ventilation by clearing away any earth lying against the outside walls and reopening any blocked air bricks.

Worm tunnels in timber floors may be aesthetically displeasing but are not in themselves a problem. Badly damaged parts of otherwise sound boards can be sawn out and replaced, and the quality of the wood usually makes up for the signs of woodworms once at work. Treatment with one of the proprietary sprays kills any live woodworm and prevents further infestation for a limited period.

Dry rot, detected by its damp smell, as well as signs (such as wood distortion) of the damage it has caused, is a different problem and often affects poorly ventilated ground floors. It must be carefully checked for and dealt with immediately when found. The fungus can spread rapidly through sound timber, plaster and even brickwork causing untreatable decay in any conditions once it has a hold. It is essential to remove and burn every bit of rot-affected timber when renovating an older house.

SOLID FLOORS

From the earliest times and into the 20th century solid floors were widely made of baked, dampened and beaten earth, patched with clay. Superior beaten earth floors could be made by mixing clay with ox blood, which dried to make a hard, smooth and gleaming surface, not unlike the quarry tiles which later replaced them.

During the 17th and early 18th centuries in Britain, the earth floors of prosperous farmers' houses were replaced with brick or kiln-burnt paviors (shaped like bricks but only about an inch and a half (4cm) thick) or square quarry tiles just like those still being manufactured today (measuring roughly nine by nine inches (23×23cm)). These are unglazed, but technically non-porous and therefore practical.

If suitable stone was available locally, huge flags would be laid instead of tiles. The various English marbles: Purbeck, Sussex, Kent and Derbyshire, were used only when the finest materials could be afforded. Many of the freestones were not suitable for flooring; but Bristol houses had blue stone slab floors, and other areas had a suitable local stone for flagging. Smarter houses reserved both flagging and tiling for pantries or other service rooms. In Devon and South Wales "pitched" floors were made from small pieces of stone cut with wedged backs and laid like street cobble-stones. These were arranged in patterns curiously like those of woven straw mats – a craft which survived into the 19th century. Local slate was successfully used for solid floors in parts of Wales and Cornwall, and this extremely waterproof material was transported to other parts of Britain in the 19th century.

Portland stone was used in big houses from the 17th century, often laid in diamond pattern rather than on the square, and with a small square of black marble at the intersection of the cut-off corners of every four meeting slabs. It was not until late in the 19th century that marble and other polished stones became available to the ordinary householder. Tessellated floors of white and black marble and coloured stone then became quite common, especially in entrance halls. From 1900 all sorts of stone, slate and ceramic tiles were used within the house to complement the tiled paths and porches which led in from outside.

1 A stone floor emulating a type made of Portland stone and marble popular from the 17thC.   CP

2 Basic stone flags have been a popular floor covering from the 17thC to the 20thC in more modest houses or servants' areas. They are serviceable but care should be taken not to leave the floor wet as salts can damage the surface. These particular huge blue stone slabs can be found in many Bristol houses of the late 18thC.

3 Lighter coloured stone flags are typical of many floors from the 17thC on. They varied according to the availability of local stone and were used extensively in the service areas of larger houses.

4 Warm coloured tiles make a solid floor less utilitarian. They look more inviting still when covered by rugs. FE

2

3

4

PROBLEMS AND SOLUTIONS

All the materials used for non-wood solid floors are hard-wearing, but some damp is nearly always present, if only rising through the joints. Although this may partly be due to condensation, which can be tolerable, or poor drainage of the site, which can be remedied outside, it will nearly always be rising through the tired fabric of the floor itself as well. The remedy is to have a damp-proof course laid (for which a local authority grant may be available). This involves removing the floor and storing it while a new base is made of hard-core, a damp-proof membrane, concrete, and a sand and cement screed onto which the floor is relaid.

You should do this for yourself only if you are experienced at building work; otherwise you should find a reliable contractor, as skill is involved as well as spadework. Although new materials of good quality are available, the signs of age are usually very much part of an old floor's charm. Some of the money you would save by re-using original materials could well be spent on the contractor's skill in relaying them, but many people still prefer to do this in order to preserve the character of the house.

CLEANING AND POLISHING

All these floors can be cleaned by scrubbing with water to which two tablespoons of washing soda have been added. When old polish has built up excessively, a cup of detergent and a cup of soda should be mixed in a pail of water, and the floor should be kept wet with this for half an hour before being scrubbed and rinsed.

Caustic soda is very effective for cleaning dirty, grease-stained quarry tiles and stone floors, used (with care) in the proportions of one tablespoon (15ml) (a wooden spoon should be used) to a gallon of water (4.5l), and well rinsed afterwards. Marble should be dried with a leather, and stains in it can sometimes be lightened with bleach, although they may reappear in time. Slate is improved by being cleaned with a 1:4 mixture of linseed oil and white spirit.

These materials are all maintenance-free, and it is simply a matter of taste whether or not they are polished.

Slate should be re-cleaned every few months to keep its lustre. Quarry tiles, paviors and stone can be given a gleam, using a polishing machine (which can be hired by the day), with a wax polish or one of the proprietary multi-purpose floor polishes, which also give some protection against stains. Liquid wax polish, well-buffed, brings life to dulled marble and polished stone but it should be used very sparingly if the floor is not to become dangerously slippery.

1

3

4

1 Reproductions of square quarry tiles. Many realistic copies of tiles dating from the 17thC in different parts of Britain and North America are now manufactured. FE

2 These original square quarry tiles have been relaid in a refurbished kitchen. PC

3 Brick paviors replaced the beaten earth floors in rural areas from the 17thC. These were popular until the late 19thC and are often used as replacements in country kitchens today.

4,5 It is possible to buy original tiles to be relaid. The tiles shown here are taken from period houses and chateaux in France prior to their being demolished. These have the advantage of a certain charm due to their age although they would not be strictly correct outside France. However, it should always be borne in mind that throughout history, particularly from the 18thC, the rich have imported period details from Europe to houses in Britain and North America PC

2

5

6

9

6, 7 *This mosaic floor was designed by George Aitchison, architect of Leighton House. It was executed by Italian craftsmen around 1879-80 and although it was probably of local English marble, the floor has proved a problem to restore.* LH

8 *Mosaic floors of white and black marble and coloured stones became very common in entrance halls in the late 19thC.*

9 *Geometric tiles were popular in entrance halls in the late 19thC. These were probably made by Maw of Coalbrookdale. The "welcome" mat is also in period.* LSH

10 *The mid-19thC "encaustic" tiles in the Minton residence in Torquay, Devon, are identical to those supplied by the Minton company to the Capitol, Washington D.C.*

11 *The tiles in the hall of the Minton residence are a form of early Victorian mosaic pavement. These tiles became increasingly popular during the 19thC especially in hallways and terraces. They added colour and interest while primarily being functional.* C

10

7

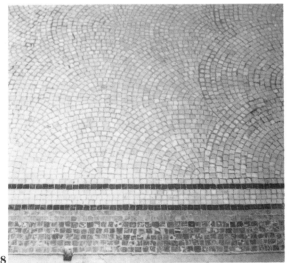

8

11

Bare walls are like giant canvases, and the impulse to decorate them is almost as old as civilization itself. But the origin of most methods of treating internal walls was functional — to make houses less damp and draughty.

The thick stone walls of medieval houses absorbed some water from outside and were hard and cold, encouraging condensation on the inside in winter. To reduce this, and to cut down draughts in the large open halls, the rich hung imported tapestries on walls and across doors. Later, woollen or canvas hangings in imitation of tapestry became increasingly common in houses of all sizes, and these were among the ancestors of modern wallpapers. Panelling was also used to line walls and act as screens. By Tudor times, this was often exquisitely carved in grand houses; in more humble ones it was developed into the fitted furniture that we find so useful in small houses today. By the 17th and 18th centuries simple oak or softwood panelling was common in the houses

2

of the gentry, and wood was further employed to add the classical detailing so much in vogue at the time.

Plastering walls began in Britain as a method of reducing heat loss or fire risk and strengthening wattle-and-daub walls. Yet colour washes of yellow ochres, blues and umbers can be found in plaster layers of early Anglo-Saxon origin. From this basic decorative start there developed the art of stucco and the parget work of East Anglia, culminating in the decorative swags of the Adam brothers in the 18th century.

Narrative scenes, patterns or simple colour washes enriched nearly all these wall coverings. The range of pigments and techniques has of course widened greatly and continues to change in line with fashion. Machine-printed rolls of paper brought quick, inexpensive decoration to every householder in the 19th century, and it is probably behind layers of this that you will find the clue to the original scheme for your house.

1

4

5

3

1 Many firms now produce wallpapers which use designs and colours to blend with a period house. Both 18th and 19thC designs are available. M. Armitage's hand-printed designs use traditional subjects in interesting new ways. MA

2 This wonderful wallscape in a house of the 1870s has, as a central feature, a bookshelf built in an unused doorway. Note too the olive green paint for skirting boards, dado and architrave. This all adds to the Victorian feel of the house. LSH

3 A faithful copy of a mid-18thC ballroom, reconstructed by careful study of original examples. IIII

4 Decorative ceramic tiles were features of many 19thC or early 20thC houses. Original examples have become expensive, but designers are now producing attractive examples such as this based on old patterns. MR

5 Plaster archways in this 18thC Bath house mirror the design of the cornice. The fake marbling on the walls is also in period. RC

PANELLING

In the 13th century Henry III imported wood from Norway and used it to line the rooms at Windsor Castle. These plain boards, unpanelled and unframed, were the first wainscots. They were intended to be painted, as were the plain plastered walls of the palaces. They were decorated with paintings of biblical stories, or stencilled (literally "starred") with gold, and whitewashed walls were "pointed" or patterned with a framework containing flowers. By Tudor times the fashion for panelling had spread in areas where timber was available. Oak panelling was used for screens, to line walls and as internal partitions to make more, and smaller, rooms within the large open walls. In these partitions, the narrow panelling boards were fixed into vertical studs, which were either split in half and fixed on each side of the boards or grooved to hold them. It was simpler to make narrow grooves, and accordingly the panels themselves were narrowed along their edges, creating the effect of raised surfaces. The middle of

such panels would be moulded with a rib as if to imitate stonework. The panels would usually also be set into a timber sill at the base and a frieze or moulded beam at the top, which gave the effect that was to develop into what is now known as linenfold.

The creation of linenfold, or "wavy woodwork" as it was called, had developed into a fine art by the early 16th century. Rectangular panels had fluted ribs placed close together, with realistic open folds at the tops, which were punched and carved to look like a needlework border. Sometimes the flowing ribs were opened out into honeycomb patterns or twined and interwoven and adorned with carved fruit and flower motifs.

By the middle of the 16th century a crude Renaissance classicism was taking over, as medallion heads and urns replaced linenfold. Sometimes, goemetric patterns with an inner square or rectangle surrounded by "L" shapes of moulding echoed those on the two-panelled doors. In the best examples different woods were used instead of painting for pattern, and by the end of the century arcading was sometimes used to

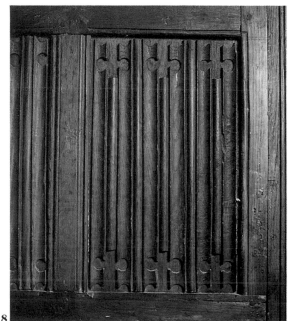

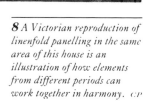

6, 7 These panels of wainscot have had a fairly adventurous history. Carved in the mid-16thC for a chapel in Kent, they eventually found their way into a late 19thC staircase made to fill the courtyard of a 17thC house. CP

8 A Victorian reproduction of linenfold panelling in the same area of this house is an illustration of how elements from different periods can work together in harmony. CP

9 Detail of a carved pilaster which is part of a careful restoration of a 16thC house in Somerset. SI separate the various panels, especially on the upper parts of the walls.

Applied pilasters began to appear on panelling in the grand houses of the 17th century. They were like those of the door cases, and were used for a similar reason – to provide an architrave which elegantly concealed the join between the stiles and the panels set into them. This device became prevalent in the big houses; like other classical borrowings it was often applied in a cheerfully unscholarly way, but sometimes the effect was very pleasing, with divisions in the length of the columns matching the divisions in the panelling itself. Applied pilasters – and columns – continued to be used in grand houses as classical architecture became a stricter discipline in the 18th century. As panelling went out of fashion pilaster strips and columns were applied to punctuate the wall surface or emphasize the window positions and give a flowing look to long rooms, as well as to divide the shelves in libraries.

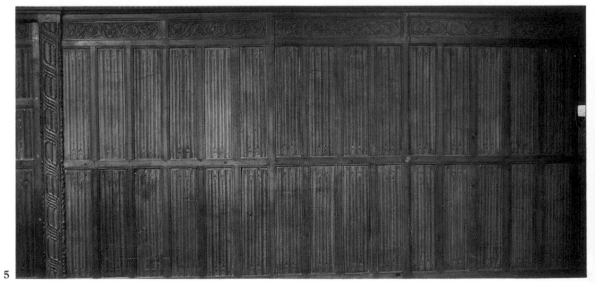

2

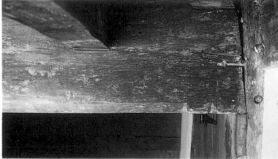

3

4

1

1, 2, 3, 4 Before decorative interior wall finishes became widely popular, it was not unusual for the boards that made up the fabric of the house to form the interior surface as well. VNS

5 Salvaged Tudor linenfold panelling with decorative pilasters and frieze has here been installed to create an authentic 16thC interior. C of SI.

5

6

8

10

7

9

6, 7, 8 *Simple panelling with sunk framed squares or rectangles was popular in the 16th and 17thC and is a particularly appropriate choice when restoring a country manor house. Such panelling is still made today using 17thC methods.* AS

9 *This room in a 17thC Oxfordshire manor had been robbed of all of its original features over the centuries, but recently it was completely restored – fireplace, panelling and ornate overmantel are all new but are faithful reproductions of the correct period of around 1640.* SI

10 *This panelling was put into a 17thC New York house about a hundred years after it was built, demonstrating how succeeding generations have always "improved" on their old houses. From the mid-17thC it was the fashion to paint not only softwood panelling, but also oak. So, if you have painted panelling in your house, do not feel you necessarily have to strip it.* BH

1, 2 The original panelling of this room of 1720 has been repainted in the style of the period, with marbled panels and authentic colours. At that period, paint for wood had a slightly glossy finish – oils, waxes or milk were included to achieve this effect. *SI*

3 Emulsion paint with a streaked effect gives the correct period flavour to the panelling of this 18thC room. *RC*

4 A George II panelled room, rescued complete from a house that was being demolished and reinstated in another house of the period. *C of SL*

5 An interior of the same period that has undergone the same happy fate. This time the panelling is waxed pine. The room has a dentilled cornice and door surrounds and a chimneypiece carved with masks flanked by drapery swags. *C of SL*

1

2

3

4

5

6

7

8

9

10

6 *Simple but elegant painted panelling is featured in a house built in the Bronx in the second half of the 18thC. The colouring is authentic.* vc

7 *An elegantly carved pediment over this door is set off by fairly plain panelling and cornice. The room is a copy of a 1760s interior. The pine panelling, unpainted in the original, has mellowed to a marvellous honey.*

8 *A late 19thC answer to the problem of concealing the heating system. This cast-iron grille conceals a hot air duct. It neatly fills one whole panel, its formal decoration complementing the chestnut and walnut.*

9, 10 *Panelled rooms of the 18thC often featured ornate carving in the form of swags, fruit, leaves and classical motifs. These are by a follower of William Kent.* cofsi.

EARLY FITTED FURNITURE

Wooden partitions and straightforward boarded or rectangular-panelled wainscotting were used increasingly in modest houses from the beginning of the Tudor period. From such features, the first fitted furniture developed. Lack of space meant that living rooms had to double as bedrooms. In the 16th century, many two-roomed dwellings consisted of two bed-sitting rooms, with the beds neatly boxed into an alcove and hidden by a curtain during the day – a tradition strong in Scotland.

During the 17th century this development was refined, with beds hidden completely behind wainscot-like panelling by sliding doors across the opening. Similarly, a fixed seat might run along the panelling, with the panelling itself acting as a settle back, perhaps decorated with a painted pattern, perhaps folding down to form a bed. Examples of this built-in furniture survive in parts of Wales, northern England and across the Channel in Brittany.

In vernacular buildings, where change was slow, the wooden partition dividing the rooms from the passage often contained seating or cupboards on the room side. Beside the fire, a built-in spice cupboard was worked in similar style, and sometimes a much larger cupboard was to be found in the same position. These handsome features, rather than filtering down from higher up the social scale, developed out of necessity and are rare examples of features which then ascended the social ladder. From early in the 18th century, the alcoves produced on either side of the fire by the chimney breast were put to use as cupboards in the new townhouses, in England and in North America, with panelled and well-proportioned doors and frames — the modern instinct to build cupboards or shelves in this position has a long history. The fireside alcoves were also adapted into niches, sometimes with covered tops of modelled plasterwork, in imitation of styles in grander houses.

1 Building furniture – particularly wardrobes – into a period house can all too easily spoil the period feel. It can be done, but the style must be chosen carefully. This wall of cupboards, drawers and glazed display cabinets, for example, would work well in a well-proportioned 18th or early 19thC bedroom. s

2 A Neo-classical room with finely moulded cornice and walls painted in one of the light shades favoured by the brothers Adam. GH

3 A cleverly faked and antiqued library in an 18thC building. The cornice (an elaborate reproduction) and also the bookcases were dragged in two shades of green . CP

4

7

4 *This panelled hall and staircase are a 19thC addition to an earlier house. This is a good example of the Victorians' habit of imposing their own taste on a building with little regard for its original character. However, it is here done with such confidence that somehow it works!* CP

5, 6 *A restored turn-of-the-century room with mahogany panelling and doors and Art Nouveau-style marquetry panels. Fortunately, there are still craftsmen able to carry out this type of work.* RDL

7, 8 *Built in furniture is by no means a recent invention. This fitted dresser and chest-of-drawers in an 18thC house in Bath look quite surprisingly modern.* GH

5

6

8

PLASTER

The plasterer's art developed alongside the use of timber. Stucco or moulded plasterwork was much used in Palladian and Neoclassical houses of the 18th century, but it had first been used some 200 years earlier in Henry VIII's palace of Nonesuch. It appeared in friezework and panels in many of the great Tudor and Jacobean houses, modelled into stylized scenes, with countryside, forests, beasts and huntsmen, or scenes from mythology, and often painted.

Modelled stucco was a European, especially Italian tradition, but in the late 16th and early 17th centuries a native style developed in England. This was known as parget work. It was executed in the plaster mix of lime, sand, animal hair and dung with which the walls were usually lined. Parget work is particularly associated with East Anglia, though by no means confined to that area, and is found on both internal and external walls for friezes, overmantels and gable ends. The craft died out at the end of the 17th century as it became difficult to obtain plasterers of high quality.

This plaster was so strong that much parget work has survived. Its formal patterns are still familiar to us with their herringbone, basket work, strap work,

2

2 *This 18thC room had several "layers" of restoration. It was refurbished during the later 19thC, and recently the two doors were added. When creating new doorways, make sure that they balance with the existing architecture. Here the proportions of the doors are correct and their symmetrical positioning within the arch is in harmony with the room.* CP

3 *A niche in a Neo-classical interior may be painted a darker shade of the wall colour to give it more definition and set off objects placed against it. The choice of a marble pillar and bust is correct for the period.* BP

4 *Around the turn of the century there was something of a classical revival in both architectural detail and wall colouring. Creams, pinks and pale greens and greys are good choices for such interiors.*

1

1 *The wallpaper border in this American house shows clearly the way in which Empire decoration has been overlaid on earlier, Federal period architecture.* MJ

3

4

combed waves and charming and naive birds and human figures, myths and fables.

Hand-modelled plasterwork was originally applied to ceilings, cornices and friezes. It was the Palladian architects who, abandoning the use of panelling, introduced wall plasterwork and plaster wall panels based on a French pattern, and framed ornament with swagged surrounds were soon to become the fashion. Examples of such plaster modelling, with scenes from mythology set within panels of plaster architrave, with pediments and swags, can be seen in the houses built in Bath from 1727.

Later in the century the Adam br ... ornament widely for inside walls. D ... appearance, their graceful decorativ ... something of an innovation. They used a mixture known as Liardet's preparation, containing gypsum or fibre and glue, the exact composition of which is not known. Instead of being modelled *in situ* it was pressed when hot into metal moulds. The Adams painted their groundwork in light tints of pink, green or blue to relieve the ornament, and sometimes the ornament itself was painted. The mass-produced mouldings of the 19th century were merely a development of this approach and can themselves be reproduced by taking further moulds.

5

6

7

8

5, 6 A good alternative to distressing walls to resemble marbling, graining and so on is the paint-effect wallpapers currently on the market. Here such papers have been successfully used in a grand 18thC interior. The plaster columns followed the classical tradition of the early 19thC. CP

7,8 The Victorians were great travellers and collectors. Lord Leighton, who lived in this grand house, travelled extensively in the Middle East and his wanderings greatly influenced the decoration. The columns in this case are marble. The screen was brought back from Damascus, and the room is hung with brocaded silk creating an opulent Arabian mood. LH

PAINT AND PAPER

The most frequently used hand-mixed paints, for over six hundred years, were simple whitewash, colour washes with pigments added to the whitewash to give ochre yellow or red, blues and greens, or limewash, which had slaked lime as a main constituent and seems to have had disinfectant qualities. A more glossy finish came from paints which contained a proportion of oils, waxes, or even milk; these were the ancestors of our emulsion paints. They were used for wainscots and indoor woodwork from the mid-17th century, and we now know that all but the finest timbers were painted – our taste for stripped pine would have seemed very odd to our ancestors.

With the increasing variety of paint pigments available during the late 1600s, it became fashionable to completely hide the timber used for panelling by covering it with cloth, paper, or even leather. At the same time silks and papers were used to decorate plastered walls in expensive interiors, backed with linen and mounted on wooden frames that were nailed to the walls. Small pieces of patterned paper, publishers' rejects, had also been made available since the 15th century in an enterprising waste-not, want-not spirit and were glued by artistic householders to the insides of cupboards and chests.

As printing developed printed wallpapers were produced to replace more expensive cloth hangings.

But even wallpaper was quite a luxury. It was made by hand from shredded cloth, and as part of the manufacturing process involved draining it in flat sieves, it was available only in quite small pieces, based on the dimensions of the sieves. Nevertheless, it was common enough to be taxed from 1694.

Elizabethan wallpapers were patterned and coloured with stencilling or hand-painted designs, often with heraldic shields, vases and flowers very similar to the plasterwork of the time. Tiny flowers on bright backgrounds were popular in the 16th and 17th centuries. By the end of the period brocades were imitated and flocked papers replaced real hangings.

Increased Eastern trade late in the 17th century meant that luxurious papers could be imported from China. These came in large pieces decorated with scenes of flowers, birds, villages, mountains and clouds and were popular in the stylish Palladian houses of the 1700s. Towards the end of the 18th century, plasterwork was again imitated with delicate Neoclassical prints, while Georgian townhouses had another treatment for walls in which paper backgrounds were "distressed" or "scumbled" with oil paints to produce the effect of marbling or clouding.

1

3

2

4

1,2 These are two examples of 20thC reconstructions of 18thC wallpaper taken from fragments discovered on the walls. These paper borders were a fairly common device in American houses redecorated in the Empire taste. MJ

3,4 Original hand-painted Chinese papers can be found both at auctions and in specialist shops. These papers were created by the Chinese for the European market and were used in English stately homes during the 18th and early 19thC. Those shown here are the "bird and flower" type – a common design on the porcelain of the period. Such papers need expert hanging and often need some restoration once they are installed. TC

5   6   7

8   9

10   11

Simultaneously, cheaper "domino" prints with little geometric designs, of the type often found again today, were produced. Their use was generally restricted to the sitting room and the best bedroom; elsewhere, whitewash or tinted whitewash was still the rule, with stencilling providing any pattern. Stencilling was extremely popular in the USA from the late 1700s and survived well into the 19th century.

Printing methods improved, and early in the 19th century a method of producing continuous rolls was patented with the result that wallpapers became much more common, and tax on them eventually had to be dropped in 1861. Nevertheless plain tinted whitewash (or distemper) continued well into the 20th century and was given a further lease of life by the restrictions caused by the Second World War.

While other manufacturers were producing cheap substitutes for stone and wood, and casting moulded plaster by the yard, Victorian wallpaper makers developed imitation panelling and moulding in embossed papers which soon completely replaced wall plasterwork. By the end of the 1900s every house had this "Lincrusta" paper up to the dado rail and machine-printed patterned paper above. Very similar, but much lighter and more pliable embossed papers are available now to give the original look to Victorian

8,9 *These hand-printed wallpapers using traditional themes and colours would be ideally suited to 18th or 19thC rooms. It is worth remembering that the effect is often more dramatic if the paintwork is painted a complementary colour.* JO

10,11 *These papers give the right feel in a period room as the blocks are cut and the paper printed by hand. This method also gives a wider colour choice as the inks are individually mixed.* MA houses, although the rich patterns and sombre colours of some of the printed papers may not be to everyone's decorative taste.

Since the practice of stripping off old wallpaper is a recent one, the layers of old papers can usually still be found in unrestored Victorian and later houses and this will give a clear idea of how the house was decorated. You are most likely to find machine-printed papers, which almost completely ousted hand-blocked prints by the middle of the 19th century. Woodblock printing was kept alive by designers such as William Morris, but their use was restricted to those discerning people who could afford to pay for hand-work. These deliberately two-dimensional prints have remained in production for over a hundred years, and are still available. Ironically perhaps, they are more often found in Victorian houses now than when they were first produced.

1 *The decoration in this Georgian mansion, built in the Palladian style, is mainly in the French Empire manner.*

The walls in the bedroom were papered and then finished with a paper border. The colour is authentic to the 18thC. MJ

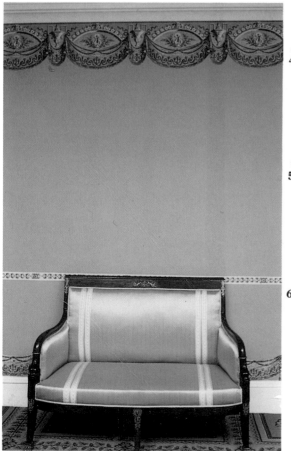

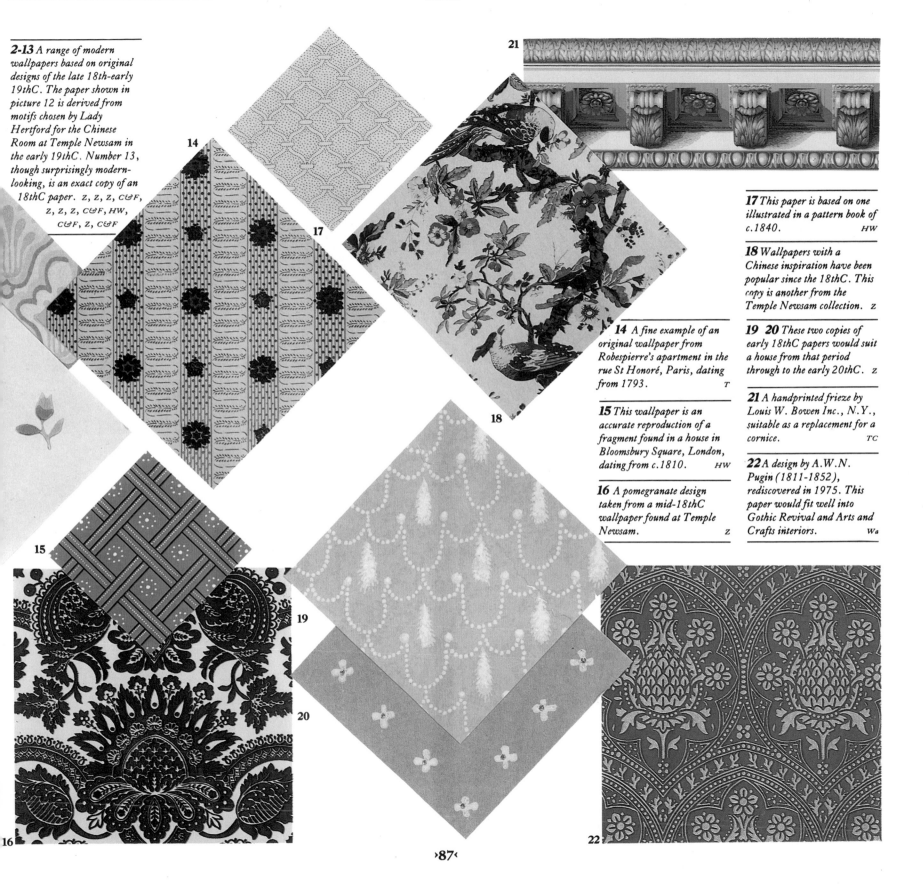

2-13 *A range of modern wallpapers based on original designs of the late 18th-early 19thC. The paper shown in picture 12 is derived from motifs chosen by Lady Hertford for the Chinese Room at Temple Newsam in the early 19thC. Number 13, though surprisingly modern-looking, is an exact copy of an 18thC paper.* z, z, z, C&F, z, z, z, C&F, HW, C&F, z, C&F

14 *A fine example of an original wallpaper from Robespierre's apartment in the rue St Honoré, Paris, dating from 1793.* T

15 *This wallpaper is an accurate reproduction of a fragment found in a house in Bloomsbury Square, London, dating from c.1810.* HW

16 *A pomegranate design taken from a mid-18thC wallpaper found at Temple Newsam.* z

17 *This paper is based on one illustrated in a pattern book of c.1840.* HW

18 *Wallpapers with a Chinese inspiration have been popular since the 18thC. This copy is another from the Temple Newsam collection.* z

19 20 *These two copies of early 18thC papers would suit a house from that period through to the early 20thC.* z

21 *A handprinted frieze by Louis W. Bowen Inc., N.Y., suitable as a replacement for a cornice.* TC

22 *A design by A.W.N. Pugin (1811-1852), rediscovered in 1975. This paper would fit well into Gothic Revival and Arts and Crafts interiors.* Wa

1

1 The Victorians had no hesitation about mixing pattern and surface decoration in their interiors. This late 19thC artist's house exemplifies how well such mixes can work. The whole interior is beautifully integrated. *LSH*

2 This wallpaper in the same house was made in Japan by an English firm, Rothman and Co. It is embossed and gilded to look like leather and was so expensive that it was used very sparingly: there is none behind the pictures or the Florentine mirrors! *LSH*

3 The dark colour under the dado rail and the darker skirting add to the enclosed feel of this Victorian interior. Note the stick rack. *LSH*

4,5 These Lincrusta papers are based on Art Nouveau and Edwardian originals *C*

2

3

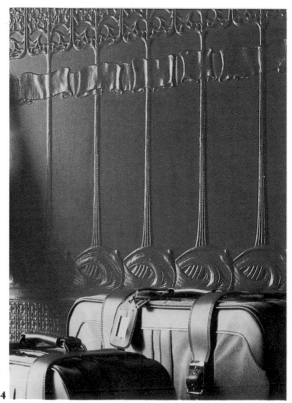

4

5

6

7

8

9

10

6 Murals, frieze paintings and trompe l'oeil *can be effectively introduced into most period houses. The decorative style of* trompe l'oeil *works best in 18th and 19thC houses.* CB

7 Figure painting was of special interest in the 18thC. It works well in period houses, but you should select the artist carefully. TP

8,9 The range of possibilities for trompe l'oeil *is extensive. Paintings of vistas, windows and furniture are popular themes.* TP

10 Stencilling is an effective wall decoration and can be used in most periods of houses so long as the general feel of the room is taken into account. It has always been popular in America and has recently come into vogue in Britain.

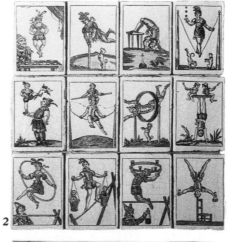

1 *These wonderful 15th and 16thC Persian tiles were brought back by a Victorian collector and now decorate a late 19thC London house.* I.H

2,3 *These allegorical tiles are based on a traditional 17thC design and made by the traditional method. This gives them the slight imperfections which blend with period settings.* PC

4 *Hand-painted tiles like these Spanish examples can be used as a panel or a border.* PC

5 *Blue and white is such a classic tile coloration that modern designs still retain a period feel.* BCS

6 *Hand-painted tiles made by traditional methods may be more expensive but successfully recreate the Dutch Delft originals. These tiles were designed by ceramic artist Doug Wilson.* PC

7,8 *Tiles can also create a trompe l'oeil effect and can give the impression of a niche in a wall. Geometric patterns and flowers are classic motifs here used in an innovative and interesting way.* SR

9 *By the end of the 19thC tiles were produced in strong colours. This modern tile has a similar inspiration and could be used to good effect in 19thC as well as 20thC homes.* MR

10 *Vases of flowers with simple borders have been used on tiles since the 18thC. These hand-painted tiles in strong colours provide excellent panels.* SR

11 *This blue and white panel successfully uses themes popular on tiles from the 18thC. As many original panels have been damaged, such hand-painted modern tiles are a useful alternative.* SR

12 *Tiles can also be used on exteriors and these highly glazed ochre, brown and deep blue tiles form an interesting archway to a late 19thClearly 20thC facade.* S of D

13 *As original 18thC English delft tiles become more expensive and difficult to find, replacements using sketchy designs can be found from firms specializing in modern reproductions.* FE

9

10

11

12

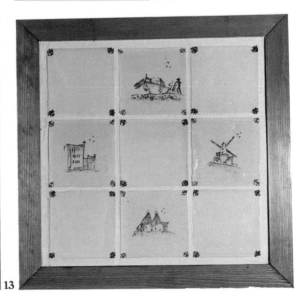

13

1 *Prints interestingly placed on a staircase wall lead the eye upwards. The plain walls in this example of a late 19thC hallway are brought to life by the prints in maple frames, some original and some reproduction.*

2,3,4 *These exuberant examples of Victorian wallscapes show great confidence in mixing dark colours, wallpapers, prints, mirrors and Chinese porcelain. The owner of this house was a noted cartoonist and obviously had a special interest in drawings, paintings, prints and photographs. But the general effect can be recreated by*

similar handling of masses of mostly monochromatic pictures. Used singly on such busy backgrounds the pictures would have been lost; but grouping them to almost cover the walls gives them unity and importance. In picture 3 it is interesting to note the combination of oil paintings, Japanese prints, silhouettes, mirrors and medallions. I.S.H

5 *Simply framed photographs (mainly of the house's owner Mr Linley Samborne) cover a bathroom wall. Again the whole effect is gained by the sheer quantity of pictures decorating most of the wall area.* I.S.H

1

2

3

4

5

1

5

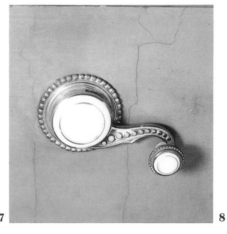

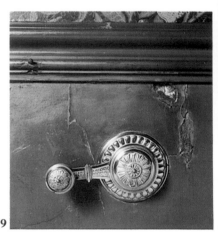

6

7

8

9

DADO RAILS

Dado rails complemented skirtings. Again they are a reminder of earlier wall treatments, being placed at the height of the middle rail in panelling. Visually pleasing but also practical, dado rails protected the wall where chairs were most likely to scrape, and thus may also be called "chair rails".

Often the dado rail was inversely related in outline to the skirting board; the greatest projection was at the upper part of the rail, whereas on skirtings it was nearest the floor. In the later 19th century, dado rails are found less frequently, except in entrance halls and on stairways, and mouldings became simpler.

When walls are being replastered to tackle damp, it is well worth keeping a record of the exact position and profile of the original skirting boards and dado rails, as even in the simplest houses these were often sensitively proportioned and deserve to be carefully replaced. Where the skirtings and rails are in plaster and you cannot match the mouldings in wood, make new ones from a mould taken from the originals: they will then blend in perfectly.

1 In the very grandest rooms in 18thC houses, walls might be covered in fine fabrics such as silk damask. Here the joins have been covered in gilded beading which serves also to define the lines of the room. There are many companies today specializing in putting fabric on walls and advising on appropriate types to use. Braid would be an apt substitute for the beading. Note the deep moulding on this dado rail which reflects the deep skirting below. RC

2 An 18thC house can have walls simply painted in a suitable colour. Here, blue walls are set off by panelling and mouldings in white. The dado is part of the panelling – a common feature at this time. RC

3 From the 17thC small geometric wallpaper designs were being used in the houses of the gentry. This paper in the bedroom of a restored 18thC house is a copy of one of the period from Temple Newsam, Leeds. Wallpaper designs in country regions lagged dramatically behind those in capital cities. Laura Ashley's early mini-prints were based on fragments of wallpaper found in a 19thC cottage in Wales. As these would have been up to a hundred years out-of-date by London standards, her designs fit well into 18thC as well as 19thC interiors. The paper is given a more authentic look in this well-researched Georgian house by the plain colour from dado to skirting. RC

4 This Georgian room has paper of a much later period, but the design successfully picks up the detail from the panelling, giving the room the correct feel. The dado here is quite elaborate with the central motif picked out in gilding. GH

5 If you cannot afford to line the walls of your 18thC drawing room with fabric, a paper which simulates a fine fabric (such as moire) is a helpful possibility. CP

6 Strong colours can work in well-proportioned period rooms – provided that they are based on authentic colours of the period. The secret is to use them with conviction. CP

7,8,9 These three examples show the interesting variety in bell pulls. The Georgians often used sashes or decorative brass pulls. The Victorians also used these but added china pulls decorated with gilding or painted with flowers. An interesting feature of picture 8 is the revival of the classical key pattern frieze under the dado. Most homeowners today do not need bells to summon up legions of servants. However, if you are lucky enough to find pulls intact in your house, leave them in as a novel period feature. LSH

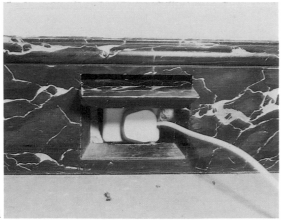

10   11   12

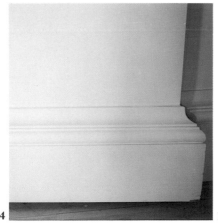

13   14   15

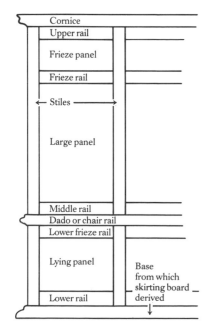

| Cornice |
| Upper rail |
| Frieze panel |
| Frieze rail |
| ← Stiles → |
| Large panel |
| Middle rail |
| Dado or chair rail |
| Lower frieze rail |
| Lying panel |
| Lower rail |

Base from which skirting board derived ↓

Panelling: THE NAMING OF PARTS

By the mid-17th century a pattern based on classical proportioning had been developed for the wainscot. A base, or *sill*, had a panel above it known as the *lying panel*. This was fixed at the top into the *middle rail, chair rail* or *dado rail*. The second level of panelling, known as the *large panel*, was fixed at the bottom to the middle rail and at the top to the *frieze rail*, above which ran a further panel, the *frieze panel*. In higher rooms the frieze panel would be surmounted by an upper rail and cornice, and extra rails would be placed above the base and above and below the middle rail. The diagram, which shows the typical arrangement for higher rooms, would make a suitable model from which to plan reconstruction work for wainscoting in 18th- or 19th-century houses.

10, 11 These marbled skirtings in an 18thC house in Bath have been skilfully adapted to conceal the electric sockets essential to 20thC life.   RC

12, 13, 14 Stripping woodwork of its painted surface is very much a modern fashion, but one which often works well in a period house. Painted woodwork is correct for most Victorian interiors, but bare wood is fine for an 18thC or early 20thC context, and is certainly easy to live with.

15 Sombre colours are typical of the Victorian period, although black woodwork like this can be a little too much to live with!   LH

SKIRTING

The skirting board was a consequence of the 18th-century preference, in grand houses, for plastered walls rather than panelling. Marble floors had a marble skirting which protected the wall when the floor was being cleaned. However, 18th-century skirting boards were usually made of wood. Plaster was frequently found in 19th-century houses.

A reminder of the sill of old panelling, these deep skirtings were moulded and often intricately carved – in keeping with the architraves around windows and doors and with the shutters of the room. Palladian houses have rich but restrained and subtly varied carving: the "egg-and-tongue" type of moulding was especially popular. Deep but simply moulded skirting boards are characteristic of Victorian and Edwardian houses, becoming shallower and more austere as the 20th century wore on.

Ceilings

When houses were chiefly one high open space the only ceiling was the inside of the roof. Timber-framed houses were usually thatched and the underside of the thatch, increasingly blackened by soot, was all that could be seen from the room below. Even when pantiles were used (as in East Anglia) a layer of thatch was put beneath as lining and insulation.

The introduction of an upper floor naturally created a ceiling in the lower room. At first the term "ceiling", or "sealing", referred to the panelling which lined or sealed the walls of a room. However, when the underside of upper floors came to be treated in the same way, the word came to acquire its current usage.

As with so many architectural elements, the earliest treatments for the undersides of floors survived in vernacular buildings long after they had been superseded elsewhere. Thatch roofs were often sealed on both sides with lime plaster, partly to reduce fire risk and partly to make them longer-lasting and even warmer. Sometimes upper floors were simply plastered rushes laid between the narrowly spaced joists. Wooden floorboards laid over the joists were often sealed on the underside with plaster too, for insulation and cleanliness, leaving the joists themselves exposed. Ceilings like this continued to be made in country houses **1**

1 Many original beamed ceilings were painted, and any traces of this should be preserved. Complete restorations should follow appropriate period colours. In this example red, cream, blue and gilding give the room a mellow "aged" feel.

for hundreds of years and still look right today.

The bare undersides of floorboards made a simpler ceiling still. However, if the original wide floorboards of oak or elm have been replaced with narrower pine boards, the visual impact may be inferior, and it will be preferable to apply a coat of plaster between the joists for sound or heat insulation between lower and upper floors. When this practice was followed in the 17th century, the space between the boards and the plaster was filled with straw. The modern version of this is to use lengths of fibre-glass insulation between floorboards and plaster-board panels on the ceiling below.

As vernacular building skills were dying out early in the 20th century, there was a curious fashion for painting joists black to give an "olde worlde" country look. However, this has no foundation in history. Fine timber in better-quality houses was usually left untreated, but for centuries in cottages and farmhouses the joists and floorboards have been limewashed, occasionally with pigments added, or patterned with flowers and leaves. With great patience you can remove 20th-century black and restore the ceiling woodwork by sanding and treating with paint stripper. Often the dark staining has penetrated the wood, so that planing may even be necessary. An alternative is to paint white or off-white emulsion directly over the black to give an acceptable and hard-wearing period effect. Limewash, which needs to be reapplied more frequently, may be used by the purist restorer.

Tudor Ornament

Timber beams and joists were at first merely functional, but the Tudors saw decorative possibilities in them. Using the limited tools available then, they began to give them champfered corners and mouldings similar to those on stone ribs. Many handsome Tudor ceilings have survived, with oak beams chiselled and gouged into smoothly flowing ribs, like those in the linenfold panelling of the same period. The undersides of beams could be carved

2

3

2 Tudor beams were often painted. Such decoration should be preserved if possible. Restoration should only be undertaken by an expert, as colours have to be carefully matched.

3 Friezes are one of the great joys of Tudor interiors. The carving often reached great heights of grotesque ornamentation.

with Gothic ornament, and gaps between them further divided by mouldings.

The Tudors also became prolific plasterers. Like the wooden ceilings, the plaster ones were at first divided into compartments by moulded ribs with plaster bosses or pendants at their intersections, just as in stone vaulting. Gradually, ribs became flatter and developed into the characteristic strapwork, with lozenges and geometric shapes, scrolls and Tudor roses. Bosses and pendants punctuated the junctions where ribs intersected. Much of the repeated background ornament was made in moulds, while figures and other ornament in deep relief were hand-modelled *in situ*.

Early in the Tudor period wooden friezes were carved and moulded to match the heavy beams. Plaster ceilings also were soon accompanied by a modelled plaster frieze. Although coving was sometimes used at the conjunction of wall and ceiling, deep plaster friezes **5**

4

6

8

were more often applied at the tops of walls. They had an even greater wealth of decoration than the ceilings themselves. There was no real precedent for the frieze, and its ornament developed freely. Dolphins and mermaids were much liked; secular and biblical narratives were told in high relief; scrolls, lozenges, acorns and flowers complemented identical motifs on the ceilings; and landscapes based on Flemish engravings unfolded around the top of the walls. Sometimes the ornament featured personifications of the Virtues or the senses. Such flourishes, naturally restricted to the greater houses, came to an end as purist classical influences were felt, although they were to enjoy a vernacular revival some hundred years later.

In lesser houses plastered ceilings also became more ornamental, though less spectacularly so. They spread over the beams and joists themselves, with ornamented

panels on the flat infilling and mouldings on the beams. Unplastered ceilings were frequently lined between the beams with tongued-and-grooved boarding, again divided into compartments by strips of moulding and sporting carved wooden bosses – when, that is, the owners could afford such embellishment. Plain timber boarding was often used for farmhouse and cottage ceilings in succeeding centuries, usually white-washed or painted and sometimes extending over the beams to form a flat ceiling.

4 Some rot has to be expected in beams that have survived 300 years. Parts of beams can be replaced, and this may well be essential with structural beams. If possible, however, you should cut back to good wood and treat with a proprietary brand of woodworm killer. Over-restoration can be totally counterproductive. CP

5 The 18thC addition to this house saw little improvement in insulation. The ceiling is just the inside of the roof shingles.

6 It has recently been accepted that the natural honey colour of oak is in itself a delight and the practice of painting or staining black is totally unnecessary. If beams have been painted, sanding is the most effective solution. Protect your furnishings adequately against the dust.

7 This 17thC New York house has a perfect example of a beamed ceiling of the time. The beams were hewn from white oak close to the house and the ceiling is merely the underside of the floorboards above.

8 When taking a ceiling down to expose the beams underneath, one is usually left with lathe marks. You can remove these by sanding, although this gives the beams a very new look. Waxing with clearwax will often create a pleasing effect.

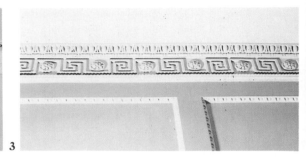

1 **2** **3**

1 Note the fine cotton damask used in the first-floor drawing room of this late 18thC house. This was usually the most richly decorated room, as it was used principally for entertaining. The cornice and frieze are original. RC

2 This pierced cornice is typical of the late 18thC. Such cornices should be vacuumed at least once a year. If the moulding is finely carved, clean with a small brush. RC

CLASSICISM

In his work for the Court in the 1620s and 30s Inigo Jones introduced smoothly plastered and often coved and painted ceilings decorated with mouldings and gilded ornament in a much more authentic classical tradition. After 1630 and as a result largely of Jones's influence, plaster dolphins, badges and pendants took over from compact fruit and flowers, ribbons and wreaths, musical instruments and suspended cherubs in many great houses. Perhaps to our eye plasterwork had lost some of its earlier verve but it remained highly decorative in Palladian houses in Britain into the 18th century and in North America up to the 1750s. By Regency times the divided ceilings of the Palladians with their heavily ornamented compartments and elaborate friezes and cornices were thought to be ponderous and ugly. The Adam brothers ridiculed them almost as much as they ridiculed the mid-century vogue for French Rococo ornament.

In Georgian houses right across the scale of wealth, relief plasterwork was very much in demand, often

4

3,4 Two examples of cornices which show the refined classical taste so prevalent in the late 18th and early 19thC. RC

5,6 Classical swags on the frieze were a popular late 18th and early 19thC design. The first example here is a modern reproduction. The second, with a Greek key pattern cornice, is original.

5 **6**

7

8

15

9

10

providing surprising contrasts to the rather plain exteriors of the houses. Italian plasterers from France took their art to Dublin and there you can find grand schemes in plaster relief with gods and clouds and birds in flight and borders of acanthus leaves. These feature even in relatively modest houses as the Italians' work was imitated and developed by local craftsmen during the 1740s.

The Adam brothers revolutionized all this with their chaste ornament in Grecian or Etruscan style for ceilings, friezes and walls. Meanwhile, owners of humbler contemporary houses contented themselves with a straightforward cornice. The very simplest houses either continued in the floorboards-and-joists tradition or, in towns, had plain plastered ceilings and nothing more.

11

12

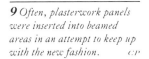

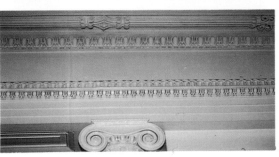

13

14

7,8 *Two cornices from a New York house built in 1765. The first picture shows some of the architectural wallpaper fashionable in the Federal period, used extensively in hallways in the 18th and 19thC. The second, in a bedroom, is a plain cornice in the style popular from the 18th to the 20thC.* MJ

9 *Often, plasterwork panels were inserted into beamed areas in an attempt to keep up with the new fashion.* CP

10 *Deep cornices such as this one are often found in high rooms. Owing to years of over-painting, such cornices may sometimes be left with no real detail. The most effective method of cleaning is by hand with a paint stripper. This often loosens pieces of plaster, and instant repairs may be necessary.*

11 *The fashion for white painted ceilings gave more light and started a new trend for a decorative plastered effect.* CP

12,13 *Two views of an elaborate cornice and pillar from the parlour of an early 19thC New York house. The cornice is accentuated by being painted in three tones.* OMII

14 *This early 18thC cornice would have been added to the house during remodelling in 1728. The leaf design is of particular interest: a new mould had to be made for each leaf. Today, we have the advantage of rubber, but such cornices are still expensive to restore.* CP

15 *In this reproduction of a mid-18thC American house the cornice decoration is in carved wood.* IIII

1 The Victorians often imitated a much earlier design, as this late 19thC ceiling shows. It is a good copy of the Chinese Chippendale style, although the cornice is slightly too ornate. CP

THE 19TH CENTURY

The *nouveaux riches* of the turn of the century tended to opt for profuse decoration in their houses. Their ceilings were stuccoed and painted with landscapes and mythical scenes. Later in the century the many new houses being built also enjoyed the luxury of decoration. Cornices and friezes were cast in moulds, and a sort of *papier mâché* was often used for ornaments so that despite their elaborateness they were light enough to be fixed in place with screws.

Compared with earlier craftwork this moulded decoration, which remained in favour into the 20th century, certainly owes more to repetition than to inspiration. Nevertheless, acanthus-leaf cornices and heavy central ceiling roses in halls, and main rooms of 19th-century houses are very much part of their imitable style. They have often been made ugly by successive coatings of distemper which have blurred their relief, and will be much improved with careful cleaning. There are specialist restorers who undertake this work; however, it can done by anyone whose affection for the original is enough to inspire endless patience. A crisp relief will repay the careful work involved, giving a marked uplift to the room.

At the end of the 19th century there was a new emphasis on craftsmanship and individualism. Rather than conforming to a predetermined model, each room was treated as a unique problem with its own solution with regard to the size, angle and enrichment of cornice, ceiling bands and other decoration. Flower and leaf ornament and scrolls and loops were sometimes used very expressively in domestic public buildings. The pattern and depth of relief were scaled to suit the ceiling height. Schemes were determined by the shape of the room and the position of the windows. The acorn was a much-loved motif. Other themes included oak trees, squirrels, daisies and even fairies; sometimes these motifs were coloured while the plaster was still comparatively moist.

At the same time new methods of mass-producing plasterwork were being found, using clay models to make jelly (gelatine) moulds. Definition was lost in the process, so that castings from such moulds were indistinct. Today, however, the jelly mould comes into its own as a way of casting replacements for damaged work to match existing ornament.

1

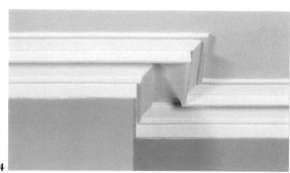

4

2

5

2 As the 19thC progressed, friezes were often incorporated into other features to augment the decorative effect. CP

3, 4 These simple but elegant Greek Revival cornices were used in both Britain and America from the late 18th to the end of the 19thC. Their very simplicity contributed to their longevity. BP

5,6,7 The simple classical cornice in the main reception room of a New York house built in 1875 is in direct contrast to the plaster columns and arches (pictures 6 and 7).

6

7

12 Cornices in bedrooms were usually simpler than those in the main rooms of the house. However, this elegant pattern would have been considered suitable for the living room in a lesser early 19thC house. OMH

8,9,10,11 The 19thC saw a tremendous revival of interest in all things classical. In many houses columns, both Doric and Ionic, suddenly appeared as purely decorative features. They could be wooden, stone or marble. LH, LH, CP, OMH

In the 19thC the ceiling rose became an essential adjunct of a tastefully decorated room. The size and complexity of the rose was dictated by the room's importance. There are many different types, often needing careful cleaning to show the true magnificence of the plasterwork.

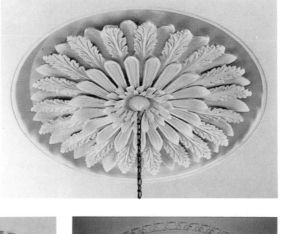

1

2

1 These ceiling roses would be quite acceptable for use in houses built between the later years of the 18thC and the end of the 19thC. You have to bear in mind the size and proportion of the room when adding a ceiling rose. It is also worth checking throughout the house or, if possible, in similar houses to see the style and size of rose used. The top two examples on this page and the top four opposite are original cornices from 19thC houses in America and Britain. The other roses shown are modern, designed to blend with 18th and 19thC styles; these particular examples are made by Hodkin and Jones.

2 New cornices are available in wood, resin and plaster. It should be noted that good plaster cornices which are moulded to a specific design can be expensive. However, the above are good examples of standard designs.

Cornice cleaning

Distemper paints are water-bound and can be removed with water. You can use water-soaked rags or sponges to wet the old distemper, but this is a messy job and cannot easily be done without also soaking the walls and floor. A steam spray (which can be hired), more often used for stripping wallpaper, does the job with less fuss.

When distemper is thoroughly damp you can scrub it out of crevices with a bottle brush or nail brush – and sometimes you can use a small spoon to gently clean out the hollows. For intricate work, you may need to use wood-carving tools bought from an art shop.

It is not advisable to paint distemper-laden plaster relief work with emulsion paint as a stopgap until you can find time for a proper cleaning job. First, the emulsion cannot get a proper "purchase" on top of the flaky distemper; and secondly it will ultimately make the distemper much more difficult to remove.

These views of an early 19thC cornice show a three-stage restoration process. The first shows the uncleaned cornice, with the detail totally obscured by layers of distemper. The second shows the same cornice after hours of painstaking cleaning, using a wood-carving tool. The result is really quite dramatic. The third example was produced by a specialist plaster firm who took a mould from a restored section. Each leaf is made up of two parts, as is each flower; the back is produced in lengths.

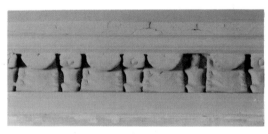

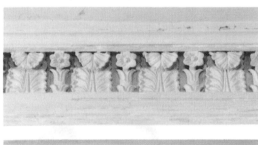

2

1

3

4

5

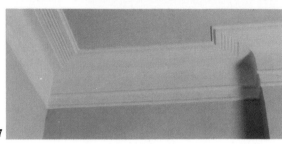
6

7

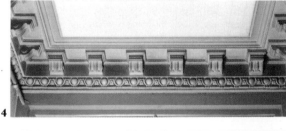
8

1,2 These friezes in a late 19thC house are reminiscent of earlier designs, in theme if not in execution. Period styles tend to be cyclical. I.H

3 This ceiling offers an excellent example of early anaglypta wallpaper. The cornice is lincrusta, a pioneering material in the mass production of period detail. I.SH

4 The authentic feel of this late Victorian cornice is achieved by using a classic period green with gold. I.SH

5 This "wedding cake" ceiling was introduced into a Georgian drawing room by exuberant 1880s craftsmen. CP

6,7,8 Modern cornicing, readily available in standard lengths, can be used with reasonable success in period rooms from the end of the 18thC, especially if the rooms themselves are plain. Alternatively, if parts of the original cornice are intact, restoration is possible from a mould (picture 8).

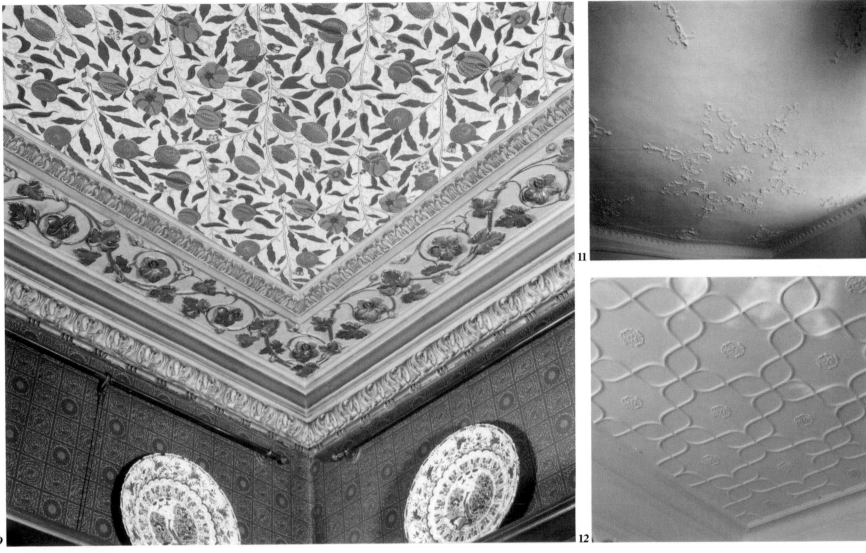

9

10

9,10, *As the 19thC progressed, the style changed from light classical to the heavy late Victorian. Wallpaper was often used on the ceiling, and numerous colours and textures added to the overall impression of confident vulgarity.* LSH

11 *The late Victorians did, on occasion, emulate 18thC motifs, as in this copy of a Chinese Chippendale style.* CP

12,13 *By the end of the 19thC, even grand ceilings could be wallpapered to give the impression of plasterwork.*

11

12

13

Early houses often had no stairs at all: the upper floor was reached by a ladder. Stone houses, however, were likely to have one or both of two simple stair types: a flight of stone steps ascending on the outside of the house, or a winding flight set into a wall inside. The former type persisted in vernacular buildings, especially in northern England and in Scotland, for over five hundred years. Sometimes it provided access to separate quarters for people employed by the house; sometimes, in the Norman tradition and especially on sloping sites, storage rooms were on the ground floor and the steps led to the living quarters above.

WOODEN STAIRS

The upstairs rooms that became a feature of late medieval halls were reached by ladders, even when the rooms were used for living rather than storage space: they were easy to move and took up very little space. When wooden stairs first appeared, early in the 16th century, they were little more than fixed, solid ladders made of oak blocks set against the wall and cased on the open side with bare, functional panelling.

As galleried show houses began to be built for courtiers and gentry during the course of the century, it was realized that stairs could be handsome features, although they remained simple compared to those of the following century. Gradually, they became

1 This early newel post, somewhat crudely carved, is in a style extensively used in the 17thC.

broader. They were usually of oak, in keeping with the other parts of the house. Sometimes the steps were made of solid blocks instead of the separate treads and risers now normal. Running from floor to floor in a succession of straight flights, they had stout newel posts supporting a balustrade of sturdy balusters and a broad handrail, moulded like the beams. The newel posts had big carved terminals, or extended up to the ceiling and acted as structural supports for the floor above. Sometimes they were carved with strapwork designs that reflected the ornamental plasterwork of the

ceiling. In less grand houses where solid, hand-carved balusters were inappropriate, craftsmen instead produced flat balusters with similar outlines but in two dimensions and often perforated to give a lighter effect.

2 When the central chimney was removed from the heart of the house, it was normally replaced by a staircase or "pair of stairs". The dogleg stair first appeared in the mid-17thC and has remained a firm favourite, especially in terrace houses, to the present day.

1

2

17TH-CENTURY STAIRS

Beginning with the work at Knowle House, Kent, in 1605, the 17th century saw much more magnificent stairways in the great houses, and scaled-down grandeur in big farmhouses. At the same time smaller houses were moving more and more towards built-in and cased flights of stairs instead of ladders.

Long straight flights with right-angled dog-leg changes in direction gave way to shorter flights punctuated by landings – an arrangement which had a dramatic visual impact. Stairs could be articulated round to form a well or could lead in separate stages to a gallery above. The balustrade and the string running along the side of the stairs at its base were painted in complex colour schemes. Newel posts in the best houses terminated in carved heraldic beasts, symbols of the owner's family. Balusters were now often rectangular but highly carved, and the stair handrails were flatter. Sometimes balusters were replaced with ornamentally carved panels, casing in the stairs to handrail level. This panelling, of painted pine or oak, would be matched by panelling up to the dado rail on the wall.

Inigo Jones introduced many fine staircases in the Italian manner and stairs with marble steps and pretty iron balustrades – ironwork was often used for balustrading after the Restoration. Jones's stairs might be curved round in a sweep instead of rising in angular straight flights, but even so they could still occupy a confined space. However, by the end of the century the tendency was for stairs to occupy key positions as they rose up the two storeys of the hall, the grandest room of the house.

3

3 This secondary staircase in a 16thC house is a good example of a simple form of stairs. It is often a mistake to use over-elaborate features in an early house.

4,5 Early stairs were often beautifully joinered, balustraded and enriched with carving. If a stick is missing, a local wood turner should be able to make a replacement.

6 Although the newel post on this 17thC stairway is highly decorative, the actual sticks are flat.

4

5

6

THE 18TH CENTURY

The concept of the magnificent entrance hall in which the stairs had pride of place was fully developed by Palladian architects in the houses for the wealthy built from around the 1720s in Britain and the United States. Marble steps were flanked by exquisitely worked iron balustrades and the ceiling above the staircase was singled out for superlative treatment, such as *trompe l'oeil* coffering. The walls along the stairs were also treated grandly, perhaps painted with architectural subjects from classical antiquity. Many fine new town houses were built on a smaller scale, but still following the same principles, with the stairs designed to make a major impact on entrance .

In houses with wooden stairs the chunky look of earlier examples would now have been quite out of keeping and newel posts were much slimmed down. Balusters were made finer too, and were evenly spaced, two or three per stairs. Handrails were generally narrower, to team up with the lighter newel posts. The barleysugar twist, which had first appeared around 1690, came into vogue for balusters and long remained fashionable, even though there were many other imaginative designs by the middle of the century. In England classically fluted and vase-shaped balusters were applied to elegant mid-18th-century stairs, and, of course, wrought iron was used in grand houses with stone stairs; however, in the United States barleysugar continued in popularity until the end of the century.

1,2 This type of turning on the sticks was extremely popular in England in the 18thC and was mirrored by a similar development in America. Often one or several sticks have been broken. If this involves complicated turning, a perfect stick may have to be removed and taken to a wood turner to be copied.

3,4 The panelling and decorative elements on this staircase are typical of grand houses of the mid-18thC. The use of three different patterns of turning on the balusters is common in America.   HH

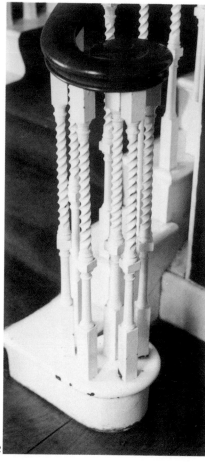

5

6

9

10

7

8

9,10 *Stair turning in the 18thC developed into a fine art form, with turners producing either intricate or plain designs. Many local forms developed, which makes it difficult to replace sticks with mass-produced items. It is also worth pointing out that much decoration on stairs is hidden by layers of paint. To reveal original carving, paint must be stripped back to bare wood.*

5 *Classic 18thC wooden stairs like these can be found in town houses in both Britain and America. Many have been vandalized or replaced by plain sticks, and thus need restoring to their original condition.* RC

6 *This mid-18thC stairway in a New York house is a fine example of simple but elegant balusters.* VC

7,8 *Many 18thC houses had quite plain staircases with straight sticks and a minimum of carved decoration.* MJ

1 These cast-iron sticks were popular in the 18th and 19thC. They were frequently painted. GH

2 Stairs were often built in stone. Old stone steps which are beginning to break up are very dusty, and should be vacuumed regularly. GH

3 An interesting example of a secondary staircase added to a 17thC New York house in 1820. BH

4 A classic example of an early 19thC staircase in a terrace house. Note the plain square sticks.

5 The wooden newel post of this period had lost its 18thC flamboyancy. In less grand houses in the early 19thC it was a purely functional end to the handrail.

6 In an 1830s New York house, the hole left by the bolt that holds the post into the floor joist is capped with a mother-of-pearl coat button. The story is that, when the mortgage was paid off, the button would be replaced with a silver coin.

7 An interesting solution, in a 1830s New York House, to the problem of how to make a handsome staircase without expensive turned elements. The newel post is not turned, and the simple balusters are set at an angle in the plain round banister.

8 This interestingly carved mid-19thC newel post at the top of the cellar steps actually faces the front door. BP

9,10 This excellent staircase has been well restored in a Neo-classical stone mansion built between 1837 and 1846. The cluster of sticks forming the newel post is a common 19thC device. BP

THE 19TH CENTURY

The fashion for balusters with complex shapes died out at the end of the 18th century, and square-sectioned wooden bars had become common. Panelling in place of balusters had disappeared, and so, in general, had the solid string. In the 19th century, balusters (three per step in good houses, but two in smaller ones) almost always rested directly on the stairs themselves, and in most houses of the period they were accompanied by smooth mahogany handrails, which were characteristically oval in section.

Many 19th-century houses had a two-storey rear extension, making the stairs even darker than they had been in the Georgian period: the half-landing at the first level now led to the back extension, so there was no possibility of a window. Sometimes such staircases would be lit by a skylight, with the light filtering down the well to the ground level.

4

5

6

7

8

9

10

1

5

2

4

6

1 *This 1830s New York staircase is a perfect example of the period.*

2 *A highly decorative newel post from the 1830s. The original builder of this New York house used many details from pattern books of the time. This design was probably meant to be executed in stone; but here it was made in oak.* OMH

3 *This first-floor landing newel post is much simpler than the previous ground-floor example.* OMH

4 *By the last quarter of the 19thC, although the staircase could often be quite small, the newel post was still a major feature.*

5 *These cast-iron staircases, with all their intricate detail, are very much a part of the late Victorian terrace. The greens and browns which predominate in this 1870s house accentuate the Victorian character.* LSH

6 *This Arts and Crafts house is a good example of the reintroduction in the late 19thC of the grand staircase.*

In the simplest Victorian houses, with front doors opening into the small front room, the staircase was a cased-in and extremely modest flight leading from the corner of the back room to a tiny landing between the two rooms on the upper floor. The large new terraced and semi-detached houses of the time still managed to give a flourish to the stairs, sometimes with a moulded nose extending along the exposed sides of the treads as well as along the front, and often with the bottom step broader from side to side than the rest and curving round at the ends. This feature, and the handrail sweeping round above it, were fashions developed from the grander houses of the preceding century. With them went ornate cast-iron balusters or balusters turned in soft wood on a square base; the latter became standard in smaller houses by the 20th century.

In comfortable private houses of the early 20th century, the traditional wooden staircase with turned balusters and broad moulded handrail enjoyed a final moment of glory before being ousted by the trend towards modernistic simplification.

7

10

11

8

9

7 *The central courtyard of this essentially Elizabethan house was filled with the staircase hall in the 1880s. Late Victorian taste demanded a spectacular stairway in a house of this importance.* CP

8,9 *This late 19thC staircase in Leighton House, London, was designed by George Aitchison. The balustrading is oak which has been stained and lacquered, the detailing in gold. The carpet is modern but woven from the original cards, based on the pattern "The Tree of Life" from a historic rug.* LH

10 *By the turn of the century, sticks were being mass-produced. If you are replacing damaged sticks, always have at least one extra turned.*

11 *Many firms produce new staircases with an acceptable period feel. This example is admirable.* WB

A fireplace is one of the obvious things to install or replace when you set about restoring a period room. The right choice can bring the whole interior together; a mismatch, on the other hand, can absolutely destroy the whole carefully wrought effect.

However, distinctions between "right" and "wrong" are not always clear-cut. There is a bewildering range of original and reproduction fireplaces available but not so much guidance on where to use them.

It is relatively easy to replace a Victorian or even an 18th-century fireplace correctly, as such interiors are well-documented. More difficult, however, is the question of what you put into a 15th-century house – few of us really want a central hearth with a hole in the roof to let out the smoke! In such cases you have to accept a compromise, matching materials and styles that are as sympathetic as possible. Whatever type of house you are restoring, your choice will be governed by its position on the social scale and the particular room with which you are concerned.

The Saxon tradition of a central open fire was still the norm in most houses until the beginning of the 16th century.

In the great houses of medieval times the fire was placed at the upper end of the large communal living hall and the burning wood was controlled by an iron fire-dog (an endiron or andiron) which also served as a spit. The basic fireplace was established when a hood was introduced to minimize smoke: this was most easily supported by a wall, so the fire was moved from a central to a lateral position. An indentation was made to accommodate the fire, and a chimney was provided, with flues that conducted smoke to holes in the wall or to a louvre in the roof. However, chimney building was inhibited by a tax imposed by Rome. Until the Reformation smoke still left many houses through a hole in the roof, whether the fire was against a wall or against a plaster-covered wooden reredos (usually of elm, which does not ignite easily) with a wattle-and-daub canopy and funnel.

From the 16th century a single central chimney normally heated the whole of the house. When a further room was added to the basic plan, this would be provided with its own fireplace and chimney on the end wall.

1 Even in the 16th and 17thC many fireplaces were imported from Italy, Spain, Portugal and France. These extended chimneypieces became very popular.

2 The typical 16thC inglenook fireplace which provided the family with heating and cooking facilities. It may take quite a bit of detective work to find an original fireplace, as many were filled in over the centuries. Note: the original fireplace may look out of place in a "Georgianized" room.

3 The inglenook (from the Scottish Gaelic aingeal, and nook meaning corner) may well need quite extensive renovation. Old bricks should be used where possible and care must be taken in choosing an acceptable colour. The main beam or mantel has sometimes been removed. It is possible to find old beams in most areas.

FIRE SURROUNDS

The simplest form of fire surround was a hood set in the wall over the fire, supported either by piers or by a stone lintel bracket. This survived through more than three centuries, while grander or more elegant chimneypieces were being developed. In Tudor houses the deeply recessed fireplace was given a Tudor arch of stone and otherwise treated as part of the panelled wall.

4

5

6

4,5,6 *The fire surround and overmantel provided the perfect surface for incorporating the decoration that was a measure of wealth and status in the 17thC. These beautifully made examples are modern reproductions.* SI

7 *A fine Continental carved marble overmantel of hybrid taste, 16thC, set over a more classically orthodox fire surround. Imports were sometimes of whole fireplaces, but often of finely carved panels to set into locally made surrounds.*

However, the mongrel classicism of European craftsmen soon influenced the decoration. Grander houses had a carved wooden ledge above the stone arch and richly carved panels above that.

In the Elizabethan great houses the fireplace, framed with columns and an entablature with highly ornamented carved wooden panels above, was the focal point of an already much decorated room. This type of surround was elaborately applied in showy Jacobean houses too, with the owner's coat of arms carved in the panel above the fire. Inigo Jones and his pupil John Webb were later to handle this same treatment with a better understanding of classicism and Italian Renaissance models. However, their work was confined to important buildings and was not taken up generally until the 18th century.

CHANGES IN THE 17TH-CENTURY

In some country districts twigs, peat, furze or even dung were still being burnt in the middle of the room in the old manner, with the occupants seated on low stools under the smoke. In more prosperous and forested areas the fuel was wood, and fireplaces were high and wide to accommodate it. When coal was introduced it produced still more smoke than timber; however, coal was not in common use until the 18th century in Britain and the 19th in North America.

To reduce smoke a chimney cloth was placed across the mantle and this soon became a decorative feature of

1 A 17thC Baroque chimneypiece in Verona marble, originally intended for a grand Italian house. Many such fireplaces were imported into England from Italy and many more were made in England by Italian craftsmen.

2 When considering the fireplace, one of the most important decisions is whether you are going to have a modern reproduction, put in a genuine period fireplace which is not original to the house or try to restore what is there. This example is authentic, but an import: a 17thC Italian chimneypiece in pale yellow Verona marble, beautiful and rare.   C/OFS.I.

3 A wonderful example of a George II (1727-1760) Siena marble chimneypiece taken from a substantial English house in Wiltshire. These fire surrounds are extremely rare and have *frequently cost a great deal to restore. It is worth noting that such a fireplace demands a prestigious setting and would look out of place in anything but a grand room. As always, scale is crucial.   C/OFS.I.*

4

5

8

9

the fireplace. It continued to appear in Victorian homes, even though by this time fires had supposedly been cured of smoking.

With the introduction of coal came a narrower grate placed in the wide hearth. In new buildings the fireplace itself was now set further back. This meant that in thinner-walled brick buildings the chimneystack formed a projection on the outside wall. Fireplaces in older homes tend to have been modified over the years and have often been made narrower, but if building work is being done on houses with chimneys like this, it will almost certainly reveal that the house originally had a wide fireplace.

Another feature dating back to the 17th century which may still be found in country houses, even of very modest size, is the clay bread oven, an early ancestor of the kitchen range. This was a British invention, found especially in Devon and Cornwall, but exported to North America soon after the Pilgrim Fathers. And you still may find in country kitchens the built-in box in which salt was kept to dry beside the fire, and the lockable fireside spice cupboard.

7 A detail of the mantel in 6, right, showing the intricate carving and classical ornamentation that was becoming popular in both Britain and America in the late 18thC. vc

7

6

4 This example is from a mid-18thC New York house. The fireplaces in the servants' quarters or, as in this case, the children's nursery, were usually simple in style. vc

5 A simple fireplace with no mantel and surrounded by panelling – typical of mid-18thC New York. The paint is modern but an authentic colour. vc

6 In the same house, a splendid fireplace of late 18thC style. It would have been added around 1780. vc

8,9 This mid-18thC fireplace is set into the panelling with Delft tiles surrounding the opening. Tiles like these have frequently been damaged either by heat or over-zealous workmen. It is interesting to discover if the tiles in such fireplaces are English or Dutch and also their date: the glaze and colour can be quite different depending on origin. vc

FIREPLACE FURNITURE

Where wood was the fuel, fire dogs continued to be necessary as a means of propping up logs and keeping them in place. The early fire dogs had been permanently joined together at the base by a low bar which went across the front of the fire. By the 17th century the two dogs stood separately, one at each side of the fire.

A detachable spit was still placed between them at the front, often with a tray beneath to catch the hot fat and juices from roasting meat.

To solve the problem of damage to brickwork, a cast-iron fireback was produced with designs which range from simple to immoderate. Stout bellows and cast-iron tongs, sometimes with a shovel for heaping up the wood ash, completed the furniture of the fireplace. Today it is possible to obtain authentic cast-iron reproductions of fire dogs and backs, bellows and tongs from specialist founders.

THE 18TH CENTURY

In the bigger Tudor and Jacobean houses the fireplaces were all placed centrally, so that the smoke left the building through one chimneystack. But when classically inspired houses became the only acceptable fashion the central chimneystack was a problem in the design: it looked ungainly. One solution was to place fireplaces at the four corners of the house, and to hide the chimneytops as much as possible behind the parapet. These corner fireplaces were given very lavish treatment in early 18th-century stately homes, while simpler corner fireplaces are found in smaller houses of the time. Even when fireplaces were not set in the corners of the rooms, chimneys at the gable ends of the house became standard.

At the beginning of the century many town houses simply had a stone or brick hearth and fireback. The hearth was often given a daily whitening. But with the growth of streets of fashionable new houses, fireplaces become more sophisticated, reflecting those of the great houses. Inigo Jones's designs were at this time being circulated, along with many pattern books showing classical details. Accordingly, fireplaces were given classical frames, with columns or pilasters, and consoles supporting an entablature topped by a picture panel, the whole planned to echo the door case of the room.

In simpler houses the frames were at first in wood. Soon they were lined or made completely with marble or stone. The picture panel above the fire was widely copied in houses for the well off, while grander people were beginning to prefer mirrors.

As coal was increasingly used for fuel, the fireplace opening was made smaller. The fire basket came into being for holding the coals in the old wide hearths, while in new houses the trend was to install a cast-iron coal-burning hob grate with urn-shaped sides – this is the familiar grate of Georgian interiors. Unlike the earlier free-standing grates and contemporary fire baskets, Georgian cast-iron grates were fixed and took up the whole width of the new narrow fireplace, in the manner which persisted into the present century.

This type of grate, its front patterned with classical motifs, its curved sides developing into the double-U shape, suits Georgian and Regency rooms perfectly. Old grates can be restored, and new or restored replacements can be obtained. Even if central heating is more appealing than the thought of carrying coals up and down narrow Georgian stairs, a fireplace in the original style can be cherished for its looks. Unused chimneys need ventilation to keep them dry and should never be sealed without the provision of air vents.

Because the new grates raised the height of the fire, a fender became necessary to catch any falling coals. A poker was also essential. Both fenders and pokers were made in brass, with matching tongs and shovel.

1 After James Gibbs published his Rules for drawing the several parts of Architecture *in 1732 his designs were copied and embellished in both England and America. In this example the picture frame has been replaced by a mirror.* CP

2 From the mid-18thC white marble was considered the most prestigious material for the fireplace in the drawing room – not only in the grand houses but increasingly in smaller houses. This fireplace in a first-floor drawing room is in fact a Victorian copy. CP

3 An 18thC fireplace with a classical broken pediment and additional 19thC embellishments. CP

1

2

3

Restoring marble fireplaces

Before attempting to restore a marble fireplace, ensure that you allow yourself plenty of time. It is certainly not a job to be done in a hurry. A point to remember before you begin cleaning is not to use any acids, dyes or alcohol: marble is a porous substance, and fluids such as these will soak into it and stain, or eventually cause the marble to rot.

There are three main problems to be overcome when restoring marble. First, it is likely to be broken or chipped; secondly, it may have been painted; and lastly it may be heavily stained. If you are unlucky you may have to deal with all three!

If the fireplace has been badly damaged, and is in pieces, you will have to break it open and reassemble it from scratch. To do this you will need a special marble glue and extra pieces of marble to make good the breakages. Often a fireplace will be only slightly chipped, in which case it is only necessary to mix up a coloured marble glue to blend with the surrounding marble. Apply this to the damaged area, allow to set and then rub down in turn with a fine wet and dry sandpaper until the surface takes on the same decorative form as the original marble.

You can quite easily remove paint from marble using "Nitromors" stripper. Working on only a few square inches at a time, take off excess stripper with acetone on small swabs of cotton wool. Repeat this until the paint disappears. It is essential to wear rubber gloves to protect your own skin and clothing. If you are very careful, you can also do this using a paint scraper: but bear in mind that marble is easily scratched.

Staining, due to years of neglect, is the most common problem in restoring a marble fireplace. The best way to tackle it is to use a substance called Sepiolite mixed with de-ionized water to a paste of custard-like consistency. This should be applied in a ½in/1cm thickness and left for 12 hours or so, depending on the humidity of the room. When it begins to dry and crack (a process known as *craquelure*), remove the covering and wipe over the marble with de-ionized water on small swabs of cotton wool. This process should remove all stains.

When polishing marble, use a white hard polish: any colouring in the polish will stain. Rub the polish hard into the marble using a soft white cloth. (Any dye in the cloth, again, could seep into the marble.) For a matt finish use a softer polish.

After a long and laborious restoration, it is important to look after the marble. For day-to-day upkeep use a white polish such as "Pledge" to keep it clean. Remember that marble is porous, and careless placement of plantpots and glasses will cause staining.

4

4 This very pleasing marble fireplace has been introduced into an early 19thC house. The marble had been painted, but a professional firm stripped the paint before installation. Putting in a marble fireplace is a heavy, dirty, skilled job, not to be undertaken lightly.

1

2

3

4

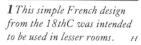

5

6

7

1 *This simple French design from the 18thC was intended to be used in lesser rooms.* H

2 *By the late 18thC, cameos of fine ceramics were often applied to chimneypieces. Such fireplaces were intended to be painted.*

3 *This popular mid-18thC design in the William Kent style is suitable for a grand room. Such fireplaces could be used in houses dating from the 1740s through to the turn of the century.* H

4,5 *Modern reproduction fireplaces are available in marble. It is interesting to remember that, in the 18thC, fireplaces were often made in marble workshops which the 18thC architect or home owner visited to choose from the many designs available – just as he would today.* MII

6 *Consideration of proportion is essential when choosing a mantelpiece. This classic Georgian design with square fluted frieze and jambs is ideal for a smaller room where a more ornate, heavily carved example would look totally out of place.* H

7 *An inlaid marble chimneypiece decorated with Wedgwood plaques. These fireplaces became very popular after 1778, when Josiah Wedgwood produced them from designs by John Flaxman. The jambs are typically in the form of architectural pilasters.* COFSI.

8

9

12

10

13

11

14

ADAM-INSPIRED DEVELOPMENTS

A visually lighter fire surround deprived of pediments was preferred in the later 18th century and was ornamented to perfection by the Adam brothers. From then on, the simple albeit enriched form of pilasters and consoles supporting an entablature with a ledge or shelf above the fire continued as the model fire surround for most of the 19th century.

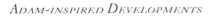

8 *This carved statuary marble and Blue John (Derbyshire Spa) chimneypiece was made in the 1780s. The delicately carved overmantel is in the manner of Grinling Gibbons (1648-1721).* C0fSI.

9-14 *As the 18thC advanced there were two main developments in fireplace design: first, a dominant taste for classical architecture encouraged by the Adam brothers; and secondly, chimneypieces became smaller in standard town houses. These reproduction fireplaces are all eminently suitable for houses built from the later 18thC until well into the 19thC.*
AB,AB,PF,PF,C0fSI.,AB

1-14 *The range of classically inspired fireplaces on the market from the 1760s on was enormous, with almost every conceivable classical motif applied somewhere or other. Swags, urns and foliage have never really gone out of style* *since. Poor modern reproductions are frequently discernible by the hesitant application of undersized motifs. 1-5 are original fireplaces in 18thC houses, and 6-14 are modern reproductions.*

GH,RC,RC,RC,HH,H,MH,
H,H,MH,H,PF,MH,MH

1

2

3

4

5

6

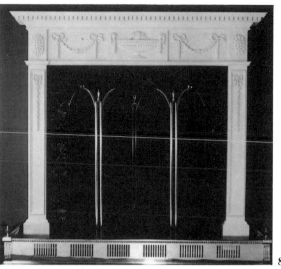

7

8

9

10

11

2

13

14

1 *A humble fireplace was a common feature of many servants' rooms in the late 18thC. This housekeeper's room in the semi-basement is typically plain but very functional.* GH

2 *This early 19thC marble chimneypiece depends for its effect on contrasting marble. Fireplaces of this style demand a grand room.* CofSL

3 *A Regency period statuary marble chimney displaying a more exuberant classical motif. The frieze is carved with Bacchanalian figures at play, the jambs in the form of Antonio Canova's dancing girls.* CofSL

4 *A Scottish white marble fireplace which shows more austere decoration, from the early 19thC.* CofSL

1

3

2

4

5

7

8

9

5 *A simple 19thC white marble fireplace imported from France.* MB

6 *By the mid-19thC in minor rooms cast-iron fireplaces like this were often used, often painted white to emulate marble examples.* BH

7 *This marble fireplace is actually French but would equally enhance a drawing room in America or Britain. It has the advantages of small size and not excessive decoration.* MH

8 *This George I period (1714-1727) fire grate was made in brass and steel. The engraved serpentine front and ball finials are typical of the early 18thC.* CofSL

9 *This Regency period, c.1810, brass and steel dog grate could be used to good effect in fireplaces of the late 18th and early 19thC.* CofSL

1

2

3

1 A marble fireplace in a New York house illustrating early 19thC trends. The slightly raised hearth is typically American. MJ

2 French influence is apparent in this fireplace in a front drawing room. White marble was universally thought to be a statement of wealth and taste. MJ

3 This fireplace with its recessed hearth is made from English fossilized marble, but is original to the New York house in which it remains. MJ

4,5 In this 1830s New York house the Greek Revival style is still very much in evidence but both these wooden fireplaces are restrained examples.

6 A wooden fireplace in a mid-1830s house. This is a reconstruction from "paint ghosts" – the traces left on the wall after a fire destroyed it completely. The more ornate surround was used in the front parlour where guests were received.

7 A much plainer wooden surround. The Franklin stove is of the period, around 1836, and would have been in the back parlour where the family spent most if its time.

4

5

6

7

8,9 *The 19thC saw a wide diversity of styles and materials. This Greek Revival Belgian black marble fireplace dominates the room when placed in an earlier New York house in the 1860s. The grate is original. The capital on the fireplace matches the capitals on the pocket doors. In this period of nostalgia, people were very aware of proportion and symmetry.* OMH

10 *By around 1840, the American taste for intricately carved chimneypieces was waning. Marble was often used in slab form and surrounds tended to be geometric – a simplification which had happened slightly earlier in Britain. This high coal grate of brass and iron is an English import. It would have been permanently fitted to the fireplace opening with masonry. It was more efficient than andirons.* BP

11 *This black marble fireplace in the same house is in the upstairs reception room. The fact that the more impressive fireplaces are downstairs would tend to suggest that this upstairs room would be for family, rather than for entertaining on a grand scale.* BP

12 *A classic Greek Revival white fireplace, very common in houses in New York in the 1830s.* OMH

VICTORIAN AND EDWARDIAN DEVELOPMENTS

In Britain experiments towards more efficient burning eventually led to "register grates", with dampers to control the supply of air to the fire, and additional dampers in the chimney throat. These grates were cast in one piece as part of the inner frame and back of the hearth, and set as an insert within the marble surround.

Fire regulations strictly controlled chimney construction in the 19th century, and the risk of fire was further reduced by the almost exclusive use of marble or cast iron in the massive and mass-produced fire surrounds of *piano nobile* rooms in Victorian houses and in the minor fireplaces provided in most of their other rooms. Now that plate glass was readily available, the huge ornamental mirror descended the social scale and replaced the picture or stucco panel over the fireplace. This was a forerunner of the overmantel with side mirrors and shelves around a mahogany-framed central mirror.

Gothic and Picturesque influences affected fireplace design later in the century, and the Arts and Crafts movement's nostalgic yearnings led to a taste for wide hooded hearths, with stone frames and wood surrounds, in which to burn wood again. Most fireplaces, however, became smaller, with surrounds in painted pine or slate – marble was becoming too expensive. At the same time ornament became heavier from the 1860s on. Painted and glazed tiles were fixed into the sides of the cast-iron insert, and tiled hoods became an integral part of the construction. At the turn of the century Art Nouveau brought opulent curving motifs to the tiles, which until now had been patterned rather formally.

With the introduction of gas and electric fires, the outer surround became less and less imposing, simply serving as a frame for a wide area of plain coloured tiles. By easy transitions this became the very modest "modern" fireplace, with free-standing grate and brick back and a surround entirely composed of tilework in mottled buff or beige.

Luckily, when central heating or portable electric fires and 1950s taste conspired to banish older fireplaces, they were as frequently boxed in as removed. You may be surprised how easy it is either to restore the original or put in a replacement to create an authentic focal point in your home.

Before having a new fireplace installed, have the chimney swept and light a fire to make sure that the chimney is sound. Before doing anything in a downstairs room check that the chimney breast has not been removed upstairs – an obvious precaution, but one which the enthusiast may overlook with distressing results!

1,2,3,4,5 By the late 19thC there were as many fireplace designs as there were designers. In the reception areas they tended to be quite grand, while in the servants' areas they were simple and usually small. The size of the fireplace was scaled to that of the room and the degree of ornament was in strict proportion to the room's social importance. CP

3

2

4

5

1

6

8

7

9

6 *While the actual surrounds were frequently simple, much decoration was added to the wrought-iron grates in the later 19thC.* CP

7 *Early 19thC tiles like these should be retained if at all possible. Some damage is totally acceptable and can often add to the period feel, whereas new tiles frequently detract.*

8,9 *In small rooms, cast-iron surrounds were common. These were frequently painted white, as were carved timber or plaster fireplaces. The Victorians would have found our love for stripped pine very amusing: it was a cheap timber which was always concealed.* CP

1 *This small fireplace in the hallway of an 1870s terraced house is given prominence by a gilt and mirrored overmantel. The 17thC chimney cloth reappeared at this period: it may have helped to reduce the smoke but was mainly a decorative feature.* LSH

2 *The late Victorians used marble for their most prestigious fireplaces. While the fireplace itself could be quite understated, the brass fire accessories were quite the opposite.* LSH

1

2

3 The actual fireplace here is quite small but the overall impression is of a massive, extended chimneypiece. *I.SH*

4 Many of these simple Victorian cast-iron grates still survive. The tiles are often earlier than the grate.

5 To recreate a Victorian fireplace you need to attend to more than merely the fabric. The colours, clutter and general confusion are all necessary parts of the Victorian mood. *I.SH*

6 A detail of a small cast-iron grate with brass hood. These fireplaces were both efficient and highly decorative. *I.SH*

1 *This type of wooden surround with all its classical inspiration fits quite easily into the larger rooms of most substantial 19thC houses.* LSH

2 *A small simple stripped pine fireplace which was standard in many small homes or in secondary rooms in grander houses from the mid-19thC. The English delft tiles assist with the rustic feel, as does the original mass-produced cast-iron grate.* FE

3 *Late 19thC cast-iron fireplaces were frequently painted white. These functional items were also highly decorative. Note the ash drawer at the base – enhanced with a painted tile.*

4 *In America, as in Britain, the decorative qualities of materials such as matt black slate were fully utilized. This example had been painted white in the 20thC and had to be painstakingly stripped.*

5 *Toward the end of the 19thC it became increasingly popular to break up the solid mass of black slate or marble with inset panels – tiles, ceramics and marble were ideally suited.*

6 *This black slate fireplace in the same 1875 house has inserted Minton tiles.*

7 *This squat white marble fireplace is strangely positioned under a window. The situation is attributable to Lord Leighton, who placed it there as a joke. Note the mirrored shutters – is the window a mirror or not? and where does the smoke go?* LH

4

6

5

7

2 *The whole feel of a Victorian fireplace must be enhanced by the surroundings as a whole, as in this evocative ensemble. Although the fireplace is classically Victorian, the real impact is derived from the collection of old glass, treen, porcelain and dried flowers.*

3 *This reproduction sand-blasted fireplace, cast from an old mould, is ideal for a house built at the end of the 19thC or the beginning of the 20thC.* AF

4 *By the end of the 19thC, fire surrounds could be marble, wood (painted and unpainted) or metal. They were sometimes simple and elegant – sometimes highly decorated and charmingly vulgar. Tiles were used to good effect. The actual grate by this period had become small, and the fire was thus more efficient. This reproduction fireplace used in a Victorian or Edwardian house would add considerable character to a room.* AF

1 *The permutations of decorated cast fireplaces and multi-coloured tiles are innumerable. Such features have frequently been despised and are only now receiving due attention.* MH

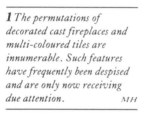

2

1

3

4

5,6 *These chimneypieces are in an Arts and Crafts house, but have a light, classical feel. The Victorians did not feel the need to rely simply on one style. This philosophy created some interesting interiors along with some very incongruous designs.*

7 *The solidity of Victorian design is often mistaken for lack of taste. This grand but simple fireplace has stature and elegance.*

5   6   7

8 *This Arts and Crafts house entrance hall fireplace depends much on the Renaissance revival.*

9 *These solid carved wood late Victorian fireplaces have sometimes been most inappropriately sited. Their quality is undeniable but they require careful consideration of their environment to be in keeping.*   I.H

8   9

STOVES

Stoves in glazed earthenware or cast iron were much more common in the United States and Europe than in Britain, perhaps because the winters are more consistently extreme outside the British Isles and because wood was widely available for fuel. The completely closed European stove was adapted in Pennsylvania by Dr Benjamin Franklin, whose designs for an open-fronted box stove were imported to England. These extremely functional objects were available from the 1750s to the end of the century, but stoves were never widely adopted in Britain.

1,2,3,4,5 In the 19thC, stoves were more popular in America and Europe than in Victorian England. These reproductions can be used to good effect in any 19th or early 20thC house. They combine the decorative elegance of their Victorian and Edwardian predecessors with modern heating technology. They not only heat the room and provide a hot plate, but they also provide a focal point without the mess associated with an open fire.

S&W,CF,CF,H&S,H&S

6

7

8

6 *Radiators can always be concealed. This screen with a marble top was a late-Victorian way of hiding the massive, ugly but useful heating contraption. The grilles could be either painted or brass.* CP

7,8 *These original 19thC cast-iron radiators look more in keeping with a period house than modern slimmer versions.*

9 *This squat radiator is unusually low and long. This type of radiator, although not authentic, does not look out of place in a large period room.*

10

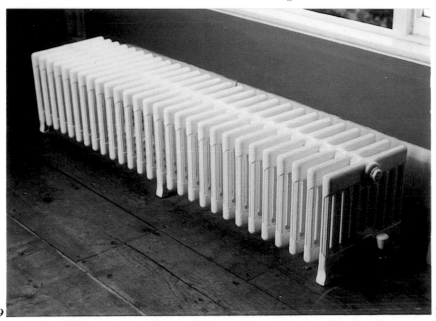

9

11

10 *This black-painted radiator is actually inset into the wall. The loss in heating efficiency is balanced by a gain in aesthetic appeal.* I.H

11 *There are firms now producing efficient and modern look-alikes of the original cast-iron Victorian radiators which are fast disappearing from architectural scrap yards.* B

It was not until the 1880s that bathrooms existed as we know them. Anyone restoring an older house therefore has the choice of simple modern sanitary ware, which need not jar whatever the surroundings, or a Victorian or Edwardian style bathroom which will have a "period" look, even though the period may be different from that of the house.

Cleanliness, of course, was valued long before the 19th century. Soap was made in England from the 14th century, and the highest classes in the Middle Ages had decorated jugs and basins in gold or silver, with brass and pewter for the slightly less well-placed. Obvious ancestors of the washstand existed as gilt and copper ornamented lavers, which had a top for the metal wash bowl, a little water vessel and tap above the bowl, a shelf for soap below, and a fixed towel rail.

Bathing in a tub was a sociable activity for nobles and their ladies. Although the tub was usually round like a barrel, longer versions more like the baths of today were also known. Medieval palaces even had precursors of the modern bathroom, with tiled floors and plumbed-in baths supplied with water from a lead tank. Queen Elizabeth I possessed vast bathing rooms lined with wainscotting and mirrors. These early models may serve as fanciful inspiration, but only the jugs and bowls, and perhaps the lavers, can really be borrowed as practical ideas for houses today, when pools and jacuzzis supply the modern equivalent of social bathing.

1

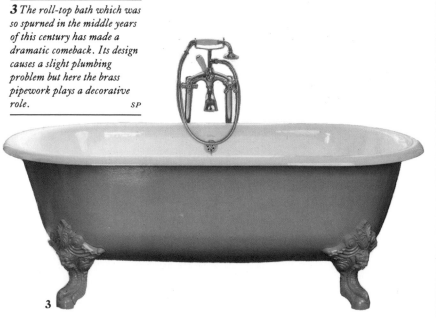

2

1 This reproduction Victorian bathroom ware has as its central feature a roll-top bath set in a mahogany panel surround. The pedestal basin, the cistern on brackets and the bidet all have a Victorian or Edwardian feel. This effect is accentuated by the lighting, marbled walls and hanging antique lace. BCS

2 It is worth remembering that there are alternatives to brass finishes when you are considering bathroom fittings: nickel, chrome, antique copper, antique bronze and, as here, black chrome are some of the many available. This bath filler and rack are part of the Edwardian range. CS

3 The roll-top bath which was so spurned in the middle years of this century has made a dramatic comeback. Its design causes a slight plumbing problem but here the brass pipework plays a decorative role. SP

THE BATH

By 1730 communal pumps and aqueducts supplied water to the towns, while some large country houses had their own water supply. Very occasionally, a grand house could also boast a marble-walled bathroom with a large sunken marble bath and piped water. Portable metal baths were quite widely in use by this time – made of tin, flat-bottomed, roll-topped, and filled and emptied by hand. They were not unlike the simpler tin baths, with a handle to carry and suspend them by, which were filled with hot water from the kitchen range in many houses until relatively recently.

Baths as we know them could not become widespread until water tanks were installed in lofts and enamelling and cast-iron techniques had been developed. In France, the wealthiest few had huge "theme" bathrooms with plumbed-in baths, rather like sofas in design, draped with fine cloth in a most unfunctional way. Usually, baths were still portable tubs, painted outside and in.

It was from the 1850s that sheet-metal baths were plumbed in and a small bedroom given over to their use. The style was decorative, with flower-sprigged wallpaper and gathered curtains. The outside of the bath would be stencilled or painted to look like wood. No attempt was made to conceal the plumbing – a blessing to anyone who wishes to recreate a bathroom of this period.

Even in the 1880s flowery wallpaper was still

4

5

8

6

4 Few people living in an 16thC beamed house would want to live with bathroom furniture of the period – you can carry authenticity too far! Victorian fittings, either original or reproduction, will give a period feel combined with modern comfort.   OR

5 Sponged and marbled walls with classical-motif stencils are a good choice for an 18thC or early 19thC house with large high-ceilinged rooms. The design of the pedestal basin and lavatory is from the first half of the present century, but their simple lines suit the formality of the setting.   SI

6 This room successfully recreates the feeling of the late Victorian taste for opulence and elaborate decoration. The bath is enclosed in a lavish mahogany surround and is further decorated with insets of decorated tiles. The basin too is set into a washstand-type unit.   VN

7 A Victorian-style roll-top bath is a much more convenient choice than the portable metal ones more usually found at the time.   OB

8 The elegant proportions and drag-painted finish on these built-in bathroom units sympathize with the proportions and style of the Georgian house.   SI

1,2 *These are faithful reproductions of late 19thC fittings. The roomy high-sided basin has a shape that is practical as well as decorative. Often such basins were made in even more elaborate forms of crouching lions or dolphins. Attention to detail is reflected here in the brass and porcelain lavatory chain and ornamental brackets holding the basin and cistern.*

TB, AS

4 *Following a practice begun around the 1850s, a bedroom in this Victorian house has been turned into a bathroom. The lavatory and pedestal basin are of modern design but echo the rounded line of the roll-top bath. As the room is spacious enough, the owners have added some original Victorian furniture – the mahogany mirror and the chest of drawers with its old lace cloth.*

TB

3 *This house built in the 1870s still has its original fittings and decoration. Flushing lavatories were well-established by this time and the embossed pedestal is* typical of the period. The deep tub made from slabs of marble would have been cold-fill only: cold baths were a normal part of life until well into the 20thC.

LSH

5

7

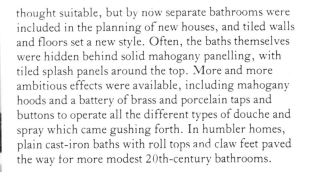

8

6

9

10

thought suitable, but by now separate bathrooms were included in the planning of new houses, and tiled walls and floors set a new style. Often, the baths themselves were hidden behind solid mahogany panelling, with tiled splash panels around the top. More and more ambitious effects were available, including mahogany hoods and a battery of brass and porcelain taps and buttons to operate all the different types of douche and spray which came gushing forth. In humbler homes, plain cast-iron baths with roll tops and claw feet paved the way for more modest 20th-century bathrooms.

5,6,7 *Three bathrooms which follow the mid-19thC fashion of decorating the outside of the bath. They also reflect the fashion then and later on in the century of adopting a bedroom style of decoration — flowery wallpaper and gathered curtains. This style of bath was produced well into this century, and works with a variety of styles of basin and lavatory.* BCS, CPH, TD

8 *Classic square pedestal basins like this were still being made thirty or so years ago, and work especially well in houses built between the wars. A black and white colour scheme has a particularly good feel of the period.* OB

9 *Whether you are renovating a cottage or a Victorian townhouse, painted fittings like these are a good choice. Their fresh blue and white colouring works well against stronger designs or with beams, low ceilings and white-painted walls.* TB

10 *The choice of tiles is important. The colours here — dark green with cream — are typical of the late 19thC and early 20thC. So are the border designs used at skirting, dado and cornice level and the design of patterned tiles arranged in a diagonal trellis.* TB

1

4

1 *A reproduction roll-top bath which gives an excellent period feel without the discomfort. No attempt has been made to hide the pipework which, with the taps and shower mixer, is an attractive as well as authentic feature.* BCS

2 *A Spanish portable bath of the 18thC with carrying handles on either side. It was not until the 1850s that plumbed-in baths began to appear in any other than very grand houses. In humbler homes portable baths were still in use until quite recently. However, this solid marble bath is quite a grand affair. A bath like this can be plumbed-in and would look splendid in a large room, perhaps with marbled walls with a stencilled Greek key border and fittings housed in mahogany cabinets.*

3 *This roll-top bath with brass feet as well as fittings solves the plumbing problem in an interesting way. The shower fitting and porcelain taps are all that are visible, the pipework being hidden by panelling.* SP

4 *By contrast, this roll-top bath displays the brass furniture as part of its decorative appeal. Note also the towel rail and bath rack, which all add to the nostalgic feel. The marble floor and painted brick walls also add to the general mood but could make the bathroom rather cold.* CS

5 *An ordinary shower curtain would strike a jarring note in a period-style bathroom. An etched-glass screen like this one is a more appropriate choice.* BCS

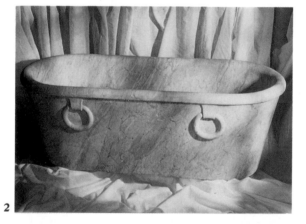

2

3

5

WASHSTANDS AND BASINS

Tripod washstands made of wrought iron with pewter basins appeared in the 1750s. From the 1770s superior dressing-room furniture included elegant mahogany or rosewood washstands designed by Sheraton or Hepplewhite or their imitators. Set in a quarter circle, so that they could stand in a corner, they had raised, shaped backs, circular bowls and round indentations for the soap. Very soon, even washstands and gentlemen's shaving tables were disguised to look like other furniture, with tops and shelves which opened out, as if their inner workings were slightly indecent. The bidet, also for the dressing room, was introduced from France and was even more convincingly concealed in cabinetwork, while the bedroom chamber pot was hidden away in a beautifully made bedside table or cabinet.

In the 1830s washstands became larger and rectangular, with marble tops which had round openings for deep bowls, and slop pails on a low shelf. They developed into the late Victorian stands which could readily be found in junk shops until quite recently. These had patterned tiled tops and splash-

6 *Even when piped water became fairly common, basins were still set in dark mahogany cabinets with marble tops like washstands. If you are thinking of installing a basin in the bedroom of a Victorian house, copying this idea is an authentic solution.* LSH

7 *Setting deep bowls into marble surrounds was a practice which continued into the 20thC. The classic simplicity of this one on chrome legs, dating from the 1920s or 30s, works well in a Georgian house.* CP

8 *A fascinating example of Victorian ingenuity. This sink, still in its original marble surround, does not look particularly unusual – until you notice that it has no waste outlet. The basin is pivoted: after use you simply swing it over to empty the water into a bucket below – which is then emptied by a menial!* LSH

9 *From the late 18thC, elegant washstands were made in the shape of a quarter-circle to fit in a corner. Here is a Victorian plumbed-in extension of the same idea. Notice how well the marble splashback surround has kept its original good looks.* LSH

10 *The interior of this Neo-classical mid-19thC stone mansion is in the Greek Revival style. This pedestal washbasin with its pedestal in the shape of a column mirrors the overall design. The mirror surround is also classically inspired.* BP

backs with cupboards underneath. A variety of prettily decorated jugs and bowls, perforated soap dishes and false-teeth holders went with them.

As piped water became more common, plumbed-in wash basins were still given surrounds in dark mahogany. Bathrooms sported extravagantly patterned ceramic basins which complemented the water closets and cisterns and opulent gleaming brass taps. By the end of the century, however, plain white ceramic ware was beginning to take precedence over patterns, and by the time the pedestal wash basin was developed in the early 1900s hygenic white was universal.

1 *From the early 20thC pedestals which hid the pipework began to be fashionable. It is therefore quite allowable to use reproductions such as this.* BCS

2,3,4 *Late Victorian inventiveness produced all sorts of elaborate systems for douches and sprays, whose style is reflected in these brass and porcelain reproductions.* TB, WA, CS

5 *Attention to small details is important when putting in a bathroom. If you can find original taps like these, so much the better.*

6 *An unfussy traditional shape like this works well in a variety of settings from the 18thC to the 1940s* CPH

7 *A modern pine reproduction of a Victorian washstand intended to be plumbed in.* TB

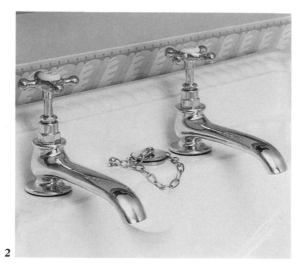

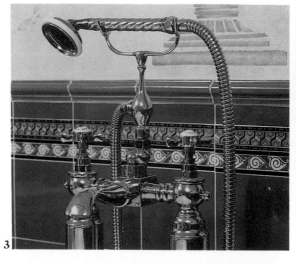

LAVATORIES

A version of the flushing lavatory was invented in 1596 by Sir John Harington, and supplied to Queen Elizabeth herself. After a long and insanitary delay, water was piped to Georgian town houses, and brick drains and public sewers were built. Closets were supplied in the gardens, sometimes flushing and sometimes connected to the main drain, but more often emptying into a cesspit. Proper water closets with traps and valves were introduced in the late 1700s. By the 1840s substantial country houses, at least, were usually well supplied with flushing pans.

Glazed clay pipes made by Doulton were replacing the London brick sewers at the same time. Lavatories too were increasingly made of various kinds of glazed earthenware, and the early types were surrounded by substantial wooden framing. The inside of the bowl was treated as an opportunity for decoration, and was florally adorned in all but the very cheapest models. The outside of the new pedestal lavatory was also decorated. Doultons and Twyfords led the field, and throughout the rest of the century, in Britain and the United States, an astonishing variety of designs and decorative treatments became available.

Pedestals could take the form of crouching lions or dolphins, or were embossed with classical fluting on the outside. Both outside and inside, the bowls might be painted or printed with fruit, flower or willow-pattern designs before being glazed. Blues, reds and pinks were commonly used, and gilding was not unknown. Several reproductions of these designs, with matching basins, bidets and cisterns, are now available.

Seats were usually of polished mahogany or other wood. Porcelain handles, paper-holders (often set into the back of the lavatory itself) and matching porcelain cisterns added to the decorative effect. Cisterns were also made in cast iron, mahogany or other wood (lined with lead or copper) to match the bath panelling. Push-button flushes became available at the end of the 19th century, and surprisingly, low-level suites were first made as early as 1825.

8, 9, 10 Three modern reproductions suitable for period bathrooms. The first shows that with a simple rounded shape plus a natural wood seat you can achieve an attractive period effect; the second has a certain Edwardian feel; the third is a versatile classic shape.
CS, BCS, CPH

11 From the 1840s lavatories were made of glazed earthenware and were usually set in handsome wooden framing, as in this example. Here the pull for the flush is also housed in the surround.
LSH

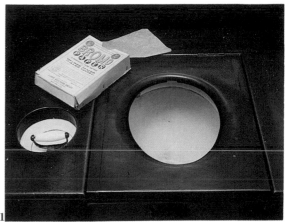

8

9

10

11

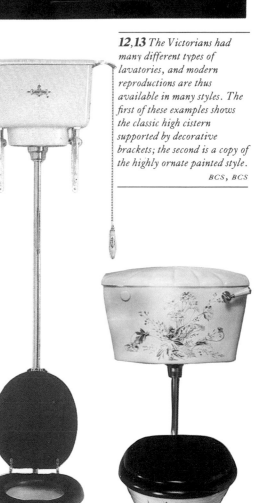

12, 13 The Victorians had many different types of lavatories, and modern reproductions are thus available in many styles. The first of these examples shows the classic high cistern supported by decorative brackets; the second is a copy of the highly ornate painted style.
BCS, BCS

12   13

itchens in old houses worked well because they had to. Perhaps the standards of ventilation, light to work by and even hygiene would not satisfy us today, but as domestic workshops old kitchens simply had to be efficient in terms of layout and furnishings because of the almost total lack of labour-saving devices.

The ways in which old kitchens were planned, furnished and equipped are of interest for two reasons. If you are restoring a period property, a kitchen which looks as if it belongs to the appropriate era is likely to be more visually compatible with the remainder of the building than wall-to-wall plastics. But many people are also realizing that in planning today's multi-user family kitchens there are many practical lessons to be learned from the kitchens of a century or more ago.

Consider sinks, for example. Thirty years ago everyone wanted to get rid of their Butler sinks and get the latest stainless steel models instead. Then came the Germans with small round coloured bowls. Today the practical advantages of the old Butler sink are being appreciated anew and there is a trend towards big sinks in cast iron, plastics, stone or terrazzo, or even towards reusing old china sinks in good condition.

Period kitchens, designed around a large central working table, contained a large walk-in larder for food storage. Dresser shelves and racks were used for items in constant use. Function dictated the form of the furniture, which was always plain and easy to keep clean.

Floors and shelves were scrubbable and walls and ceilings were generally lime-washed until Victorian times.

1

2

1 It is quite practical to restore an inglenook fireplace for cooking, as this example in an Elizabethan house in Kent illustrates. This "down hearth" was recreated with a mixture of antiques and reproduction ironwork hand-forged from old iron with hand tools. Attention to detail is the key to success. For instance, the ropes for the spit drive were traditionally spun at Hawes in Wensleydale. ST

2 The National Trust of Scotland have completely restored this magnificent Georgian kitchen at No. 7 Charlotte Sq, Edinburgh, and it contains a host of reference details which are very useful to the student of period kitchen restoration. The kitchen range is typical of models which were produced in many Scottish iron foundries at this time and can still be found in kitchens all over Britain.

3

5

4   6

3 *In the classic domestic kitchen, such as this delightful Victorian example which is preserved by the National Trust at Uppark, West Sussex, everything revolved around the central working table. This was served by dressers and cooking areas, larders, still rooms, pantries and a scullery for dishwashing and wet food preparation. Note how simple and functional the furniture is and how it is the kitchenwares which create such decoration as there is. The basic table top was of ash but pine planks were fitted at a later date as it wore away and these would have been replaced from time to time.* ST

4 *When this kitchen was restored it was decided to keep as many authentic details as possible, such as the brick floor and rough plastered walls and ceiling. The table was made of English oak with a top of elm and the rack above is a copy of a Yorkshire "bacon flake". The walk-in larder was created from a disused entrance porch. A dishwasher and microwave oven are completely hidden in cupboards when not in use.* ST

5 *The swing towards "unfitted" kitchens is noticeable in the market generally but it started among people refurbishing kitchens for old houses. Here a "gamekeeper" sink has been pressed back into service, together with a mixture of real kitchen antiques and objets trouvés. The snag with old sinks is that they do not accept waste disposers or basket strainer fittings but new versions which do are now available.* ST

6 *In this kitchen for a rebuilt barn in Suffolk, elements of traditional thinking were used to create an attractive but practical sink area. As a dishwasher is used for all washing up, the rack above the sink is mainly used to store and display chinaware in regular use. The china sink by Imperial with brass taps from Czech & Speake are set in an oiled solid maple worktop.* ST

The fascination of old kitchens is that, compared with main living areas, no effort was made in most cases to dress them up for appearance's sake. So what you will find, unless someone has done a thorough job of "renovation", is an inbuilt record of all the ideas and changes which have come and gone since the kitchen was first built. That record can provide the clues you need to plan your restoration.

Every lump in the walls, every odd stump of iron and every piece of joinery has a tale to tell. For example, if in the Georgian period the cook needed a new shelf, the local joiner took the first piece of wood of about the right size that came to hand and pressed it into service: it may have been part of some Queen Anne or Jacobean wall panelling stripped out of another part of the house a few years before. Authentic old kitchens often present a patchwork appearance of this kind.

In our heritage of remaining period kitchens we have the purest examples of vernacular design, influenced to a far greater degree by local traditions of craftsmanship and style passed down from one generation to the next than by any awareness of passing fashion. Details of moulding in old pieces of kitchen furniture, the materials used in floors and for working surfaces and the design of incidental items such as hanging racks and fireplace ironwork vary from one county or state to the next and sometimes even from town to town. Sadly, the trade in antiques and kitchenalia has displaced much valuable evidence of local traditions in the half-century or more of modernization following the advent of factory-made kitchen furniture between the wars. In trying to reconstruct how the kitchen originally looked, a little detective work will be necessary. The original may be

still there, walled up in a hidden inglenook. A big open chimney is probably evidence of a "down hearth" for a wood fire. Look for signs of an old "chimney crane" or marks to indicate where a weight-driven "spit engine" may have been mounted. Iron stumps in the sidewalls may indicate a later coal-burning roasting hearth.

Try to work out how the kitchen was laid out in earlier times. Clues may be offered by blocked-up doorways, changes in floor levels or materials or apparently pointless notches and breaks in beams. Consider the facilities such as pantries and sculleries needed in the days before fridges and dishwashers.

It is worth checking any sheds or barns you have where old wood is stored. Old cupboards, shelves and other joinery may have been stripped out of the backstairs areas many years before. With care such fittings can be restored to use.

KITCHENS BEFORE THE 18TH CENTURY

The kitchen as we understand it today was born in the Georgian era with the arrival of early cooking ranges in many homes. Before that, most cooking took place at various types of open fires and hearths, and water was obtained from a pump in the back yard or from a communal source.

From the 15th and 16th centuries onwards, inglenook fireplaces (or whatever they are called in the part of the country where you live) were being added to existing houses and incorporated in new buildings. At

about the same time we begin to see early sculleries, initially little more than a roofed-over space to make access to the water pump more convenient.

Until Georgian times, most inglenooks were entirely woodburning. They had huge chimneys which worked well enough because the fire was never let out between the end of the summer and the middle of spring. The warmth of that fireplace meant that this room was the centre of all family life.

Unless you are exceptionally fortunate, no indications will now be left of how such a kitchen was originally furnished because any furniture there was (and it did not amount to much in most cases) would

1 The kitchen is frequently the area of a house which remains virtually unaltered. This mid-18thC house was much modernized in the 19thC but as the kitchen was below stairs it was left with its original features. *MJ*

2 This mid-18thC open hearth fireplace in a New York house is filled with the many kitchen implements in use during this period. *VC*

3 Kitchens were frequently below ground level and were often dark and gloomy places. These oak beams were whitewashed to add some light. *VC*

4 This 17thC open hearth in a New York house is backed by a beehive oven. These provide a multitude of cooking possibilities along with the main source of heat and light. *BH*

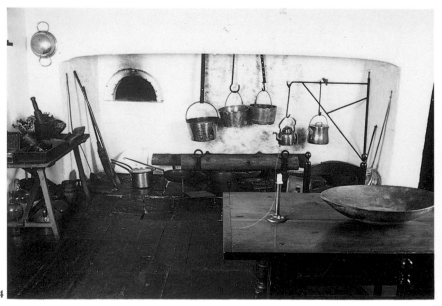

have been freestanding. The one essential piece was a big central table, but there might also have been a sideboard and later a dresser. People sat on benches mainly, with perhaps two "back stools" for the husband and wife.

The key to restoring such a kitchen today is simplicity. Closed cupboards are completely out of place, though for practical reasons most people will nonetheless consider them essential below the sink. A walk-in larder solves most food storage problems but you must disguise any modern equipment or hide it away when not in use or the effect will be spoiled.

GEORGIAN AND VICTORIAN KITCHENS

The arrival of coal as fuel for cooking led initially to raised roasting hearths. At first these still used spits and many of the other familiar fittings of the woodburning down hearth, but later they began to evolve into enclosed cooking ranges. In the Georgian period we also begin to see sinks and indoor plumbing: it is thus quite realistic to consider restoring such a kitchen to something like its original appearance and layout.

The first built-in kitchen furniture dates from this period as the increasing range of kitchenwares and utensils created a need for much more storage space. Most such furniture was very simply made from softwood using traditional joinery methods. All was painted for ease of cleaning, apart from working surfaces which were regularly scrubbed or sanded and had to be replaced periodically.

The main items of furniture would still have been the centre table and dresser (or dressers), but tall cupboards for dried goods, preserves and the storage of reserve china and kitchenwares became commonplace. Usually such items were styled to match the wood wall panelling which gradually took over from lime-washed plastered walls. The design and construction of panelling and built-in furniture varied greatly from one part of the country to another and also at different dates. It is thus invaluable as an accurate dating guide.

In practice it is almost impossible to remove such furniture from the room in which it was made without considerable damage. That means that much of it has been destroyed during subsequent "improvements", and that much of what we are now offered as kitchen furniture of Georgian times is nothing of the sort.

A century later the Victorians were embarking on the hunt for labour-saving devices, and the number and sophistication of the cooking ranges which came onto the market in late Victorian and Edwardian times were quite remarkable. Many are still in excellent working order and can be incorporated in a restored kitchen.

Furniture styling depended very much upon whether the kitchen was also the parlour in a smaller one-family house; if so, its styling became gradually more complex, although plain painted finishes were still the norm. In larger establishments, the furnishings became ever more utilitarian as the importance of ease of cleaning increased.

5 This "tin" kitchen sink was actually made of soapstone and was part of the 1850 update of this 1830 house. OMII

6 This fireplace of c.1790 was discovered behind a Victorian wall. The fittings are in period. In the late 18thC there would have been several small fires rather than one large fire. VNS

7 This kitchen range would have been the height of fashion when put in place in 1850. It was made by Abendroth Bros. in 1845. The fireplace crane was left in place. OMII

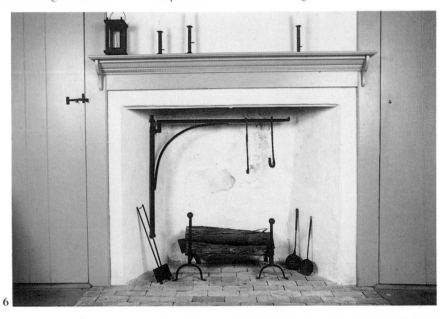

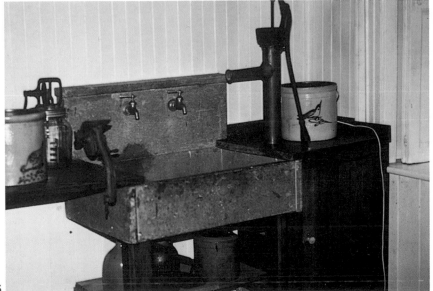

NEW KITCHENS IN THE TRADITIONAL IDIOM

Of course, the "traditional" kitchen furniture which is manufactured today is waywardly inauthentic. Generally, it is modern system unit furniture fitted with wood or painted fronts which ape certain elements of period style. Such ideas as "wall units" (which make things more difficult to get at, not easier) and working surfaces covered with tiles would have been laughed to scorn by any sane Victorian cook and the sheer impracticality of many of today's fanciful paint finishes would have been regarded in the same light. The essence of the traditional British kitchen in its heyday was the practical combination of certain key elements – a big centre table as the main working area; a carefully planned larder where most food was stored; dressers and hanging racks for those items most in use; deep drawers for other kitchenwares and utensils; and finally a really large sink surrounded by large scrubbable surfaces and a plate draining rack. When creating a kitchen which will be compatible with the style and atmosphere of a period house, always bear in mind that a real traditional kitchen was utterly practical and functional as well as warm, friendly and inviting.

It was the most important place in the house, even if normally used by servants. It is unrealistic to expect a modern housewife to dispense with her dishwasher, food mixer, microwave and refrigerator. However, these can be hidden away in period kitchen furniture. **2**

1 Interest is increasing in "unfitted" kitchens involving little or no unit furniture at all and specialist companies such as John Lewis of Hungerford are making careful copies of old items of kitchen furniture which work well in such settings. This is their Bakers Table. JL.

2, 3 Two views of a "high Victorian" kitchen with some later practical additions in a mansion at Duns near the Scottish border. Allowing for differences in scale, there are lessons to be learned from such kitchens in layout, constructional and practical details and even the materials used. Local hardwoods have been used almost throughout for cupboards and surfaces, though the working table shown here is of pine and of an earlier date.

4 Some of today's specialist kitchen furniture workshops are very skilled at recapturing the spirit of past ages. This inset cupboard by Hathaway Country Kitchens will be appreciated by anyone with a taste for that type of Victorian furniture which mixed design ideas from a dozen sources with such abandon. HA

5 The alternative to restoring a kitchen with old furniture or with reproduction joinery styled to match the period and locality concerned is to use the traditionally-styled kitchen furniture which is now offered by a number of companies. This Smallbone dresser in bleached oak, for instance, would not look out of place in a kitchen dating anywhere from the 17th to the early 20thC. S

6 The atmosphere of a traditional British kitchen is recaptured in this apparently casual but in fact thoroughly practical dresser setting. A dishwasher lives behind one of the centre doors. Much of the woodwork here has been adapted from other uses, just as most "backstairs" joinery was a century or so ago. ST

7 This Continental Art Deco stove can indeed be used for decorative purposes, but it is just as practical and efficient for every day use as the modern day Aga.

CUSTOM-BUILT AND READY-MADE KITCHENS

The traditional kitchen discussed above is the purist's answer to restoration. However, many people will find the prospect of working in an original kitchen distinctly uninviting. We have become accustomed to fitted units and work surfaces. Fortunately, many firms produce a wide range of kitchen furniture compatible with a period house. Many are styled after traditional patterns and some use old timber. There is a broad spectrum to choose from – innumerable colours and designs, textures and accessories. It is, however, vital to remember that country cottages demand a different style of kitchen from Georgian town houses.

1 This old pine kitchen has been carefully planned to give a modern design an old feel. The central Aga is a convenient modern day equivalent of the Victorian cooking range. The solid pine table imitates the central table which was the hub of the period kitchen. This pleasing modern design would not jar in a period house. S

2 A modern Aga can be given a period feel with suitable accessories. Note in particular the clock and the lighting. AR

3 Not everyone is an advocate of unpainted solid wood kitchens, especially as many kitchens are in dark areas. Smallbone of Devizes have a wide range of painted kitchens based on dresser designs. S

1

2

3

4

6

4, 5, 6 *There are many examples of solid wood kitchens, ranging from dark solid mahogany to light honey-coloured pine. Some kitchens use old wood, others are totally new although deriving from old designs. Plate racks, spice cupboards and traditional utensils give a pleasingly authentic look.*

M, S, PV

7 *An Art Deco house allows yet another design solution to kitchen planning. Note how the design on the doors is mirrored in the window glass. (Woodstock Furniture, Pakenham St, London WC1.)*

W

5

7

Today we are spoilt by the convenience and design possibilities offered by electric light in the home. This is a recent luxury. Despite the introduction of gas and electricity, candles and lamps were still widely employed at the beginning of the 20th century, especially in country regions.

Gas was first introduced in the 1780s. Electric light suitable for domestic purposes was not available until the late 1870s. Even oil lamps were not very useful until the invention in the 1780s of an improved reading lamp in which a current of air and a gravity feed made the wick burn ten times more brightly than before. Paraffin was not available until the middle of the 19th century. Few people restoring a period house are likely to want to return completely to the old laborious, dirty and inefficient methods, although a candlelit dinner will always hold its charms.

What you can do, however, is adapt the early fittings to electricity or use them as supplementary lighting.

3

2

1 *This free-standing iron candlestand is an accurate replica of early lighting. Candles can give out a surprising amount of heat and light.*   SI

2 *By 1877 this house was illuminated by gaslight pendants (except in the dining room). The decorative ceiling rose served a useful purpose, the holes in the grille providing an outlet for noxious gas fumes.*   LSH

3 *This brass three-tiered chandelier would be equally at home in an 18th or 19thC environment.*

4,5 *Accurate reproduction Art Deco lamps help to create an instant atmosphere of the cool, contrived style of the 1930s.*   EDL

1

4

5

EARLY CANDLES AND RUSH LIGHTS

In the great halls of medieval tradition, a big central fire was supplemented by torches thrust onto iron spikes or by light from cressets – metal baskets high up on poles, in which oil or pitch were burnt. Cressets were much used in Elizabethan times. Piques (or spikes), used to impale the soft wax or tallow candles, either were small, holding a single candle, or stood four or five feet high with spikes for many candles. "Candle beams", usually of wood, with four stout bars to hold the candles (sometimes two per bar) radiating from a central bar suspended from the ceiling, were the handsome predecessors of elegant chandeliers. Brass candelabra were also used. Candles were also held aloft in staffs by servants or placed on spikes in wall sconces and on stands. Sometimes light was supplied by strips of rushes, dipped in oil and held in a simple iron stand and clip with a wooden base. Candles were much too expensive for ordinary cottagers, who used rush lights, sometimes dipped in mutton fat rather than less readily available oil.

The socket candlestick emerged in the 16th century, and sturdy brass candlesticks were made. During the 17th century candleholders of all kinds became objects for display. The idea of a six-or twelve- branched candelabrum in brass was borrowed from the Low Countries. Candelabra were also produced in carved and gilded wood and ornamental wrought iron. Snuffers were of brass and precious metals as well as iron. Silver sconces were now set against the wall to help increase the spread of light.

In areas where fish oil was available, the poor used small oil lamps from shallow vessels with rough wicks, perhaps of twisted rag.

6

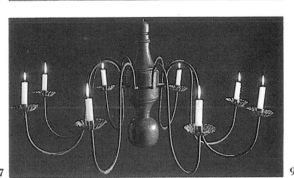

7

8

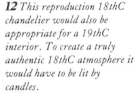

9

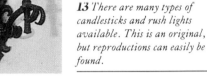

13

13 *There are many types of candlesticks and rush lights available. This is an original, but reproductions can easily be found.*

6 *This traditional-style wrought-iron and wood chandelier has a simplicity which is exactly right for a building of the 16th or 17thC. Such items can also be used in rustic or less sophisticated houses of a later date. They are ideal with candles but can be wired for candle-like bulbs. Wrought iron has a naturally rustic look and should never be over-polished or buffed.* SI

7,8,9 *There is a movement back to more authentic-looking fittings. Specialist companies make wall fittings that give the right feel to early houses while still using electricity. These examples are from Stuart Interiors.* SI

10,11 *These chandeliers, also from Stuart Interiors, are particularly well-matched to their period settings.* SI

12 *This reproduction 18thC chandelier would also be appropriate for a 19thC interior. To create a truly authentic 18thC atmosphere it would have to be lit by candles.*

14 *An original Regency lamp that has been restored and re-gilded. This would fit perfectly into any Egyptian Revival interior.*

10

11

12

14

18th-Century Styles

Fine, handsome candlesticks contributed to the character of Georgian interiors, even though they provided little light. At first sturdy holders were still created, in a variety of metals but especially in brass and bronze, to hold one or several candles. Slimmer, more elegant candlesticks were preferred by the middle of the 18th century, and although solid-looking ones later came back into fashion, these were plainer and often made of sheet iron or burnished steel.

This century saw more use of lanterns, which could be suspended or set against the wall (and, of course, carried). Their horn panels protected the flame from draughts. By the 1790s we find huge oil-burning lanterns, with a brass or iron frame housing six or eight glass panels, hung in halls and stairways and welcoming guests at the front of the house.

Pendant light fittings ranged from the relatively modest brass candelabrum, with a bowl-shaped body and six curved, branching candle holders, to the most exquisitely ornate chandeliers. The latter hung, huge, glittering and splendid, from the ceilings of ballrooms and drawing rooms, or with as few as six candles springing from a little shower of sparkling cut glass in less grand though still substantial surroundings. On the walls of these interiors, elaborately backed sconces held yet further candles: scores would be burnt in the course of an evening. In less wealthy homes tall, thin taper stands were common. These either had tripods, or round or square bases, and came complete with attached scissors for snuffing the rush tapers which were burnt in them.

1 *Chandeliers occupy a lot of space and should only be used in a generously proportioned room. This example is a perfect copy of a Regency original.*

2 *Looking-glass lights between the windows of an early 19thC house would have shed a fine, even light.* OMH

3 *A late 19thC wall light need not look incongruous in an 18thC house. As lighting developed, homeowners would install the most modern and practical form of lighting without necessarily changing the decorative aspects.*

4 *A wrought-iron outside lantern, made in the 1930s but a perfect replica of mid-18thC style.* HH

5 *Hall lanterns give a warm and welcoming atmosphere to a hallway. This type would fit well into most late 18th and 19thC houses.* BP

6 *Gas chandeliers were a common sight in the parlour of a 19thC house. This example, typically High Victorian, has a "water-slide" system enabling the apparatus to be lowered.* OMH

7 *This 19thC hallway is devoid of the furniture and fabrics which would create the "upholstered" feel of a Victorian interior. However, 19thC lighting is enough to evoke the period.* OMH

THE 19TH CENTURY

Plain steel candlesticks continued to be fashionable during the early 19th century, when the recently discovered wax-hardening process made the candles burn more steadily and with less mess. Spermaceti candles, a product of the whaling industry, gave an even better light; and oil lamps, not much used in the 18th century, were also improved.

During the 19th century, despite gas light and even individual gas plants for some country houses, oil lamps were the most common source of light. When mineral oils became available in the middle of the century, they represented a huge step forward. Many Victorian paraffin lamps are still gently illuminating dinner tables and sitting rooms. Wicks can still be obtained for them, and so too can replacement chimneys and shades, should the originals get broken. Despite the limitations imposed by their working methods, Victorian oil lamps, or excellent reproductions of them, are found in an apparently endless range of designs, in glass as well as brass and other metals.

Gas was widely used in upper-middle-class homes during the second part of the 19th century, until it was eclipsed by electricity. Gas light fittings took their form from oil lamps, but could of course dispense with the reservoir. Pendant oil lamps with three or four burners fed from a central container for the oil were produced contemporaneously with suspended gas lights of similar appearance. However, gas lamps could easily be fixed to the wall as well, and piped gas lent itself perfectly to the European *fin de siècle* look, with sweeping curves and sinuous ornamentation.

10

12 An Edwardian rise-and-fall hanging lamp with opaline glass lampshade. The great advantage of electricity was that light was thrown downwards where it was most needed. LSH

12

8 An electric bracket light in the style of a 19thC gas fitting. The glare of light bulbs can be hidden behind translucent frosted, coloured or engraved shades to create the mellow lighting of the era. EDL

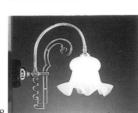

8

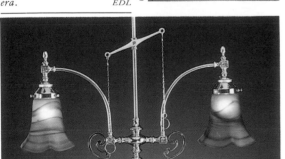

9

9 A good example of a reproduction 19thC ceiling pendant. The original would have been fitted for gas or oil; however, adaptation to electricity does not detract from the period feel. EDL

10 This Venetian chandelier does not look out of place in a 19thC house, but really belongs to the less cluttered, classical style of the 18thC. It requires a high room. LH

11 Gas fittings often remained in place even when electricity had largely superseded gas. Their hollow pipes made them easy to convert. LSH

11

13

13 A typical Victorian lamp, evocative of the clutter and cosiness of the period. LSH

ELECTRICITY

From the 1880s Edison lamps in the United States and Swan lamps in Britain brought the blessings of clean, controllable and odour-free electric light into the home. Electric light gave all possible scope to designers. Some stuck rigidly to the candle theme, and placed the light bulbs on candle-like stalks set in traditional candelabra or table-standing burners. The advantage (if it was one) provided by the new source of light was that the bulbs could now be dressed in little shades, whether plain or pleated and frilled.

Electric lights were also set in wrought-iron fittings of branches, leaves and flowers. They were equipped with shades in glass and metal, the glass fluted and shaped like bluebells and harebells, or in the form of simple globes and cones. European Art Nouveau contributed its characteristic curves and milkily opaque glass in subtle colours. Perhaps most spectacular of all were the American Tiffany lamps in their glowing stained-glass shades.

These and their coolly 20th-century Art Deco successors are now available in perfect reproductions from specialist manufacturers. Those whose purse cannot stretch to handmade reproductions will find that a search through antique and second-hand shops may still yield derivative period light fittings. An Edwardian mottled glass bowl suspended by a brass chain or an Expressionist faceted wall light in metal housing would complete a well-contrived interior.

1

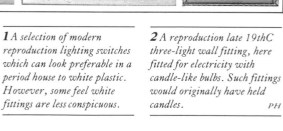

6

2

3

4

5

1 *A selection of modern reproduction lighting switches which can look preferable in a period house to white plastic. However, some feel white fittings are less conspicuous.*

2 *A reproduction late 19thC three-light wall fitting, here fitted for electricity with candle-like bulbs. Such fittings would originally have held candles.* PH

3 *Wall lights of the 19thC characteristically had brackets with etched globe or upturned shades. Even when gas-fuelled, they still followed the styles of oil or candle power. These are now usually converted to electricity.*

4 *A Regency gilt metal hanging lantern, now fitted for electricity.*

5 *Hall lanterns were still being used to light the way for guests in the late 19thC, but they had become much more ornate.* PCA

6 *Standard rise-and-fall pendant lights of the late Victorian and Edwardian periods can still be found intact in their original settings.*

7,8,9,10 *Art Nouveau lamps have become highly desirable in recent years. Many of the best were made by the firm of Tiffany in New York, as illustrated by the examples here. These are originals. Similar lamps are to be found in auction rooms and antique shops.*

11,12,13,14,15 *Art Deco lamps can add greatly to the atmosphere of a 1920s or 30s flat or house. These examples are reproductions but follow the lines and colours of the originals.*

EDL

The visual pleasure we derive from the outsides of period houses comes partly from the architectural elements – the doors, windows and so on – and the ways in which they are treated and related to each other. Enjoyment also comes from the materials – weathered limestone, shining granite, knapped flint or bricks of every type, size and arrangement, whether Elizabethan herringbone or 19th-century polychrome, perhaps dressed up in contrasting stone on the corners (quoins), pilaster strips and window surrounds. The hardened oak of half-timbering, the ornamental impact of plasterwork, the soft contours of clay daub: all have their own characteristic "feel". Additionally, the personality of a house is expressed in its immediate surroundings, the nature of the boundaries (walls, fences, railings, hedges), the materials and detailing of access points (gates, paths and steps), and features such as window boxes.

1 A stone pineapple offers a sign of welcome beside an entrance. Although such ornaments are always called pineapples, they are in fact pine cones, ancient symbols of fertility and wealth.

2 One of the interesting features of architecture is the recurrence of themes. These sphinxes and obelisks reflect the fascination with Ancient Egypt in the Regency period (1812-30).

3 This doorway combines many features from the late 18th and early 19thC. The classical pediment seems somehow to vye with the decorative ironwork on the door and holding the lantern.

4 Exterior lead pipework was formerly treated as part of the decoration of a house.

5 Decorative ironwork on balconies was popular in both the 18th and 19thC.

6 When designing this house in New York – a replica of one of 1760, built in the 1920s – the architect included some elements salvaged from old houses. However, most features here are faithful copies. The ornate carving over the entrance includes the beaver symbol of New York State. HH

SCROLLS, URNS AND STATUES

The Tudors elaborated doorways with terracotta panels and stucco coats-of-arms, roses and animals. Then the Jacobeans continued this tradition and developed it, sometimes covering whole facades of half-timbered houses with plaster ornament. Patterns could be simple scrolls set in large panels or, in East Anglia, swirling "parget work" decorated with clumsy but charming classical motifs such as swags.

With the Restoration came the fashion for classical facades, though usually without the parapets of later classical houses. Ornament was rather in the form of bold pediments partly concealing the sloping roofs and decorated with stone swags and emblems and stone pilasters with elaborate capitals. The niches of the Palladian mansions of the 18th century were occupied by stucco figures in contemporary dress, in place of the classical statues in stone that were favoured previously.

In the early 18th century, gardens of grand houses were still designed formally in the French manner, with broad avenues and *rond-points* (intersections). Main avenues were flanked with trees, but urns, vases and classical statuary along the paths also made an important contribution, and these features were continued in the facade niches, along the tops of walls and set into parapets. Stone garden urns were often encrusted with swags and cherubs, more ornamental than the plants themselves.

Later in the 18th century the Picturesque landscape superseded the formal garden, but niches were still provided for classical statues, for example in clipped yew hedges, and stone lions overlooked the parkland from the balustraded terrace next to the house.

Gardening and plants had become a passion at all levels of society from the middle classes upward. In an age when pattern books were disseminating details of classical design among builders, gardening manuals were also widely distributed, with advice on all subjects, including ideas for tubs and window boxes for houses without gardens.

In the 19th century many of the older features were revived. The parget work and stucco of the period have a vigour which makes them hard to distinguish them from their 17th-century models, while houses built in the same spirit as the Palladian mansions have classical statuary in the same manner, with the niches inhabited by figures such as Venus and Apollo.

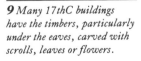

7 This Victorian house has ornamental balustrading which dominates the roof and is mirrored by that around the top of the bay window. Note also the popular scroll design .

8 Classically inspired eagles are often later additions.

9 Many 17thC buildings have the timbers, particularly under the eaves, carved with scrolls, leaves or flowers.

10 It is still possible to buy garden ornaments made from old moulds or based on 18th and 19thC patterns.   CS

BOUNDARIES

Small country houses may be bounded with picket fences – simple wooden slats placed quite closely together and driven into the ground or fixed to supporting posts with wire, or often nailed to wooden horizontal bars themselves fixed to posts.

Larger country houses with roots still in the vernacular tradition consort well with low walls of local brick or stone in front of dense box or yew hedges – which may be clipped into extraordinary shapes.

RAILINGS AND GATES

Ironwork was introduced to Britain by William and Mary when they brought the French Huguenot smith Tijou to work under their patronage in 1689. He made beautiful gates, balustrades and garden screens in sheet iron embossed into scrolls, gilded flower and acanthus leaves in a way not seen in England before. Subsequently ironwork became enormously popular, and with good reason. The gates might be set within stone piers, perhaps with niches and topped with eagles or covered urns, or fluted and bearing proud gryphons. Charming pastoral figures in lead were found on gate piers by the end of the 17th century and were in vogue during the 18th. Wrought iron might also be used for the piers themselves and for delicate overthrows across the top of wide gateways.

With the passage of time, upper-class styles in ironwork filtered down to the less privileged social strata. Wrought, *repoussé* (hammered) and eventually cheaper cast iron were used for plain and decorative railings, gateways and other features right up to the 20th century. In the 18th century simple, well-proportioned cast-iron work was as much favoured as more elaborate wrought-iron scrolls and curves. Even simple town houses had plain cast-iron railings round

their areas (that is, the enclosed spaces between the street and the drop to the basement) and up the steps to the front door. In the Regency period wrought iron flourished in England in the form of elaborate balconies, verandas and porches. Door hoods were revived, but now made in curving sheets of lead like the veranda canopies of the same period. All such flourishes, however decorative, were still accompanied by plain boundary railings at the front of the house.

Throughout the 19th century similar plain cast-iron railings continued to be provided at the front of countless new houses, and sometimes also for little balconies above the porch. By the turn of the century even the smallest houses had such railings at the front. Often they still stand, set into a low wall in front of the privet hedge which the builder planted as part of the complete package.

Towards the end of the 19th century, grand houses in the Queen Anne style, though so different in appearance from these terraced rows, also had iron-work boundary fences. In keeping with their attachment to old traditions, these were usually wrought, not cast. Fortunately the art of the smith is still flourishing today, and there are many architectural metalworkers who can restore wrought- and cast-iron work to make replacements in keeping with the style of the house.

1 Ornate wrought-iron balustrades, terminating in lantern-shaped newel posts, flank the stone steps at the entrance to this Federal-style American house. OMH

2,3 Two views of the fence and gate of an 1830s house in Roslyn, New York. The white painted picket fence has elaborate spear tops and the supporting posts of the gateway with their vase decoration have the importance of columns. The close-up shows the original iron hinges and shutting mechanism.

4, 5 Wrought-iron railings are a delightful and interesting adjunct to houses of the 18th and 19thC. On smaller houses they were often quite plain but in grander houses they used many classical themes such as the pineapple or pine cone.

6

7

8

9

10

11

12

13

14

15

6-14 Wrought-iron and, later, cast iron balconies and railings were common in both grand and simple houses. It is essential to the look of our streets that terraces retain a feeling of continuity. Blacksmiths can reproduce perfect copies, and these do improve the overall appearance of the exteriors of period houses. Your local historical or architectural society should be able to advise on the style of balcony or railing which would have been original to the house. Otherwise, copies of neighbouring styles will suffice.

15 On a Neo-classical stone mansion built between 1837 and 1846 the wrought ironwork sweeps down on either side of the steps to curve around the newel posts. *BP*

1 Plain railings were not always mirrored in the treatment of balconies and ironwork around windows. Houses develop piecemeal, as owners decide to introduce more up-to-date features.

2 The entrance porch of a late 19thC house is given greater importance with pillars, arches and a balcony above.

3, 4 Whether in a simple terrace or grander entranceway the Georgians had a feeling for proportion and the continuity of classical themes.

5 Wrought and plain ironwork provide a useful security device for this basement of an early 19thC house.

STEPS AND STAIRS

The great Palladian houses had magnificent double staircases curving or angling up to a terrace along the house. On a smaller scale, the front doors of town houses (however close to the street) were from the late 17th century almost universally approached by stone steps the breadth of the doorcase. No fine house, however handsome, would be quite so imposing without the steps leading up to its front door.

When the entrance was at a sufficiently high level, the flight of steps could be longer. However, until well into the 19th century often as few as two or three treads were needed. The builder's or architect's skill in judging proportion came fully into play: it is surprising how harmonious two steps can be. The lower step in 18th-century houses may rise only slightly above the street; sometimes it is wider than the step above and curved at the sides; and often a moulded nose finishes the edge of each step.

Railings round the basement area usually continued up the sides of the steps to the porch or front door. In smarter houses, the railings included lamp holders and conical link extinguishers, which may still survive .

Houses of the 19th century may have lacked the finely judged proportions of their predecessors but their broader entranceways, set higher up from street level and farther back, enabled them to have impressive flights of stone steps. These might have simply moulded noses, continuing round the rounded-off corners, or be flanked by wide stone flat-topped or solidly balustraded ramps, in keeping with the solid, comfortable houses. Later Victorian houses with semi-basements and set close to the road have ended up with an awkwardly steep flight of inelegant steps, compensated for, perhaps, by the lofty rooms inside. Edwardian family houses, their main rooms and entrance halls at ground level, may lack this lofty spaciousness, but their prettily tiled paths leading up to timbered porches are friendly and inviting.

6

8

5

7

6 A long flight of steps leads up to the side door of a 1748 Bronx mansion. The lattice work under the steps is to facilitate a good flow of air.

VC

7 A Victorian house in London where cast-iron railings and gate are matched by low rails in front of the bay windows. The areas too have simple railings cutting them off from the approach to the house. The front door is reached by a flight of stone steps, flanked by flat-topped balustraded ramps terminating in pillars and flower urns. LSH

8 Steps to the front door were standard even in the simple terrace. These steps are tiled. Note also the highly decorative ironwork on the upper floor.

We generally think of the conservatory as a Victorian invention, and indeed it had its heyday in the 19th century. However, it was first popular in the 18th, in the form of the elegant orangery. The advantages of a conservatory, not only as a place for growing plants but also as a living area with a summery atmosphere, remain undiminished today.

The orangery was a gracious extra room in the Palladian mansion. Its transitional role between house and garden satisfied the Georgian passion for the pastoral – a terrace would often run along the outside, adjoining the garden – and as the name implies it was a place where exotic fruits could be grown. These would be raised in tubs so that they could be set out or even planted in the summer. Orangeries were designed and built in the same manner as the rest of the house. Although the walls consisted of glazed windows on three sides (the fourth often being joined to the house), the parapets usually concealed a conventional slate or tiled roof. After cast iron began to be used in the 1770s, the orangery retained its noble, restrained form. It was at this period a carefully proportioned, unobtrusive building, very different from its showy Victorian relative, which bristled with cast-iron ornament and flaunted huge sheets of polished glass.

By the end of the 18th century the metamorphosis had begun. Robert Adam designed orangeries with slighter glazing bars and coved ceilings. Some wooden-framed glass roofs were also to be found at this time.

However, it was Joseph Paxton and his contemporaries in the 1830s who completed the

1

2

3

1,2 These two large conservatories are essentially glass houses in the tradition of Paxton and his followers. It is a modern convention to paint conservatories white: Victorian examples would more often have been green. Green canvas awnings give excellent shade while retaining a period feel. ML

3 A conservatory that joins two sections of a house in the form of a corridor with roof and frontage aligned. ML

4

5

6

8

7

4 In townhouses where there is no space to put a conservatory in the garden, one answer is to add one at first floor level over a protruding downstairs room. ML.

5 An original Victorian "window-box" type of conservatory. These are close relations to the "Wardian cases" in which travellers transported ferns and other exotics from foreign places. LSH

6,7 A Victorian-style conservatory that completely fills the space between an L-shaped house and an adjacent outbuilding. Notice how the transitional feel between indoors and out is accentuated by using the same tiling on the conservatory floor and the terrace: if you do this, make sure the tiles will stand up to the weather. ML.

8 A conservatory must harmonize with the building to which it is attached. Here, the stone and brick base blend with the main dwelling. MJ

transformation. Paxton's passion was as much for plants as it was for the new technology of glass and iron. The vogue for collecting and displaying new exotic varieties spread rapidly. In 1851, the year of the Great Exhibition in London, window tax was finally abolished; the duty on glass, which had made heavier glass prohibitively expensive, was removed in 1857. The Crystal Palace, built by Paxton for the Exhibition, thrilled thousands of visitors and helped to create a craze for glasshouses and conservatories. The demand was quickly met by prefabricated glass-and-iron structures. These provided long, high rooms with underfloor heating for tropical trees, or glazed extensions to the sitting room in which to cultivate ferns.

The new ornamented conservatories, perfect for mid-19th-century houses whose design was free from classical constraints, remained in fashion until the First World War. In larger terraced houses they sometimes provided all the garden there was, and in the smallest they were little more than exotic lean-tos. Edwardian examples were less ornate, and the simple lines of the Edwardian style might well be preferable if you are adding a conservatory onto a small house.

Although they can make the rooms from which they extend darker, conservatories are wonderfully light in themselves and remove the need for double glazing. However, they do need their own heating and shading systems to avoid extremes of climate hostile to sensitive plants. In the northern hemisphere, a south-west wall is the safest choice of situation.

If you are adding a conservatory to a pre-19th-century house, a building modelled on the orangery would be more authentic, with large windows in the same style as the house rather than a prominent all-glass room which would strike an anachronistic note. For Victorian and later houses glass and metal styles are perfectly acceptable.

Very satisfactory reproduction period conservatories are available today. They are expensive but they add a whole new living area, and provided that they are carefully integrated in style and scale they give a special atmosphere of elegance to both house and garden.

GLOSSARY

ANDIRON (OR ENDIRON): *a metal bar, supported on feet, to hold burning logs above hearth level (also called FIRE-DOG).*

ARCADING: *a series of arches on columns or PIERS which can be freestanding or attached to a wall.*

ARCHITRAVE: *the moulded frame around a window or door; or, more properly, the lowest portion of an ENTABLATURE.*

BACON FLAKE: *traditional Yorkshire Dales name for the wood rack hung from the kitchen ceiling on extended iron hooks. It was used to store cured hams and smoked bacon sides during the winter. "Bread flakes", to a somewhat different design, were used in a similar way to store loaves and the large biscuits which were traditionally cooked on iron plates over open fires.*

BALUSTER: *a banister, typically turned and undulating in form (which is why the term baluster is given to coffee pots, glass stems and so on of this shape).*

BALUSTRADE: *a series of BALUSTERS supporting a handrail or coping.*

BAROQUE: *rather heavy, flamboyant style which originated in Italy in the 17th century and appeared in England late in the same century.*

BATTEN DOOR: *a door made from rows of vertical planks, nailed or pegged to supporting horizontal planks.*

BOSS: *an ornamental knob at the intersection of ribs in a ceiling or a vault.*

BULL'S EYE: *see CROWN GLASS.*

BUTLER SINK: *a large, oblong proprietary sink of all-white or white and beige porcelain on fireclay. The name is now commonly used for all sinks of this type, though most of those offered as Butler sinks are later and much deeper laboratory sinks. The true Butler sinks were rarely more than 6in deep.*

CAMES: *the strip of metal used for leaded lights.*

CAPITAL: *the crowning feature of a column.*

CASEMENT WINDOW: *a window with the sash hung vertically and which opens inwards or outwards by means of a hinge.*

CHAMFER: *to cut or grind off bevel-wise the edge of a piece of wood or stone originally right-angled.*

CHIMNEYPIECE (OR MANTELPIECE): *the frame around a fireplace which may be made from brick, stone, marble or wood.*

CONSOLE BRACKET: *ornamental bracket, often of S-form and usually having more height than projection.*

CORNICE *a decorative projecting moulding around the top of a wall or arch (in an interior it usually disguises the join between walls and ceilings); the projecting top section of an ENTABLATURE.*

CROWN GLASS: *a sheet of glass made by blowing a bubble and spinning it rapidly on the rod; a BULL'S EYE is formed where the rod is attached.*

DAMP-PROOF COURSE: *a layer of impervious material laid in a wall to stop rising damp.*

DEPRESSED ARCH: *a shallow slightly pointed arch.*

DOG-LEG STAIRCASE: *two parallel flights of stairs with a half-landing between.*

DOORCASE: *the ARCHITRAVE enclosing a door.*

DOWN HEARTH: *Southern English name for an open fireplace in which a log fire was formed directly on the floor of the inglenook. Often used for cooking as well, using turnspits, pots and griddle plates hung over the fire from bars or cranes and three-legged gunmetal pots pushed into the edge of the fire.*

ENTABLATURE: *in classical architecture, the top part of a column made up of ARCHITRAVE, FRIEZE and CORNICE; a decoration made up in this way popular from the mid-18th century.*

FANLIGHT: *a window over a door, often semi-circular with radiating glazing bars.*

FENDER: *a low metal screen which prevents burning coals or logs from rolling into the room.*

FENESTRAL: *a lattice frame across which oiled or waxed paper or linen was stretched to keep out draughts while letting in the light.*

FIELDED PANEL: *panel with the centre raised in profile.*

FIREBACK: *a thick cast-iron panel put at the back of a hearth to protect the wall and to reflect heat into the room.*

FIRE-DOG: *see ANDIRON.*

FLAG: *stone slab used for flooring.*

FREESTONE: *stone that cuts well in any direction, notably fine-grained sandstone or limestone.*

FRIEZE: *the middle section of an ENTABLATURE: the upper part of a wall directly below the cornice.*

GRATE: *a framework of bars to hold a fire.*

INGLENOOK: *a recess for a seat beside a fireplace, often covered by the chimney breast.*

KNAPPED FLINT: *flints split and laid so that the smooth black split surfaces form the facing of the wall.*

LIGHT: *vertical opening between MULLIONS of a window.*

LIMEWASH: *a mixture of slaked lime and water used for painting walls.*

LINENFOLD: *a panelling decorated with design representing vertical folds of linen.*

LINK: *a torch.*

LINTEL: *a horizontal beam or stone across an opening.*

MANTELPIECE: *see CHIMNEYPIECE.*

MULLION: *upright dividing a window into two or more LIGHTS.*

NEWEL POST: *the upright post at the end, or at the corner, of the handrail of a staircase; on a circular staircase, the column around which the stairs wind.*

OVERMANTEL: *an ornamental structure placed over a MANTELPIECE.*

PALLADIAN: *a style of architecture taken from the designs of the 16th-century Italian architect Palladio. Inigo Jones brought the style to England in the 17th century but the great revival of Palladianism was brought about by Lord Burlington and Colen Campbell in the first quarter of the 18th century.*

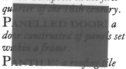

PANELLED DOOR: *a door constructed of panels set within a frame.*

PANTILE: *a roofing tile with a curved S-shaped section.*

PARGET WORK: *a style of moulded plaster decoration particularly associated with East Anglia.*

PARQUETAGE: *thin hardwood laid in patterns on a wood sub-floor.*

PAVIORS: *thin "bricks" used for flooring.*

PEDIMENT: *a low-pitched gable above a portico, door or window which may be either straight-sided or curbed; a broken pediment is one which is open at the top.*

PIANO NOBILE: *the principal storey of a house — more lofty than the others — containing the reception rooms; there is a basement or ground floor below and shallower floors above.*

PIER: *a solid vertical masonry support; the solid section of wall between openings — windows, doors etc — in a building.*

PILASTER: *a shallow column or PIER set against a wall and projecting only slightly from it.*

PITCH FLOORS: *floors made from small pieces of stone laid like cobblestones and arranged in patterns.*

PLATE GLASS: *glass used for mirrors and windows, originally made by pouring moulten glass onto an iron plate.*

QUARRY (OR QUARREL): *a small pane of glass, most often diamond-shaped, used for medieval leaded windows.*

REBATE (OR RABBET): *a rectangular recess along an edge of a piece of wood or stone to receive a tongue of another piece.*

REEDED: *decorated with parallel convex mouldings which touch one another.*

REREDOS: *a screen. The term is more commonly used for the decorative wall or screen behind an altar.*

RESTORATION: *the time of the reinstatement of the monarchy in England in 1660.*

REVEAL: *the side surface of a recess or of the opening for a door or window between the frame and outer surface of the wall. If the reveal is cut diagonally it is called a splay (or splayed) reveal.*

ROASTING HEARTH: *Georgian and later cooking hearth in which coal was burned in a grate of variable width raised well above the floor of an inglenook on horizontal bars. These hearths were the predecessors of early cooking ranges.*

ROCOCO: *the delicate and elegant style which followed the BAROQUE, characterized by S-curves, naturalistic motifs and a tendency towards asymmetry.*

SASH WINDOW: *a window composed of sliding glazed frames (sashes) running in vertical grooves.*

STENCIL: *originally "to spangle", from the Old French estinceller: now describes a method of decoration where paint is brushed over a cut-out design usually in varnished manilla paper.*

STILES: *the vertical parts of a door, window, or other frame.*

STRAPWORK: *decoration consisting of interlaced bands and shapes like fretwork.*

STRINGS: *the sloping sides of a staircase which hold the treads and risers.*

STUCCO: *smooth or modelled plasterwork.*

STUDS: *secondary vertical wall timbers.*

TABERNACLE FRAME: *a style of door surround composed of columns or pilasters surmounted by an ENTABLATURE.*

TESSELLATED FLOOR: *a floor composed of small cubes of marble, stone or glass embedded in cement.*

TRANSOM: *a bar dividing a window opening horizontally.*

TROMPE L'OEIL: *something which gives the appearance of reality by means of paint, architecture etc; literally "something that deceives the eye".*

TUDOR ARCH: *a very flattened arch coming to a definite point.*

WAINSCOT: *wood panelling on an internal wall.*

WATTLE AND DAUB: *a type of wall construction whereby laths are plastered over with mud.*

Addy, Sidney Oldall, **The Evolution of the English House.** *London*: The Macmillan Co; *New York*: Swan Sonnenschein & Co., 1898.

Airs, Malcolm, **The Buildings of Britain: Tudor and Jacobean.** *London*: Barrie & Jenkins, 1982.

Amery, Colin, **Three Centuries of Architectural Craftsmanship.** *London*: The Architectural Press, 1977; paperback edition, 1978.

Artley, Alexandra, **Putting Back the Style.** *London*: Evans Brothers, 1982.

Aslet, Clive & Powers, Alan, **National Trust Book of the English House.** *London*: Penguin Books, 1986.

Ayres, James, **The Shell Book of the House in Britain.** *London* and *Boston*: Faber & Faber, 1981.

Bankart, George, **The Art of the Plasterer: An account of the decorative development of the craft.** *London*: Batsford, 1908.

Barley, M.W., **The House and Home: a review of 900 years of house planning and furnishing in Britain.** *London*: Studio Vista, 1963.

Beard, Geoffrey, **Craftsmen and Interior Decoration in England 1660-1820.** *Edinburgh*: John Bartholomew & Sons, 1981.

Bowyer, Jack, **Vernacular Building Conservation.** *London*: The Architectural Press, 1980.

Clifton-Taylor, Alec, **The Pattern of English Building.** *London*: Faber & Faber, 1962.
— **Six English Towns.** *London*. British Broadcasting Corporation, 1982.
— **Another Six English Towns.** *London*: British Broadcasting Corporation, 1984.
— **English Stone Building.** *London*: Victor Gollancz, 1983.

Cook, Olive, **The English House through Seven Centuries.** *London*: Thomas Nelson, 1968; paperback edition: Penguin Books, 1984; *New York*: Overlook Press, 1983.

Cooper, Nicholas, **The Opulent Eye: Late Victorian and Edwardian taste in interior design.** *London*: The Architectural Press, 1976.

Cornforth, John, **English Interiors 1790-1848: the quest for comfort.** *London*: Barrie & Jenkins, 1978.

Cruikshank, Den & Wyld, Peter, **The Art of Georgian Building.** *London*: The Architectural Press; *New York*: Architectural Book Publishing Co, 1975.

Curl, James Stephens, **Victorian Architecture: its practical aspects.** *Newton Abbot*: David & Charles, 1973.

Dixon, Roger & Muthesius, Stefan, **Victorian Architecture.** *New York* and *Toronto*: Oxford University Press, 1978.

Dutton, Ralph, **The English Country House.** *London*: Batsford, 1935.
— **The English Interior, 1500-1900.** *London*: Batsford, 1948.

Edmunds, R.C., **Your Country Cottage: a guide to purchase and restoration.** *Newton Abbot*: David & Charles, 1970.

Fletcher, Banister F. & Fletcher, H. Phillips, **The English Home.** *London*: Methuen & Co, 1910.

Girouard, Mark, **Sweetness and Light: the 'Queen Anne' movement 1860-1900.** *Oxford*: Oxford University Press, 1977.

Good Housekeeping Institute, **Good Housekeeping Quick Home Repairs.** *London*: Ebury Press, 1982.

Gotch, J. Alfred, **The English House from Charles I to George IV: its architecture decoration and garden design.** *London*: Batsford, 1918.

The Guild of Master Craftsmen, **Guide to Restoration Experts.**

Hanna, Max & Binney, Marcus, **Preserve and Prosper: Save Britain's Heritage.**

Hemming, Charles, **Paint Finishes.** *London*: Macdonald.

Hill, Oliver & Cornforth, John, **English Country House: 'Caroline' 1625-1685.** *Suffolk*: Antique Collector's Club, 1985.

Hills, Nicholas, **The English Fireplace.** *London*: Quiller Press 1983, 1985.

The Historic Buildings Co, **Period Property Register.** Published 11 times a year.

Jackson-Stops, Gervase & Pipkin, James, **The English Country House – A Grand Tour.** *London*: Weidenfeld & Nicholson.

Johnson, Lorraine, **New Decorator's Directory.** *London*: Michael Joseph/Design Council; paperback edition: Mermaid Books, 1986.

Keltel, Russell Hawes, **Early American Rooms.** *New York*: Dover, 1967.

Lambourne, Lionel, **Utopian Craftsmen: The arts and crafts movement from the Cotswolds to Chicago.** *London*: Astragal Books, 1980.

Lasdun, Susan, **Victorians at Home.** *London*: Weidenfeld & Nicholson.

Le Grice, Lyn, **Lyn Le Grice's Art of Stencilling:** Viking Press, 1986.

Lloyd, Nathanial, **A History of the English House.** *London*: The Architectural Press, 1931, 1949, 1975; paperback edition, 1975.

McCorquodale, Charles, **The History of Interior Decoration.** Phaidon Press, 1983.

McDonald, Roxana, **The Fireplace Book.** *London*: The Architectural Press, 1984.

McGown, John & Du Ben, Roger, **The Book of Home Restoration.** *London*: Ebury Press, 1985

Moore, Derry & Pick, Michael, **The English Room.** *London*: Weidenfeld & Nicholson.

Muthesius, Stefan, **The English Terraced House.** *New Haven and London*: Yale University Press, 1982.

Paint Research Association, **Paint and Pretreatment Products Directory.** Second edition March 1983.
— **Evaluation of Biocidal Masonry Coatings and Guide to Paint Film Biocides.** March 1986.

Palmer, Roy, **The Water Closet: a new history.** *Newton Abbot*: David & Charles, 1973.

The Penguin Dictionary of Architecture, John Fleming, Hugh Honour and Nikolaus Pevsner, Penguin Books, London.

The Penguin Dictionary of Decorative Arts, John Fleming and Hugh Honour, Penguin Books, London.

Pilcher, Donald, **The Regency Style 1800 to 1830.** *London*: Batsford, 1947.

Plumb, J.H., **Georgian Delights.** *London*: Weidenfeld & Nicholson, 1980.

Quennel, Marjorie & C.H.B., **A History of Everyday Things in England, Vol III, 1733-1851.** *London*: Batsford, 1961.

Radford, Penny, **Surfaces and Finishes.** *London*: Macmillan, 1984.

Reid, Richard, **The Shell Book of Cottages.** *London*: Michael Joseph, 1977, 1986.

Scott, John S., **A Dictionary of Building.** *London and New York*: Penguin Books, 1964; revised edition, 1974.

Seymour Lindsay, J., **Iron and Brass Implements of the English House.** *London*: Alec Tiranti, 1970.

Summerson, John, **Georgian London.** *London*: Pleiades Books, 1945; revised paperback edition: Penguin Books 1978.
— **The Architecture of the 18th C.** *London*: Thames & Hudson, 1986.

Watkin, David, **The Buildings of Britain: Regency** (Series editor, Alastair Service). *London*: Barrie & Jenkins, 1982.

Williams, Constance, **A Continuing Tradition . . . the development of wallpaper manufacture.** Good Housekeeping, 1976.

Wilson, Everett B, **Fifty Early American Towns.** *South Brunswick, N.J.*: A.S. Barnes & Company; *London*: Thomas Yoseloff, 1966.

Wood, Margaret, **The English Medieval House.** Ferndale Editions, 1981.

Wright, Lawrence, **Clean and Decent: the fascinating history of the bathroom and the WC.** *London*: Routledge & Kegan Paul, 1960.

Bathrooms p182

Ceilings p177

Conservatories p187

Doors p170

Exteriors p188

Fireplaces and stoves p179

Floors p173

Kitchens p184

Lighting p186

Staircases p178

Wallpapers p177

Walls p174

Windows p172

Other useful addresses p190

DOORS (FRONT AND INTERIOR)

A. & H. Brass
201-203 Edgware Road London W2 1ES
Tel: (01) 402 3981/(01) 402 1854
Supply brass door and window fittings, electrical accessories, chandeliers, lights and bathroom fittings.

Architectural Components Ltd
(Locks and Handles)
4-10 Exhibition Road
London SW7 2HF
Tel: (01) 581 2401/(01) 584 6800
Three showrooms, near the South Kensington Museums and Underground station, supply a large range of period fittings used in the renovation and furnishing of property. Over 6,000 different items in stock – door and cabinet fittings, bathroom accessories, all types of locks, window fittings, hinges, curtain hardware, door closers, grilles and vents, electrical switch plates, fireplace furniture.

Bailey's Architectural Antiques
The Engine Shed
Ashburton Industrial Estate
Ross-on-Wye, Herefordshire HE9 7BW
Tel: (0989) 63015
Large stock of decorative architectural fittings. Extensive range of both original and reproduction fireplaces, mantelpieces, bathroom fittings, tiles, stained and etched glass, garden furniture, doors, gates, pews, panelling, counters, bars, etc.

Beardmore Architectural Ironmongery
Field End Road, Ruislip, Middlesex HA4 0QG
Tel: (01) 864 6811, Telex: 923111
Also: 3-5 Percy Street, London W1P 0EJ
Tel: (01) 637 7041
Ornamental period-style brassware, from electrical accessories to door furniture.

Brass Art Craft Birmingham Ltd
76 Atwood Street
Lye, Stourbridge West Midlands
Tel: (038482) 3346/4814
Period brass door and window fittings and electrical accessories. Catalogue available.

Brass Tacks Hardware Ltd
50-54 Clerkenwell Road
London EC1M 5PS
Tel: (01) 250 1971, Telex: 261507 (Ref 2871)
Manufacturers and distributors of decorative brass door fittings and accessories, the range including locks, hinges and furniture, electrical accessories and bathroom fittings. The company also produces special items and decorative grilles for covering radiators, etc. Catalogues available.

Bridgwater Reclamation Ltd
Monmouth Street
Bridgwater, Somerset
Tel: (0278) 424636
See FIREPLACES AND STOVES

Bromley Demolition Co Ltd
75 Siward Road
Bromley, Kent
Tel: (01) 464 3610
Demolition items such as bricks, doors, floorboards and joists.

Celmac Heatherley Ltd
Unit 3 Ferry Lane
Brentford, Middlesex TW8 0BG
Tel: (01) 568 7963
English porcelain door furniture, English ceramic bathroom fittings, English natural wood bathroom fittings and toilet seats.

Comyn Ching Ltd
110 Golden Lane
London EC1Y 0SS
Tel: (01) 253 8414
Telex: 296004
Showroom at 17 Shelton Street, Covent Garden, London, WC2. Specialists in door furniture, locks, hinges, door closers, sliding door gear, wholesale and export. A large range of black antique ironmongery.

Conservation Buildings Products Ltd
Forge Works, Forge Lane
Cradley Heath, Warley
West Midlands B64 5AL
Tel: (0384) 64219/(052 784) 497
See EXTERIORS

Cotswood Door Specialists (Kew) Ltd
63A Park Road
Kingston-upon-Thames
Surrey KT2 6DE
Tel: (01) 546 3621
Also: 294 Uxbridge Road, Hatch End
Pinner, Middlesex HA5 4HR
Tel: (01) 428 0155
Supply and install high quality hardwood joinery, with the emphasis on doors and entrances, with the associated mouldings, architraves, skirting, etc. A range of standard designs is offered in mahogany. A design service is also offered and doors and joinery can be made to customers' own designs, or to match an existing pattern, particularly in period and/or listed properties. Other special products include panelling, cupboards, staircases and windows.

Counterparts Demolition Ltd
Station Yard
Topsham
Exeter, Devon
Tel: (039 287) 5995
See EXTERIORS

Crittall Windows Ltd
Manor Works
Braintree, Essex CM7 6DF
See WINDOWS

T. Crowther & Son Ltd
282 North End Road
Fulham, London SW6 1NH
Tel: (01) 385 1375/6/7
Cable Address: Antiquity
See EXTERIORS

Door Controls Ltd
19-21 The Broadway
Herne Bay, Kent CT6 8LG
Specialists in door-operating equipment including floor springs, transom closers, overhead door closers.

G. & H. Products Ltd
Unit 14 Gainsborough Trading Estate
Rufford Road
Stourbridge
Worcestershire
Export Agency: A.D.N. Products
Radnor House
93-97 Regent Street, London W1
Manufacturers and suppliers of electrical fittings in three ranges: Georgian, Regency and Victorian, all complemented by a full range of door and cabinet fittings.

Glover & Stacey Ltd
Head Office: Oaklands House
Solartron Road
Farnborough
Hampshire GU14 7QL
Tel: (0252) 549334
Telex: 265871
Yard and Workshops: Malthouse Premises
Main Road
Kingsley
Nr Bordon, Hampshire
Tel: (042 03) 5754/(042 03) 89688
An architectural salvage company specialising in oak beams, stained glass, doors, period fireplaces and chimneypieces, flooring, pine, oak and mahogany panelling, stair accessories, ironwork gates and railings, garden stone and statuary, etc. Also specialist joinery workshops manufacturing, in old materials, pews, kitchens, doors, bookcases, windows.

Grandisson Doors
Grandisson Court
The Cottage
Ottery St Mary, Devon EX11 1DQ
Tel: (040 481) 2876
Specialized joinery, i.e. hand-carved doors (standard and non-standard), fire surrounds, doors, windows, staircases, etc designed and built to customers' specifications.

Charles Harden
14 Chiltern Street
London W1
Tel: (01) 935 2032
Specialists in brass, glass and china door furniture, bathroom fittings in brass, chrome and gold-plated finishes. The firm has been in existence for 58 years and is a one-man business.

Havenplan's Architectural Emporium
1 The Old Station, Station Road
Killamarsh, Sheffield S31 8EN
Tel: *Day* (0742) 489972 *Evening* (0246) 433315
See FIREPLACES AND STOVES

E. A. Higginson & Co Ltd
1 Carlisle Road
Queensbury, London NW9 0HD
Tel: (01) 200 4848
Specialists in the manufacture of timber products including staircases, balustrades, doors, frames, windows and mouldings, etc. All items tailor-made to requirements in hardwoods, left ready for polishing, or softwood for painting.

Hope Works Ltd
Pleck Road
Walsall WS2 9HH
Tel: (0922) 27175
Telex: 338917
Manufacturers of Lionheart decorative hardware in iron and brass. 16th- to 19th-century designs in door and window hardware.

The House Hospital
68 Battersea High Street
London SW11
Tel: (01) 223 3179
Specialists in second period fireplaces, doors, basins, baths, W.C.s, cisterns, garden fencing and gates, brass door handles, brass taps and many other items of architectural salvage.

Interntrade Network
Unit 9 Spring Road
Ettingshall
Wolverhampton
Tel: (0902) 404788
Manufacturers of a wide range of Victorian, Georgian and Edwardian door furniture.

Kentel Joinery Ltd
Unit 27 Smiths Industrial Estate
Humber Avenue
Coventry CV3 4JL
Tel: (0203) 449621
See WINDOWS

Knobs & Knockers
Contract and Trade Division
36-40 York Way
London N1 9AB
Tel: (01) 833 0841/4
Telex: 8954474
Leading retailers of architectural ironmongery with over 50 branches throughout the United Kingdom, also providing a full scheduling and estimating service.

Langham Architectural Materials
Langham Farm
East Nynehead
Wellington, Somerset TA21 0DD
Tel: (082 346) 297
See FIREPLACES AND STOVES

W. & R. Leggott Ltd
East Parade
Bradford BD1 5HA
Tel: (0274) 392716
Brass founders and manufacturers of period door furniture and specialist fittings.

B. Lilly & Sons Ltd
Baltimore Road
Birmingham B42 1DJ
Tel: (021) 357 1761
Craftsmen in brass including the Sadler architectural hardware.

The London Architectural Salvage and Supply Co
St Michael's Church
Mark Street, off Paul Street
Shoreditch, London EC2A 4ER
Tel: (01) 739 0448
Providers of a full range of good quality materials, fixtures and fittings for the refurbishment and decoration of commercial and domestic period buildings, including chimneypieces, panelled rooms, fencing and gates, flooring in oak, ash, pine and marble, bathroom fittings, kitchen furniture, doors and joinery, shop and bar fittings, lampposts and lanterns, carved stonework, York flagstones, garden furniture and statuary.

The London Door Co
165 St John's Hill
London SW11 1TQ
Tel: (01) 223 7243
A wide range of doors including hardwood front doors, security doors, carved and traditional doors, made-to-measure for people needing unusual size doors. Also stock stained-glass panels for leaded lights. A complete fitting service is available.

Magnet Southerns plc
Royd Ings Avenue
Keighley, Yorkshire BD21 4BY
Tel: (0535) 661133
One of the largest home improvement companies in the country, manufacturing and selling goods from doors and windows to kitchens and bedrooms.

M. & A. Main
The Old Smithy
Cerrig-y-Drudion
Corwen
Clwyd LL21 9SW
Tel: (049 082) 491
And at 44 Argyle Street, Birkenhead
Tel: (051) 647 8000
Supply period doors, fire surrounds, pews and panelling, brassware, pub fittings, sanitary ware, stained glass, spindles, newel posts, handrails, reclaimed timber. Restore woodwork in own workshops and on site.

Malvern Studios
56 Cowleigh Road
Malvern
Worcestershire WR14 1QD
Tel: (068 45) 4913
See LIGHTING

Midland Veneers Ltd
Hayseech Road
Halesowen
West Midlands B63 3PE
Tel: (021) 550 6441
Telex: 334205
Manufacturers of veneered panels and flush doors to specification. Manufacturers of preformed plywood curved components for the furniture and construction industry.

Mounts Hill Woodcraft Ltd
The Depot, Mounts Hill
Cranbrook Road
Benenden, Cranbrook, Kent
Tel: (0580) 240270
Specialist joiners, producing staircases, panelling, doors, fencing, etc made to customers' requirements or to standard designs.

Newman Tonks Consumer Products Ltd
71 Allesley Street
Birmingham B6 4ND
Tel: (021) 359 8911
Telex: 338280

The Original Choice
1340 Stratford Road
Hall Green, Birmingham B28 9EH
Tel: (021) 778 3821
See FIREPLACES AND STOVES

Perkins & Powell
(A subsidiary of Samuel Heath & Sons plc)
Leopold Street
Birmingham B21 0UJ
Tel: (021) 772 2303
Telex: 336908
Manufacturers of architectural, builders and marine brassware. Producers of a wide range of door and window fittings.

Posterity Architectural Effects
Baldwins Farm
Dymock Road
Newent
Gloucestershire
Tel: (0531) 85 597
See EXTERIORS

A. L. Rattray
Craighall
Blairgowrie, Perthshire
Scotland
Tel: (0250) 4749
See BATHROOMS

Relic Antiques
Brillscote Farm
Lea, near Malmesbury
Wiltshire
Suppliers of garden ornaments, iron and stone items, acid-etched, bevelled and cut-glass panels, stained-glass windows, doors and entrance ways. Shop fittings, period bar backs, counters, screens, doors, etc. Stockists of architectural items such as doors, panelling, corbels, finials, pediments, decorations in wood, iron and stone, overmantel mirrors. Also available: reproduction glass work, acid-etching, gilding, cutting, etc.

Rothley Brass Ltd
Merridale House
Merridale Street
Wolverhampton WV3 0RB
Tel: (0902) 27532
Suppliers of brass door furniture and electrical fittings. A comprehensive collection including the Victorian, Windsor, Georgian and China collections, also the Knockers and Numerals collection which covers ancient and traditional patterns.

John Sambrook
Part House, Northiam
E. Sussex TN31 6PA
Tel: (079 74) 2615
Makes fanlights.

Smith, Widdowson & Eadem Ltd
296 Penistone Road, Sheffield S6 2FT
Tel: (0742) 349371
Telex: 547545
Door and window ironmongery in brass, BMA, plastic, antique iron, etc.

Solopark Ltd
The Old Railway Station
Station Road, near Pampisford
Cambridgeshire CB2 4HB
Tel: (0223) 834663
Specialist suppliers of reclaimed building materials including bricks, internal and external doors, staircases, window frames, panelling, mouldings, oak and hardwood rafters and floor panels.

Stuart Interiors
Barrington Court, Barrington
Ilminster, Somerset TA19 0NQ
Tel: (0460) 42003
One of the country's leading specialist designers, recreating 16th- and 17th-century England. Run by five partners and a consultant, Victor Chinnery, whose book Oak Furniture – The British Tradition *has become the definitive work on the subject. Stuart Interiors offer a complete design and furnishing service for clients with early houses or those looking for a period style. This includes panelling, doors, staircases, stonework, furniture and a vast range of accessories. Barrington Court aims to create a national centre for all aspects of early English interior design in both a commercial and an academic context. An exclusive range of "early" fabrics has just been launched in conjunction with Tissunique in London. A shop in Williamsburg, Virginia, in the name of Stuart Interiors U.S.A. has recently been opened. The company intends to nurture an interest in interior design pre-1730 through the showrooms and with*

regular lectures and exhibitions relating to the social history, domestic life, architecture and house interiors of the period. Colour brochure available.

Thistle Joinery Ltd
73-77a Ilderton Road, Bermondsey
London SE16 3JZ
Tel: (01) 232 1553
Producers of purpose-made joinery, designed to suit customers' requirements and specifications.

Robert Thompson's Craftsmen Ltd
Kilburn, York YO6 4AH
Tel: (034 76) 218
Manufacturers of individual items executed in seasoned English oak, i.e. staircases, panelling, interior and exterior doors.

A Touch of Brass Ltd
123 Kensington Church Street
London W8
Tel: (01) 221 9256
210 Fulham Road
London SW10
Tel: (01) 351 2255
61 Fulham High Street
London SW6
Tel: (01) 731 6100
Suppliers of quality brass goods, with many different ranges to suit every period of architecture from the 16th century. Over 2,000 items in stock at each branch.

Verdigris Art Metalwork Restorers
Clerkenwell Workshops
Unit B18, 31 Clerkenwell Close
London EC1R 0AT
Tel: (01) 253 7788
Renovate and make brass-ware.

Verine Products & Co
Folly Faunts House
Goldhanger
Maldon, Essex CM9 8AP
Tel: (0621) 88611
See FIREPLACES AND STOVES

Walcot Reclamation
108 Walcot Street
Bath, Avon BA1 5BG
Tel: (0225) 66291
See FIREPLACES AND STOVES

Whiteway & Waldron Ltd
305 Munster Road, London SW6
Tel: (01) 381 3195
See WINDOWS

Winther Browne & Co Ltd
Nobel Road
Eleys Estate
London N18 3DX
Tel: (01) 803 3434
Suppliers and manufacturers of period home products including authentic styled beams, available in dark oak, light oak, grey or unstained finishes. Doors, staircases, windows and mouldings also available.

C. H. Wood (Security) Ltd
221 Wakefield Road
Bradford BD4 7PE
Tel: (0274) 725072/727960
Restorers and repairers of locks, key cutters and manufacturers.

Woodstock (Totnes) Ltd
Station Road
Totnes, Devon PQ9 5JG
Tel: (0803) 864610
General architectural salvage, doors, windows, toilets, timber, fire surrounds and staircases.

W. Woolaway & Sons (Builders) Ltd
Joinery Division
Junction Yard
Barnstaple, North Devon EX31 2AE
Tel: (0271) 74191
Non-standard joinery manufacturers, with a small selection of architectural salvage items, including doors, slates and fire surrounds, and staircases.

WINDOWS

Architectural Components Ltd
(Locks and Handles)
4-10 Exhibition Road
London SW7 2HF
Tel: (01) 581 2401/(01) 584 6800
See DOORS

Bailey's Architectural Antiques
The Engine Shed
Ashburton Industrial Estate
Ross-on-Wye
Herefordshire HE9 7BW
Tel: (0989) 63015
See DOORS

Bridgwater Reclamation Ltd
Monmouth Street
Bridgwater
Somerset
Tel: (0278) 424636
See FIREPLACES AND STOVES

Brighton Architectural Salvage
33 Gloucester Road
Brighton
Sussex
Tel: (0273) 681656
See FIREPLACES AND STOVES

Cantabrian Antiques
16 Park Street
Lynton
North Devon
Tel: (0598) 53282
See FIREPLACES AND STOVES

Peter Chapman Antiques
10 Theberton Street
London N1 0QX
Tel: (01) 226 5565
See FIREPLACES AND STOVES

Crittall Windows Ltd
Manor Works
Braintree, Essex CM7 6DF
Steel, aluminium and UPVC windows and doors. For refurbishment of period buildings, steel windows in traditional styles with hinged or pivoted opening casements supplied with the glazing bars sub-dividing the lights as required, including the classical "Georgian" proportion of panes. Curved, raked and shaped frames provided. Catalogues available.

Glover & Stacey Ltd
Oaklands House
Solartron Road
Farnborough
Hampshire GU14 7QL
Tel: (0252) 549334
Telex: 265871
See DOORS

Goddard & Gibbs Studios
41-49 Kingsland Road
London E2 8AD
Tel: (01) 739 6563
Telex: 297701
Install stained and decorative glass, ranging from windows, interior panels and murals to domes and roof lights using techniques of dalles-de-verre, acid etching and sand-blasting. Design service available.

Grandisson Doors
Grandisson Court
The Cottage
Ottery St Mary
Devon EX11 1DQ
Tel: (040 481) 2876
See DOORS

Hartley Wood & Co Ltd
Portobello Glass Works
Portobello Lane
Monkwearmouth
Sunderland
Tyne and Wear SR6 0DN
Tel: (0783) 672506
Manufacturers of stained glass and both hand-blown antique and rolled glasses.

James Hetley & Co Ltd
Beresford Avenue
Wembley, Middlesex HA0 1RP
Tel: (01) 903 4151
Stockists, distributors and exporters of antique glass including a full range of Pilkington, laminated and silvered float glass, hand-blown and reproduction bullions, glass lampshades in Art Nouveau, Art Deco and Tiffany styles, also antique and rolled glass.

E. A. Higginson & Co Ltd
1 Carlisle Road
Queensbury
London NW9 0HD
Tel: (01) 200 4848
See DOORS

Hope Works Ltd
Pleck Road
Walsall

WS2 9HH
Tel: (0922) 27175
Telex: 338917
See DOORS

Illumin Glass Studio
82 Bond Street
Macclesfield
Cheshire SK11 6QS
Tel: (0625) 613600
See LIGHTING

Kentel Joinery Ltd
Unit 27
Smiths Industrial Estate
Humber Avenue
Coventry CV3 1JL
Tel: (0203) 449621
Architectural and industrial joinery manufacturers specializing in reproducing constructional joinery such as sliding sash windows, Georgian windows, doors, stairs, etc. Services include the grinding of cutters to exact profiles, to carefully reproduce original mouldings on frames, glazing bars, skirtings, dado rails, architraves, picture rails etc.

Ed. King Stained Glass
37 Northfield Road
London EC2 AJ
Tel: (01) 472 2507
Designer of stained-glass windows and restorer of windows. Own designs available as well as traditional styles.

Magnet Southerns plc
Royd Ings Avenue
Keighley
West Yorkshire BD21 4BY
Tel: (0535) 661133
See DOORS

M. & A. Main
The Old Smithy
Cerrig-y-Drudion
Corwen, Clwyd LL21 9SW
Tel: (049 082) 491
Also 44 Argyle Street
Birkenhead
Tel: (051) 647 8000
See DOORS

M.S. Glass Decorators
51 Enterprise Drive
Streetly
Sutton Coldfield
West Midlands B74 2DY
Tel: (021) 352 0434
Sandblasting, engraving, acid etching, stained glass, gilding and screen printing.

Mumford & Wood Ltd
Joinery Manufacturers
Hallsford Bridge Industrial Estate
Ongar, Essex CM5 9RB
Tel: (0277) 362401/362675
Manufacturers of double-hung sash windows in period Georgian, Victorian and Regency styles.

The Original Architectural Heritage of Cheltenham
Boddington Manor
Boddington
near Cheltenham, Gloucestershire GL51 0TJ
Tel: (024268) 741
See WALLS

The Original Choice
1340 Stratford Road
Hall Green
Birmingham B29 9EH
Tel: (021) 778 382
See FIREPLACES AND STOVES

A. & H. Pemberton Ltd
63 Shaw Street
Liverpool L6 1HN
Tel: (051) 207 1678
Specialists in design mirrors, acid-etched or sandblasted, or both, glass, gilding and painting designs or lettering, stained glass or leaded lights made to order.

Posterity Architectural Effects
Baldwins Farm
Dymock Road
Newent, Gloucestershire
Tel: (0531) 85597
See EXTERIORS

Relic Antiques
Brillscote Farm
Lea, near Malmesbury, Wiltshire
See DOORS

Smith Widdowson & Eadem Ltd
296 Penistone Road
Sheffield S6 2FT
Tel: (0742) 349371
Telex: 547545
See DOORS

Solopark Ltd
The Old Railway Station
Station Road
near Pampisford
Cambridgeshire CB2 4HB
Tel: (0223) 834663
See DOORS

SW82 Designs
104 Valetta Road
London W3 7TW
Tel: (01) 740 0707
Specialists in design and production of decorative glass including external and internal door panels, windows, conservatories with decorative double glazing. Finger plates etched in four classic designs – lattice, ribbon, geometric or tassel.

Andy Thornton Architectural Antiques Ltd
Ainleys Industrial Estate
Elland
West Yorkshire HX5 9JP
Tel: (0422) 78125/6
Large range of reproduction architectural antiques.

Tomkinson Stained Glass
52 Islington Park Street
London N1
Tel: (01) 359 0893/(01) 267 1669
Specialists in restoration of stained-glass windows and manufacture of stained-glass windows and Georgian leaded lights. Stockists of antique windows and doors and architectural items.

Townsends (London) Ltd
1 Church Street
London NW8
Tel: (01) 724 3746
81 Abbey Road
London NW8
Tel: (01) 624 4756
36 New End Square
Hampstead, London NW3
Tel: (01) 794 5706/7
Specialists in salvage and supply of architectural antiques, restoration and fixing of fireplaces and leaded stained-glass windows, stockists of antique tiles and glazed doors.

M. Tuckey Joinery
20 Cherry Street
Warwick CV34 4LR
Tel: (0926) 493679
See KITCHENS

Walcot Reclamation
108 Walcot Street
Bath
Avon BA1 5BG
Tel: (0225) 66291
See FIREPLACES AND STOVES

Whiteway & Waldron Ltd
305 Munster Road
London SW6
Tel: (01) 381 3195
Stained-glass and architectural fittings, including doors and fire surrounds.

Winther Browne & Co Ltd
Nobel Road
Eleys Estate
London N18 3DX
Tel: (01) 803 3434
See DOORS

Woodstock (Totnes) Ltd
Station Road
Totnes
Devon PQ9 5JG
Tel: (0803) 864610
See DOORS

FLOORS

Don Bateman
Home Farm
Pulham St Mary
Norfolk
Tel: (037 976) 784
Suppliers of old beams and studs, pamment, bricks, tiles, flooring and oak barns for re-erection.

Bridgwater Reclamation Ltd
Monmouth Street
Bridgwater
Somerset
Tel: (0278) 424636
See FIREPLACES AND STOVES

Bromley Demolition Co Ltd
75 Siward Road
Bromley
Kent
Tel: (01) 464 3610
See DOORS

Campbell Marson & Co Ltd
36 Maxwell Road
Fulham
London SW6 2HS
Tel: (01) 736 3635/4777
Specialists in supplying and laying hardwood flooring, e.g. strip, strip overlay, tongued and grooved, mosaic panels, wood block, parquet, cork tiles.

Candy Tiles Ltd
Heathfield
Newton Abbot
Devon TQ12 6RF
Tel: (0626) 832641
Ceramic wall tiles, frost-proof vitrified floor tiles of Swiss origin, terracotta floor tiles, suitable for period kitchens, French origin.

Capital Tile Supplies
Designer Studio
P.O Box 80
Albion Works
Endemere Road, Coventry CV6 5SE
Tel: (0203) 58391
Telex: 312339
Suppliers of a wide range of wall and floor tiles, including specialized service for designers, architects and specifiers. Catalogue available.

Carvall Group
Ceramic Tiles and Flooring
Norman Road
Rangemoor Industrial Estate
Tottenham N15 4NE
Tel: (01) 801 5331
Importers of Italian ceramic tiles, Cisa and Cerdisa.

Castelnau Tiles
175 Church Road
Barnes, London SW13
Tel: (01) 748 9042/(01) 741 4159
Suppliers of marble, terracotta and Mexican floor tiles. Wide choice of Italian and French tiles for walls and floors.

Ceramic Consultants Ltd
The Old Brewery
6 Wish Ward
Rye, Sussex TN31 7DH
Tel: (0797) 223038
Hand-decorated wall and floor tiles made to order. Export orders welcome Contract and hotel work as well as decorators and private customers.

Ceramique Internationale Ltd
The Porticos
386 Kings Road
London SW3 5UZ
Tel: (01) 351 3467
Telex: 291745
Stockists of a wide range of ceramic wall and floor tiles including hand-made. Advice on special installations, e.g. swimming pools, patios, external claddings, restaurants and other commercial uses.

Conservation Building Products Ltd
Forge Works
Forge Lane
Cradley Heath
Warley
West Midlands B64 5AL
Tel: (0384) 6429/(0527 84) 497
See EXTERIORS

Criterion Tiles Ltd
The Criterion Tile Shop
196 Wandsworth Bridge Road
London SW6 2UF
Tel: (01) 736 9610
A range of English and Continental ceramic tiles with a variety of effects, including hand-applied transfer and stencilling, relief moulding and in-glaze hand-painting, screen-printing in special colours for floors, fine terracotta, slate and large quarries, both glazed and unglazed. Creative advice given. Catalogues available.

Croft Bros (London) Ltd
7a Coppetts Road
Muswell Hill, London N10 1NP
Tel: (01) 444 0222/3/4
Ceramic wall and floor tiling specialists. Also all types of marble work.

Domus Tiles Ltd
33 Parkgate Road
London SW11 4NP
Tel: (01) 223 5555
Telex: 916339
Showroom: 266 Brompton Road
London SW3 2AS
Suppliers of glazed and unglazed floor and wall ceramic tiles, plain and patterned, refined porcelain stoneware frostproof heavy-duty tiles, including relief finishes, polished finishes, anti-slips, step treads and skirtings, natural rustic terracotta tiles, patterned resin bonded marble tiles.

Fired Earth
Head Office and Warehouse:
Middle Aston
Oxfordshire OX5 3PX
Tel: (0869) 40724
Oxford Showroom:
Arena
Thomas Yard
6 Rectory Road, St Clements
Oxford
Tel: (0865) 726505
London Showroom:
102 Portland Road
London W11

Tel: (01) 221 4825
Designers and manufacturers of ceramic tiles, made and fired by craftsmen using centuries-old methods and techniques. Over 35 different types of terracotta tiles in stock. Suitable for kitchens, dining rooms, halls, conservatories, patios, etc. Also reproduction early English delft tiles and other glazed tiles. Catalogue available.

Forbo-Nairn Ltd
Leet Court
14 King Street
Watford, Hertfordshire WD1 8BZ
Tel: (0923) 52323
Linoleum and contract vinyl floorcovering in sheets and tiles.

Glover & Stacey Ltd
Head Office:
Oaklands House
Solartron Road
Farnborough, Hampshire GU14 7QL
Tel: (0252) 549334
See DOORS

Heritage Woodcraft
14 Carlyon Road
Carlyon Road Industrial Estate
Atherstone
Warwickshire CV9 1JE
Tel: (082 77) 4761
Manufacturers and suppliers of all types of hardwood flooring, large stock of reclaimed woodblock flooring, strip flooring and planking. Hardwood flooring machined to customer requirements.

H. & R. Johnson Tiles Ltd
Highgate Tile Works
Tunstall, Stoke-on-Trent ST6 7BQ
Tel: (0782) 85611
Manufacturers of encaustic and geometric tiles for the restoration of 19th-century floors.

Kibblewhite & Blackmur Ltd
Long Reach Road
Barking, Essex IG11 0JN
Tel: (01) 594 5591
See EXTERIORS

The London Architectural Salvage and Supply Co
St Michael's Church
Mark Street (off Paul Street)
Shoreditch, London EC2A 4ER
Tel: (01) 739 0448
See DOORS

Francis N. Lowe Ltd
The Marble Works
New Road, Middleton-by-Wirksworth
Derbyshire DE4 4NB
Tel: (062 982) 2216/7
Telex: 377106
International: 44 332 382028
Specialist designers and manufacturers in natural marble, granite and slate.

Petit Roque Ltd
5a New Road
Croxley Green, Hertfordshire WD3 3EJ
Tel: (0923) 779291/720968
Designers and installers of individual fireplaces. Also produce period Adam-style fireplaces, vanity units, worktops, marble flooring, marble wall tiles, gas, log/coal fires, all fireplace accessories.

Daniel Platt & Sons Ltd
Brownhills Tileries
Tunstall
Stoke-on-Trent ST6 4NG
Tel: (0782) 86187
Manufacturers and exporters of floor tiles and quarries. Catalogue available.

Posterity Architectural Effects
Baldwins Farm
Dymock Road
Newent, Gloucestershire
Tel: (0531) 85597
See EXTERIORS

Ramus Tile Co Ltd
Palace Road
London N11 2PX
Tel: (01) 889 4631/(01) 881 2345
Ceramic wall and floor tiles for all situations and décors. Distribute Sumara tiles.

Reclaimed Materials
Northgate
White Lund Industrial Estate
Morecambe, Lancs
Tel: (0524) 69094
See EXTERIORS

Rogers Demolition & Dismantling Service Ltd
Belgrave Road
Portswood
Southampton
Tel: (0703) 449173
See EXTERIORS

Dennis Ruabon Ltd
Hafod Tileries,
Ruabon, Wrexham,
Clwyd LL14 6ET, North Wales
Tel: Sales & Technical (0978) 843484
Manufacturers of unglazed floor quarry tiles, for refurbishment and renovation. Also worldwide distributors for Art Tile products. Catalogue available.

H. & E. Smith Ltd
Van Delft
Britannic Works
Broom Street
Hanley
Stoke-on-Trent, Staffordshire ST1 2ER
Tel: (0782) 281617/260370
Restore and install Victorian and Edwardian tiles, Art Nouveau tiles, for walls and floors, internal and external fixing. Also hand-painted and embossed Victorian tiles for fireplaces. Catalogue available.

Solid Products
5 Royalty Studios
105 Lancaster Road
London W11 1QF
Tel: (01) 229 9498
New hardwood flooring and other specialist architectural components such as ironwork, light fittings, etc.

Solopark Ltd
The Old Railway Station
Station Road
near Pampisford
Cambridgeshire CB2 4HB
Tel: (0223) 834663
See DOORS

Sphinx Tiles Ltd
Bath Road
Thatcham, Berkshire RG13 4NQ
Tel: 0635 65475
Telex: 848207
Manufacturers and suppliers of ceramic wall and floor tiles.

Stuart Interiors
Barrington Court
Barrington, Ilminster
Somerset TA19 0NQ
Tel: (0460) 42003
See DOORS

Studio Two (Interior Design) Ltd
3A Town Street
Thaxted, Essex CM6 2LD
Tel: (0371) 830234
See KITCHENS

Tiles, Tiles, Tiles
Cornwise Ltd
168 Old Brompton Road
London SW5
Tel: (01) 373 6890
Range of ceramic and marble tiles, including traditional styles. Design and fixing service.

Tiles of Newport and London
Head Office:
Dumfries Place Estate
Lower Dock Street
Newport, Gwent
Also: The Talina Centre
Unit 9 23a Bagleys Lane
off New King's Road
London SW6
See BATHROOMS

The Tile People
4 The Green
Winchmore Hill
London N21 1AJ
Suppliers of Sally Anderson, Elon, Cedit, Carre and numerous other tiles. Suppliers and installers of granite.

Verity Tiles Ltd and Verity Fabrics
7 Jerdan Place
Fulham Broadway
London SW6 1BE
Tel: (01) 245 9000
Suppliers of a range of hand-glazed ceramic floor and wall tiles, with over 16 standard tile sizes and shapes, supplied in about 500 different glaze colours and designs. To complement the tiles, there is a special range of hand-formed ceramic pieces for use as dado rails, arch surrounds, mouldings and covings, available in any glaze colour. Offer a service to architects and designers involved in projects of restoration or novel creation.

Walcot Reclamation
108 Walcot Street
Bath, Avon BA1 5BG
Tel: (0225) 66291
See FIREPLACES AND STOVES

Wicanders (G.B.) Ltd
Maxwell Way
Crawley
West Sussex RH10 2SE
Tel: (0293) 27700
Suppliers of a wide range of cork-based materials to the specialist flooring trade, working with interior designers and other specifiers.

Anna Wyner
2 Ferry Road
Barnes, London SW13 9RX
Tel: (01) 748 3940
Specialist designer of mosaics, either precast or fixed on site. Materials used range from clay and slate to Italian smalti, with an almost limitless range of colours. Fees for designing, supplying and fixing are relative to the size, design and materials involved.

WALLS

David M. Ackroyd
Bleathwood Manor Farm
Bleathwood, Ludlow
Shropshire SY8 4LT
Tel: (0584) 810726
Repair and replace existing woodwork, services from repairing and re-polishing veneered and inlaid rosewood doors to making oak window frames, skirting, panelling, etc. Also turning, inlaying, carving and a complete range of specialist paint finishes including ragging, rolling, stippling, marbling and woodgraining.

Sally Anderson (Ceramics) Ltd
Parndon Mill
Harlow, Essex CM20 2HP
Tel: (0279) 20982
Ceramic tiles, hand decorated to order. Range begins with 40 plain colours and combinations of up to five of these are used to create modular designs and system murals.

Authentic Interiors Ltd
Queen's House
Queen's Road
Buckhurst Hill, Essex IG9 5BX
Tel: (01) 506 1577
Suppliers of 15th-19th-century panels, G.R.P. panels, brickwork and timbers, embellishments, special fireplaces, caryatids and architectural panels, clients' own timber or stone mouldings reproduced for repair and restoration work. Specialist interior design service for all architectural periods. Specialist joinery service. Catalogue available.

Bailey's Architectural Antiques
The Engine Shed
Ashburton Industrial Estate
Ross-on-Wye
Herefordshire HE9 7BW
Tel: (0989) 63015
See DOORS

Jaqueline Bateman
7 Rylett Crescent
London W12 9RP
Tel: (01) 749 3596
Murals, trompe l'oeil, stencils, friezes and pastiche for hotels, restaurants and private houses. Interior and exterior work.

Christopher Boulter
43 Goodrich Road
London SE22
Tel: (01) 299 2219
Full mural service, plus all paint finishes. Any design work undertaken.

Andrew Bradley
24 Kensington Gardens
Bath BA1 6LH
Tel: (0225) 317025
Decorative finishes, marbling, stippling, rag-rolling, dragging, design and cutting of stencils for specific interior finish. Designs and paints murals to requirements.

Simon Brady
8a St Quintin Avenue
London W10 6NU
Tel: (01) 960 2631
All forms of specialist paintwork, in particular, trompe l'oeil panels and murals. Works in Britain, Europe and the U.S.A.

Bridgwater Reclamation Ltd
Monmouth Street
Bridgwater, Somerset
Tel: (0278) 424636
See FIREPLACES AND STOVES

Brighton Architectural Salvage
33 Gloucester Road
Brighton, East Sussex
Tel: (0273) 681656
See FIREPLACES AND STOVES

Cantabrian Antiques
16 Park Street
Lynton, North Devon
Tel: (0598) 53282
See FIREPLACES AND STOVES

Capital Ceramics
Priors House
Beaumont Road
London E13 8RJ
Tel: (01) 471 8121
Telex: 8955730
Importers and distributors of ceramic tiles from Italy, Holland, France and Japan. Suppliers to retail outlets, architects, designers as well as direct to the public, offering a technical information service. Catalogue available.

Carlton Smith Joinery
Harewell Lane
Besford, Worcestershire WR8 9AP
Tel: (038 65) 555770
Purpose-made joinery manufacturers, specializing in joinery for period buildings.

Carvers & Gilders
9 Charterhouse Works
Eltringham Street
London SW18 1TD
Tel: (01) 870 7047
Decorative carving to commission, original and period designs to customers' specifications. Catalogue available.

Castelnau Tiles
175 Church Road
Barnes, London SW13
Tel: (01) 741 2452/(01) 748 9042/(01) 741 4159
See FLOORS

Ceramic Consultants Ltd
The Old Brewery
6 Wish Ward
Rye, East Sussex TN31 7DH
Tel: (0797) 223038
See FLOORS

Ceramique Internationale Ltd
The Porticos   386 Kings Road
London SW3 5UZ
Tel: (01) 351 3467
Telex: 291745
See FLOORS

Naomi Colvin
16, Malford Road
Camberwell, London SE5 8DQ
Tel: (01) 274 2843
Hand lacquering, water gilding, oil gilding, carved lacquer, raised gesso and all kinds of painted finishes.

Conservation Building Products Ltd
Forge Works, Forge Lane
Cradley Heath, Warley
West Midlands B64 5AL
Tel: (0384) 64219
See EXTERIORS

Croft Bros (London) Ltd
7a Coppetts Road
Muswell Hill
London N10 1NP
Tel: (01) 444 0222/3/4
See FLOORS

Crown Decorative Products Ltd
P.O. Box 22
Queen's Mill
Hollins Road
Darwen, Lancashire BB3 0BD
Tel: (0254) 74951
Embossed wallpapers.

T. Crowther & Son Ltd
282 North End Road
Fulham, London SW6 1NH
Tel: (01) 385 1375/6/7
Cable Address: Antiquity
See EXTERIORS

Crowther of Syon Lodge Ltd
Busch Corner
London Road
Isleworth, Middlesex TW7 5BH
Tel: (01) 560 7978/7985
Telex: 8951308
See EXTERIORS

Davies Keeling Trowbridge
3 Charterhouse Works
Eltringham Street
Petergate
London SW18 1TD
Tel: (01) 871 3565
Specialist paint finishes and effects including marbling, stippling, graining, trompe l'oeil, murals, stencilling and graphic work.

Decarte
268 Gloucester Terrace
London W2
Tel: (01) 727 8294
Also: 74 Calvert Road, Greenwich, London SE10
Specialist painters, artists and gilders – moulding, stippling, graining and other paint effects, gilders and restorers.

Exclusive Art
4 Nettleshead Cottages
Maidstone Road
Paddock Wood, Kent TN12 6DB
Tel: (089 283) 4794
Specialists in murals, mainly for children.

Fireplaces of Yesteryears
(Incorporating Art Tile Distributors)
Showroom: Railway Station Platform
Station Road
Knaresborough, North Yorkshire
Tel: (0423) 863739
Office: 5 Albans Close
Bardsey, Leeds 17
West Yorkshire
Tel: (0937) 84288
See FIREPLACES AND STOVES

David Gillespie Associates Ltd
Dippenhall Crossroads
Farnham, Surrey GU10 5DW
Tel: (0252) 723531
See CEILINGS

Glover & Stacey Ltd
Oaklands House
Solartron Road
Farnborough, Hampshire GU14 7QL
Tel: (0252) 549334
Telex: 265871
See DOORS

Eleanor Greeves
12 Newton Grove
Bedford Park, London W4 1LB
Tel: (01) 994 6523
Design and hand-printing of ceramic wall tiles, specializing in repeating foliage patterns, supplied direct from workshop in any of ten alternative colours. Special designs and other colours to order. Catalogues available.

Hallidays
The Old College
Dorchester-on-Thames
Oxfordshire OX9 8HL
Tel: (0865) 340028
Also: 28 Beauchamp Place
Knightsbridge
London SW3 1NJ
Tel: (01) 589 5534
See FIREPLACES AND STOVES

Hampstead Decorative Arts
Flat 4 82 Belsize Park Gardens
London NW3
Tel: (01) 586 1810
An association of artists and craftsmen for decorative paint finishes.

Hand Painted Stencils
(Felicity Binyon and Elizabeth Macfarlane)
6 Polstead Road
Oxford OX2 6TW
Tel: (0865) 56072/(01) 701 5647
Stencil cutters for borders, friezes or overall designs on walls and floors. Samples given for clients' approval.

Havenplan's Architectural Emporium
1 The Old Station, Station Road
Killamarsh
Sheffield S31 8EN
Tel: *Day* (0742) 489972
     Evening (0246) 433315
See FIREPLACES AND STOVES

Herbert Read Ltd
Wynards Works
Old Rydon Lane
Exeter, Devon EX2 7JS
Tel: (0392) 87 4335
Design and construction of traditional woodwork, both in houses and churches. Conservation a speciality.

Inside Story Ltd
Crest, Ducks Hill Road
Northwood, Middlesex HA6 2SQ
Tel: (65) 22858/27371
A team of master decorators trained for all work including specialist paint finishers, joiners, plumbers, electricians, tilers and plasterers.

G. Jackson & Sons Ltd
Rathbone Works
Rainville Road
London W6 9HD
Tel: (01) 385 6616/(01) 381 5297
Telex: 8814525
Founded by the Adam Brothers in 1780, craftsmen in building finishes including fibrous plaster, joinery, composition enrichment, decorating and gilding, reinstatement and repair of decorative work. Design services available.

H. & R. Johnson Tiles Ltd
Highgate Tile Works
Tunstall, Stoke-on-Trent ST6 4JX
Tel: (0782) 85611
Encaustic and geometric tiles for restoration purposes.

J.S.R. Joinery Ltd
Poole Street
Great Yeldham
Halstead, Essex CO9 4HN
Tel: (0787) 237722
Specialist joiners working to customers' own drawings or photographs and producers of building requirements for development projects or replacement work.

Catherine Lalau-Keraly
104 Hereford Road
London W2 5AL
Tel: (01) 727 4998
Art Deco, geometric approach to murals, sculptures and relief, together with interior decoration.

The London Architectural Salvage & Supply Co
St Michael's Church
Mark Street (off Paul Street)
Shoreditch, London EC2A 4ER
Tel: (01) 739 0448
See DOORS

M. & A. Main
The Old Smithy
Cerrig-y-Drudion
Corwen, Clwyd LL21 9SW
Tel: (049 082) 491
Also: 44 Argyle Street, Birkenhead
Tel: (051) 647 8000
See DOORS

Maw & Co Ltd
342 High Street
Tunstall
Stoke-on-Trent ST6 5EL
Tel: (0782) 817341
Telex: 367419
Manufacturers of ceramic wall tiles and bathroom accessories. Catalogue available.

Sally Miles
37 Englewood Road
London SW12 9PA
Tel: (01) 675 4264
Painted murals and trompe l'oeil *for stately homes, luxury homes, restaurants and night clubs.*

K. Neophytou (Carlos)
131-133 Cloudesley Road
London N1
Tel: (01) 837 9451
Wood carving and antique restorations.

Oakleaf Reproductions Ltd
Ling Bob
Main Street
Wilsden, Bradford BD15 0JP
Tel: (0535) 272878
Reproduction timber in traditional period styles, including simulated oak ceiling beams, panelling and embellishments, all manufactured in rigid polyurethane foam, moulded and hand-stained. Design service offered. Catalogue available.

The Original Architectural Heritage of Cheltenham
Boddington Manor
Boddington
near Cheltenham
Gloucestershire GL51 0TJ
Tel: (024268) 741
Manufacturers and suppliers of period panelling, marble, wood and stone fireplaces, antique and original garden statuary, stained glass.

The Original Choice
1340 Stratford Road
Hall Green
Birmingham B28 9EH
Tel: (021) 778 3821
See FIREPLACES AND STOVES

Paintability Ltd
9 Heneage Street
London E1 5LJ
Tel: (01) 377 9262
A range of pre-cut stencil designs inspired by ancient ornaments, decorative stucco and plasterwork, trompe l'oeil and grisaille painted decoration. Catalogue available.

Paris Ceramics
534 Battersea Park Road
London SE11
Tel: (01) 228 5785
Specializing in ranges of floor and wall tiles, including old French tiles retrieved from period houses and restored; hand-crafted delft tiles made to traditional 17th-century designs, and others. Viewing by appointment only.

Petit Roque Ltd
5a New Road
Croxley Green, Hertfordshire WD3 3EJ
Tel: (0923) 779291/720968
See FIREPLACES AND STOVES

Phoenix Preservation Ltd
Montrose House
412-416 Eastern Avenue
Ilford, Essex IG2 6NQ
Tel: (01) 518 0921
Specialists in the in-situ treatments of timber for the eradication of wood-boring beetles and fungal decay as well as the treatment of rising damp, the supply of domestic re-humidifying equipment. Building repairs undertaken.

T. J. Plant
7 Bramham Gardens
London SW5
Tel: (01) 370 2945
Mural painter working in private homes and gardens, and commercial premises. All types of commission undertaken. Trompe l'oeil *a speciality.*

D. S. & A. G. Prigmore
Mill Cottage, Mill Road
Colmworth, Bedford
Tel: (023 062) 264
See EXTERIORS

Ramus Tile Co Ltd
Palace Road
London N11 2PX
Tel: (01) 889 4631/(01) 881 2345
See FLOORS

A. L. Rattray
Craighall, Blairgowrie
Perthshire, Scotland
Tel: (0250) 4749
See BATHROOMS

Relic Antiques
Brillscote Farm
Lea, near Malmesbury, Wiltshire
See DOORS, WINDOWS

Riva Design Ltd
'The Ryecroft' Fanavon Buildings
Warrington Street
Stalybridge, Cheshire SK15 2LB
Tel: (061) 303 0868
See KITCHENS

Sylvia Robinson
Clarence House
Winchester Hill
Romsey, Hampshire SO52 7NJ
Tel: (0794) 514930
Producing hand-painted ceramic tiles, usually to commission, for kitchens, bathrooms and fireplaces, etc, painted picture panels, trompe l'oeil panels, "Dutch" style tiles with over 50 designs, repeat pattern tiles and borders using stencils.

Rogers Demolition & Dismantling Service Ltd
Belgrave Road
Portswood
Southampton
Tel: (0703) 449173
See EXTERIORS

Maria Rosenthal, Hand Made Tiles
Kingsgate Workshops
110-116 Kingsgate Road
London NW6
Tel: (01) 328 2051
A range of original, hand-made wall tiles with raised designs, individually dipped in glazes derived from Victorian recipes resulting in rich colours and a deep gloss finish. Can be used in entrance halls and porches, conservatories, around a fireplace and in kitchens and bathrooms. A variety of colours available, plain and border tiles available to match. New designs produced periodically. Tiles made mostly to order.

Glenys Self of Kauffmans
Avonside
Brockdish
Diss, Norfolk
Friezework and wall embellishments of fine art quality. Hand-printed and painted directly onto wall surfaces and panelling.

Shaws of Darwen
Waterside
Darwen, Lancashire BB3 3NX
Tel: (0254) 71811/775111
Telex: 63401
Manufacturers of architectural terracotta and glazed faience for both refurbishment work and new projects. Catalogue available.

Shelston (Construction) Ltd
(St Giles Joinery Ltd)
Nine Yews
Wimborne St Giles
Dorset BH21 5PW
Tel: (07254) 202
Supplying individual joinery to the building industry, i.e. special items such as cupolas, etc, and specialist decorative finishing, including marbling, graining, mahoganising, etc.

Jayne Simcock Design Ltd
49 St Margaret's Grove
Twickenham, Middlesex TW1 1JF
Tel: (01) 892 9238
Interior designers specializing in tiled areas such as bathrooms, kitchens, shower and cloakrooms, conservatories, etc. Mural painting and stencilling service. Catalogue available.

H. & E. Smith Ltd
Van Delft
Britannic Works
Broom Street
Hanley
Stoke-on-Trent, Staffordshire ST1 2ER
Tel: (0782) 281617/260370
See FLOORS

Solopark Ltd
The Old Railway Station
Station Road
near Pampisford, Cambridgeshire CB2 4HB
Tel: (0223) 834663
See DOORS

Sphinx Tiles Ltd
Bath Road
Thatcham
Berkshire RG13 4NQ
Tel: (0635) 65475
Telex: 848207
See FLOORS

Stuart Interiors
Barrington Court
Barrington
Ilminster
Somerset TA19 0NQ
Tel: (0460) 42003
See DOORS

Studio Two (Interior Design) Ltd
3A Town Street
Thaxted, Essex CM6 2LD
Tel: (0371) 830234
See KITCHENS

Sumara Tiles
Distributed by:
Ramus Tile Co Ltd
Palace Road
London N11 2PX
Tel: (01) 881 2345
See FLOORS

Toynbee-Clarke Interiors Ltd
95 Mount Street
London W1
Tel: (01) 499 4472
Period-style wallpapers.

Truline Building Products Ltd
Albert Road
Buckhurst Hill, Essex IG9 6BH
Tel: (01) 504 6629
Suppliers of an extensive range of building products.

Verity Tiles Ltd and Verity Fabrics
7 Jerdan Place
Fulham Broadway
London SW6 1BE
Tel: (01) 245 9000
See FLOORS

Wansdown Joinery Works (Southern) Ltd
327 & 339 Lillie Road
Fulham Cross
London SW6 7NR
Tel: (01) 385 0351
See STAIRCASES

Whitehead & Lightfoot
Block 4
Avon Trading Estate
London W14 8TS
Tel: (01) 603 4237/(01) 602 2889
Specialist joiners also offering machining, veneering and lacquering facilities.

WALLPAPERS AND FABRICS

Marthe Armitage
1 Strand-on-the-Green
Chiswick, London W4 3PQ
Tel: (01) 994 0160
Wallpaper designers. Full range of existing designs can be seen by appointment. Commissions undertaken to design and print papers for special purposes or situations for particular clients.

Bentley & Spens
Studio 25, 90 Lots Road, London SW10 0QD
Tel: (01) 352 5685
Specialize in batik and hand-painted fabrics for fashion and interiors with a good choice of silks and cotton. A wide range of designs or artwork can be commissioned to individual requirements and advice given on suitable fabrics. Customers are able to visit the studio, by appointment, and samples can also be seen at Robin Guild Associates, 107a Pimlico Road, London, SW1, as part of their interior design service.

Blind Alley Ltd
27 Chalk Farm Road
Camden Town, London NW1 8AG
Tel: (01) 485 8030
Range includes designs to fit in with almost any style of interior from the traditional "William Morris" to exotic palm trees, from Chinese to hi-tech, and a number of designs for children's rooms. In addition to standard designs, they do hand-painted blinds to order.

Clifton Textiles Ltd
103 Cleveland Street, London W1P 5PL
Tel: (01) 323 1526
Wallcoverings and wallpapers.

Colefax & Fowler
39 Brook Street
London W1
Tel: (01) 493 2231
Two showrooms in Belgravia and Mayfair offer a range of typical English chintzes and wallpapers. Several designs still produced by hand block printing. Catalogue available.

Elizabeth Eaton
25a Basil Street
London SW3 1BB
Tel: (01) 589 0118/9
*Offers a full decorator service of advice on interior use of period houses, services of a qualified architect renowned for work on period property, joinery and cabinet making to drawings, advice on painting and decorating, preferably executed by their own team of workmen under their supervision.
Sole U.K. agents for the following American companies specializing in period wallpapers and fabrics:
Schumacher – The Williamsburg Collection, A. Diament, Philadelphia; Clarence House – French Collection; Waterhouse – Boston; Katzenbach & Warren. Catalogue available.*

Christian Fischbacher (London) Ltd
Threeways House
40-44 Clipstone Street
London W1P 8AL
Tel: (01) 580 8937/8/9
Telex: 265662
Market the fine cottons and voiles of Switzerland and are famous for their printed cotton furnishing fabrics produced in Britain and U.S.A.

Mary Fox Linton Ltd
249 Fulham Road
London SW3 6HY
Tel: (01) 351 0273
Supply wallpapers and floorcoverings.

Hamilton Weston Wallpapers
11 Townshend Road
Richmond, Surrey TW9 1XH
Tel: (01) 940 4850
Specialists in documentary reproductions of wallpapers of the 18th and early 19th centuries with designs taken from recently discovered fragments. Designs are taken from fragments dating from c.1760-1840 found in London houses. Printing to order in special colours.

K. & K. Designs
123-125 Baker Street
Enfield, Middlesex EN1 3HA
Tel: (01) 367 2011
Also: 131 Shenley Road
Borehamwood, Hertfordshire
Tel: (01) 953 2703
Distributors and manufacturers of wallpapers, vinyls and borders.

Lyn Le Grice Stencil Design Ltd
Bread Street
Penzance
Cornwall TR18 2EQ
Tel: (0736) 69881
Stencilling and designing fabrics and wallpapers. Catalogue available.

Manvel Canovas
37-39 Cheval Place
London SW7
Tel: (01) 255 2298
Manufacturers of period-style woven damasks.

Jean Monro
53 Moreton Street
London SW1
Tel: (01) 821 1860
Est 1926, specialists in reproducing period furnishings, reprinted true to document.

John S. Oliver Ltd
33 Pembridge Road
London W11 3HG
Tel: (01) 221 6466/(01) 727 3735
Reproducing wallpapers from a pattern of the client's own sample or design and, if required, in colourways of their own choice. Pattern books available.

Osborne & Little plc
Showroom: 304 King's Road
London SW3 5UH
Tel: (01) 352 1456/7/8
Offices: 49 Temperley Road
London SW12 8QE
Tel: (01) 675 2255
Telex: 8813128
Designers and manufacturers of a wide range of furnishing fabrics, wallpapers and borders.

H. A. Percheron Ltd
97-99 Cleveland Street, London W1P 5PN
Tel: (01) 580 1192/(01) 580 5156
Exclusive importers of furnishing fabrics and trimmings. A fine range of traditional damasks, brocades, velours and plain fabrics available; fabrics can be made to order for special requirements. Trimmings of all kinds from a comprehensive stock collection and made to order in any colouring.

Stuart Interiors
Barrington Court
Barrington, Ilminster
Somerset TA19 0NQ
Tel: (0460) 42003
See DOORS

Tissunique Ltd
10 Princes Street, Hanover Square
London W1R 7RD
Tel: (01) 491 3386
Telex: 21960
Wholesalers and importers of high-class furnishing fabrics and wallpapers, braids and trimmings. Specialists in historic house reproduction work, Lyon silks, producers of the National Trust Collection of Traditional Chintzes and the Historic Print Collection.

Top Layer Ltd
5 Egerton Terrace
London SW3 2BX
Tel: (01) 581 1019
Supplies wallpapers and fabrics, from any age or period.

Toynbee-Clarke Interiors Ltd
95 Mount Street
London W1
Tel: (01) 499 4472/3
Specialists in the restoration and installation of antique wallpapers, including 18th- and 19th-century hand-painted Chinese papers and French hand block printed papers, products of manufacturers such as Reveillon, Dufour, Zuber, etc.

Watts & Co Ltd
7 Tufton Street
London SW1P 3QE
Tel: (01) 222 7169/(01) 2893/(01) 1978
Offering a collection of genuine Victorian wallcoverings and damasks. The papers, to be seen in the Houses of Parliament and the National Portrait Gallery, can be hand-blocked or screen printed and all orders are coloured as individually desired. Catalogue available.

Zoffany Ltd
27a Motcomb Street
London SW1X 8JU
Tel: (01) 235 5295/(01) 7241
Manufacturers of Document wallpapers, including the hand-printed Temple Newsam Collection. Reproductions of original papers can be hand-printed to commission order on enquiry. The Red Book of Paperhangings and The Temple Newsam Collection available in the U.S.A., Schumacher.

CEILINGS

Allied Guilds
Unit 19 Reddicap Trading Estate
Coleshill Road
Sutton Coldfield, West Midlands B75 7BU
Tel: (021) 329 2874
Specializing in the manufacture, fixing and restoration of ornamental plasterwork, from Mediaeval designs to classical Georgian and Adam style, Louis XIV and Victorian. Catalogue available.

Architectural & Industrial G.R.P.
400 Ewell Road, Tolworth, Surrey KT6 7HF
See BATHROOMS

H. & F. Badcock (Fibrous & Solid Plastering) Ltd
Unit 9 57 Sandgate Street
Old Kent Road
Peckham, London SE15 1LE
Tel: (01) 639 0304
Manufacturers of fibrous plaster mouldings and enrichments, i.e. cornices, ceiling centres, columns, pilasters, etc. Repairers and renovators of damaged existing cornices, enrichments, etc.

Bridgwater Reclamation Ltd
Monmouth Street
Bridgwater, Somerset
Tel: (0278) 424636
See FIREPLACES AND STOVES

Butcher Plastering Specialists Ltd
8 Fitzroy Road, Primrose Hill
London NW1 8TX
Tel: (01) 722 9771/2
Fibrous plastering specialists, all aspects of ornamental plastering.

Clark & Kenn Ltd
681 Mitcham Road, Croydon, Surrey
Tel: (01) 689 2266
Telex: 946511
Specialists in ceilings, installation of fibrous plasterwork, suspended and integrated ceilings, design and decorating service. Catalogue available.

Copley Decor Mouldings
Bedale Road, Leyburn, North Yorks DL8 5QA
Tel: (0969) 23840
Manufacturers of decor moulding in hard polyurethane. Range includes cornices, covings, ceiling roses, corbels, dado rails, panel mouldings, etc. Catalogue available.

Delmar-R.M.C. Ltd
(Room Moods)
Manor Royal
Crawley, Surrey RH10 2XQ
Tel: (0293) 546251
Telex: 87138
Suppliers of artcove, coving, framing and ceiling centres; also reproduction old English beams. All systems available nationally from home improvement centres, D.I.Y. retailers, decorators and builders merchants. Catalogue available.

Eaton-Gaze Ltd
Office & Factory:
86 Teesdale Street
London E2 6P
Tel: (01) 739 7272
Showroom:
22 The Broadway
The Bourne
London N14
Tel: (01) 882 3132
Ornate plasterwork including cornices, ceiling centres, friezes, panel moulding, dados, columns, pilasters, niches, trusses, arches and mouldings, mantelpieces, plaster, wood and fibreglass fireplaces, brass fireplace accessories, marble trims, firebacks and canopies. Catalogue available.

G.C. Mouldings
10 West End Lane
Barnet, Hertfordshire EN5 2SA
Manufacturer of fibrous plaster mouldings, repair and refurbishment, special works castings.

David Gillespie Associates Ltd
Dippenhall Crossroad
Farnham
Surrey GU10 5DW
Tel: (0252) 723531
Specialists in suspended and decorative ceilings, screens and space-dividers, sculptures, murals, crests and emblems, domes, Islamic decoration, architectural features and textured cladding. Catalogue available.

Glover & Stacey Ltd
Oaklands House
Solartron Road
Farnborough, Hampshire GU14 7QL
Tel: (0252) 549334
Telex: 265871
See DOORS

Hammond Wholesale
(A division of Charles Hammond Ltd)
London Interior Designers Centre
1 Cringle Street
Battersea Park Road
London SW8 5BX
Tel: (01) 627 5566
Telex: 25812
Interior decorators and designers supplying interior furnishings, cornices and ceiling roses.

David J. Handley
Milton Laithe
Gargrave
Skipton, North Yorkshire
Tel: (075) 807 7576
Stockists of old oak beams, purlins, spars, scantlins, panelling, doors, floorboards and carvings. Fireplace pieces a speciality.

Hodkin & Jones Ltd
(Simply Elegant)
515 Queen's Road
Sheffield S2 4DS
Tel: (0742) 556121
Telex: 547113
Manufacturers of fibrous plaster including cornices, ceiling roses, fire surrounds, arches, corbels, etc. Catalogue available.

Jonathan James Ltd
17 New Road
Rainham
Essex RM13 8DJ
Tel: (04027) 56921/4
Plastering specialists including solid and fibrous plastering, dry lining, granolithic paving, suspended ceilings and decorative finishes. Servicing contracts throughout the U.K. and abroad. Catalogue available.

Malvern Studios
56 Cowleigh Road
Malvern
Worcestershire WR14 1QD
Tel: (06845) 4913
See LIGHTING

Oakleaf Reproductions Ltd
Ling Bob
Main Street
Wilsden
Bradford BD15 0JP
Tel: (0535) 272878
See WALLS

T. & O. Plaster Castings
7 Collier Row Road
Collier Row
Romford, Essex
Tel: (0708) 45619/46742/24633
Fibrous plasterers, ornamental plasterwork, exterior refurbishing. Contractors to the Historical Society, Grade I and II Listed Buildings.

The Plaster Decoration Co Ltd
30 Stannary Street
London SE11 4AE
Tel: (01) 735 8161
Specialists in fibrous plasterwork.

Stevensons of Norwich Ltd
Roundtree Way
Norwich NR7 8SH
Tel: (0603) 400824
A good range of standard mouldings, purpose made to any design. G.R.P. and sand and cement mouldings for external use. Fixing service, advice and guidance for restoration schemes. Catalogue available.

W. Thompson & Sons Ltd
Nobel Road
Eley's Estate
Edmonton, London N18 3BM
Tel: (01) 807 7576
Wood machining and turning including mouldings, cornices, dado rails, architraves, skirting, picture rails, etc.

Wheatley Ornamental Plasterers Ltd
Avonvale Studio Workshops
Avonvale Place , Batheaston
Bath, Avon BA1 7SA
Tel: (0225) 859678
Full range of cornices, ceiling centres, niches, panel mouldings, corbels, etc. Reproduction of existing cornices; also reinforcement and restoration of ornamental ceilings. Catalogue available.

W. J. Wilson & Son
Elm Tree Street
Mansfield
Nottinghamshire NG18 2HD
Tel: (0623) 23113
Manufacturers and fixers of fibrous plaster, moulded and ornamental cornices, ceiling centres, panel mouldings, niches, fire surrounds, arches and decorative plasterwork.

Winther Browne & Co Ltd
Nobel Road , Eley's Estate
Edmonton , London N18 3DX
Tel: (01) 803 3434
See DOORS

STAIRCASES

Albion Design of London Ltd
12 Flitcroft Street
London WC2
Tel: (01) 379 7359/(01) 836 0151
Manufacturers of cast-iron spiral and straight staircases. Catalogue available.

R. Bleasdale & Co Ltd
301 Caledonian Road
Islington, London N1
Tel: (01) 609 0934
Reproduction Victorian spiral staircases, cast railings, balconies, straight staircases, etc, balustradings.

Cantabrian Antiques
16 Park Street
Lynton, North Devon
Tel: (0598) 53282
See FIREPLACES AND STOVES

C.S.L. Davey & Jordan
The Forge , 3 Jennings Road
Kernick Industrial Estate
Penryn, Cornwall TR10 9DQ
Tel: (0326) 74762
Makers of hand-made ornamental ironwork.

The English Street Furniture Co
Somers House
Linkfield Corner
Redhill
Surrey RH1 1BB
Tel: (0737) 60986
See FIREPLACES AND STOVES

Glover & Stacey Ltd
Oaklands House
Solartron Road
Farnborough
Hampshire GU14 7QL
Tel: (0252) 549334
Telex: 265871
See DOORS

Grandisson Doors
Grandisson Court
The College
Ottery St Mary
Devon EX11 1DQ
Tel: (040 481) 2876
See DOORS

Havenplan's Architectural Emporium
1 The Old Station
Station Road
Killamarsh
Sheffield S31 8EN
Tel: *Day* (0742) 489972
 Evening (0246) 433315
See FIREPLACES AND STOVES

E. A. Higginson & Co Ltd
1 Carlisle Road
Queensbury
London NW9 0HD
Tel: (01) 200 4848
See DOORS

House of Steel Antiques
400 Caledonian Road
Islington
London N1
Tel: (01) 607 5889
Also: 28 Camden Passage
Islington London N1
See FIREPLACES AND STOVES

J. & J. Manufacturing
Burrows Lane Farm House
Burrows Lane
Eccleston
Prescot, Merseyside L34 6JQ
Tel: (051) 426 0534
Specialist joiners, making and matching reproductions and restoration work, e.g. staircases, fire surrounds, etc. Also: carving, inlaid work and polishing.

Kentel Joinery Ltd
Unit 27
Smiths Industrial Estate
Humber Avenue
Coventry CV3 1JL
Tel: (0203) 449621
See WINDOWS

M. & A. Main
The Old Smith
Cerrig-y-Drudion
Corwen, Clwyd LL21 9SW
Tel: (049 082) 491
Also: 44 Argyle Street
Birkenhead
Tel: (051) 647 8000
See DOORS

Monarch Stairways
Napton Trading Estate
Napton, Rugby
Warwickshire
Tel: (092 681) 7018
Manufacturers of cast-iron spiral staircases.

Mounts Hill Woodcraft Ltd
The Depot
Mounts Hill
Cranbrook Road
Benenden
Cranbrook, Kent
Tel: (0580) 240270
See DOORS

A. L. Rattray
Craighall, Blairgowrie
Perthshire, Scotland
Tel: (0250) 4749
See BATHROOMS

Safety Stairways Ltd
141 Field Road
Bloxwich
Walsall, West Midlands
Tel: (0215) 263133/(0922) 477722/(0922)
491341
Cast-iron reproduction staircases, including Tudor, Georgian, Regency and Victorian styles.

Solopark Ltd
The Old Railway Station
Station Road
near Pampisford, Cambridgeshire CB2 4HB
Tel: (0223) 834663
See DOORS

Spiral Staircase Systems
The Mill, Glynde
Sussex BN7 8SS
Tel: (0791) 59341
Manufacturers of spiral staircases. Design service available.

Staircraft Joinery
Unit 7
Boston Place
Coventry CV6 5NN
Custom-made joinery, staircases a speciality.

Stuart Interiors
Barrington Court
Barrington
Ilminster
Somerset TA19 0NQ
Tel: (0460) 42003
See DOORS

Studio Two (Interior Design) Ltd
3A Town Street
Thaxted, Essex CM6 2LD
Tel: (0371) 830234
See KITCHENS

Robert Thompson's Craftsmen Ltd
Kilburn
York YO6 4AH
Tel: (03476) 218
See DOORS

Wansdown Joinery Works (Southern) Ltd
327 & 339 Lillie Road
Fulham Cross
London SW6 7NR
Tel: (01) 385 0351
Specialists in period staircases, panelled rooms in old pine, limed oak, mahogany and all types of period joinery.

Weller Patents Development
1-8 Grand Parade Mews
Putney, London SW15 2SP
Tel: (01) 788 6684
Specialist fabricators of internal and external architectural metalwork, including balustrading, gates, balconies and staircases, to clients' requirements – either original designs or copies of existing designs, highlighting/matching period details.

Winther Browne & Co Ltd
Nodel Road
Eleys Estate
London N18 3DX
Tel: (01) 803 3434
See DOORS

Woodstock (Totnes) Ltd
Station Road
Totnes, Devon PQ9 5JG
Tel: (0803) 864610
See DOORS

M. Woolaway & Sons Builders Ltd
Joinery Division
Junction Yard
Barnstaple
North Devon EX31 2AE
Tel: (0271) 74191
See DOORS

FIREPLACES AND STOVES

Robert Aagaard Ltd
Frogmire House
Stockwell Road
Knaresborough
North Yorkshire HG5 0JP
Tel: (0423) 864805
Antique mantels, marble interiors, hand-carved mantels, fireplace restoration and design.

Acquisitions (Fireplaces) Ltd
269 Camden High Street, London NW1 7BX
Tel: (01) 485 4955
Reproduction fireplaces using traditional materials. Wood and cast-iron mantels, cast-iron inserts, some incorporating hand-painted tiles from a wide range of designs.

Agaheat Appliances (Boilers and Ranges)
P.O. Box 30, Ketley
Telford, Shropshire TF1 1BR
Tel: (0952) 51177
Telex: 35196

Amazing Grates
Phoenix House
61-63 High Road, London N2 8AB
Tel: (01) 883 9590
Manufacturers of fireplaces, also mantels, marble surrounds, cast-iron grates and a wide range of accessories.

A. Andrews & Sons (Marbles and Tiles) Ltd
324-330 Meanwood Road
Leeds LS7 2JE, Yorkshire
Tel: (0532) 624751
Contractors in marble, mosaic, terrazzo and ceramic tiling. Specialists in restoration and renovation of period marble fireplaces and associated work.

Antique Fireplace Warehouse
194-196 Battersea Park Road
London SW11
Tel: (01) 627 1410
Specialists in cast-iron fireplaces, pine surrounds and marble chimneypieces. Restoration and installation service available.

Architectural Antiques Ltd
133 Upper Street
London N1
Tel: (01) 226 5565
Specialists in architectural antiques such as fireplace surrounds in wood, cast-iron and marble, cast-iron tiled fire inserts, fireplace accessories, tiles, doors in pine, oak and mahogany, with stained-glass or cut and etched panels, leaded lights, railings, gates, wrought-iron work, statuary, bathroom fittings and plasterwork. Restoration and repair service available.

Architectural Components Ltd
(Locks and Handles)
4-10 Exhibition Road, London SW7 2HF
Tel: (01) 581 2401/(01) 584 6800
See DOORS

Ashburton Marbles
6 West Street
Ashburton, Devon TQ13 7DU
Tel: (0364) 53189
Marble, timber and cast-iron fireplaces dating from 1790-1910, all fully restored. Also stocked: antique fireplace accessories including fenders, fire irons, scuttles and overmantels.

Bailey's Architectural Antiques
The Engine Shed
Ashburton Industrial Estate
Ross-on-Wye
Herefordshire HE9 7BW
Tel: (0989) 63015
See DOORS

Baxi Partnership Ltd
Brownedge Road
Bamber Bridge
Preston
Lancashire PR5 6SN
Tel: (0772) 36201
Manufacturer of gas and solid fuel domestic heating appliances.

A. Bell & Co Ltd
Head Office, Showroom and Works:
Kingsthorpe Road
Kingsthorpe
Northampton NN2 6LT
Tel: (0604) 712505
Designers and manufacturers of fine fireplaces, stoves and accessories since 1899, using a wide range of materials: brick, marble, slate, stone, steel, copper, bronze, brass and wood. Catalogue available.

La Belle Cheminee Ltd
85 Wigmore Street
London W1H 9FA
Tel: (01) 486 7486
Specializing in the installation of antique marble chimneypieces, with a range of brass and steel fire-grates, fenders, screens, fire-dogs and accessories.

Bisque
244 Belsize Road
London NW6
Tel: (01) 328 2225
Also: 15 Kingsmead Square
Bath BA1 2AE
Tel: (0225) 69600/69244
A wide selection of radiators in many colours and designs – tall, short, old-fashioned, bath panels, skirting radiators, all from specialist manufacturers like Zehnden and Runtal. Will also design the whole of the central heating system for a home and give advice on the most economical system, boiler size, positioning of heaters etc.

Bridgwater Reclamation Ltd
Monmouth Street
Bridgwater, Somerset
Tel: (0278) 424636
Architectural salvage items including architraves, moulding, marble and cast-iron fire surrounds, panelling, sinks, doors and door furniture, windows, sanitaryware, skirtings, wood block flooring (hardwood and softwood), structural and decorative timbers and beams. Also tiles, bricks, decorative ridges and finials. Joinery facilities for repairing and restoring, stripping and sand-blasting service.

Brighton Architectural Salvage

33 Gloucester Road
Brighton, East Sussex
Tel: (0273) 681656
Architectural antiques, including fireplaces and surrounds, stained glass, panelling, decorative ironwork, light fittings and garden ornaments.

T. F. Buckle (London) Ltd

427 King's Road
Chelsea, London SW10 0LR
Tel: (01) 352 0952
Specializing in antique mantelpieces in pine, marble and stone; reproduction mantelpieces in old and new pine; reproduction Victorian spiral staircases in cast iron. Reproduction grates. World-wide shipping arranged. Catalogue available.

Cantabrian Antiques

16 Park Street
Lynton, North Devon
Tel: (0598) 53282
Internal and external decorative architectural antiques, specializing in fireplaces and surrounds. Also bathroom fittings, doors, oak beams, panelling, stained glass and staircases.

The Cast Iron Fireplace Co Ltd

Showrooms: 99-103 East Hill
Wandsworth, London SW18 2QB
Tel: (01) 870 1630
Foundry Works: 1 Franciscan Road
Tooting, London SW17
Tel: (01) 767 3438
Supply original and reproduction cast-iron and brass fireplaces, grates, dogs, fire-chairs and wooden surrounds. Also reproduction hand-coloured Victorian tiles for use in a fireplace or hearth.

R. & J. Castings Ltd

Unit 69 Faircharm Trading Estate
Evelyn Drive, Leicester
Tel: (0533) 892163/892310
Manufacturers of fireplace equipment, fireside accessories and gas fires. Also reproduction Victorian register inset fireplaces.

Peter Chapman Antiques

10 Therberton Street
Islington, London N1 0QX
Tel: (01) 226 5565
Supply period fittings, including fireplaces, stained glass, bathroom fittings, etc. Restoration and installation service.

Chiltern Timber Heating

Trinity Farm House
49 Worminghall Road
Oakley, near Aylesbury
Buckinghamshire HP18 9QU
Tel: (0844) 238020
Retail and wholesale distributors of wood and coal stoves, cookers, boilers, plus flue and chimney materials.

Chimneypieces

227 Westbourne Grove
London W11 2SE
Tel: (01) 727 0102
Specializing in period-style fireplaces, Victorian and French marble and stone chimneypieces, carved marble fireplaces, cast-iron grates, stone reproduction surrounds. Commissions undertaken. Full shipping and export services. Installation service.

Chiswick Fireplaces

62 South Parade
Acton Green, London W4
Tel: (01) 994 2981
Victorian and Edwardian cast-iron fireplaces and original tiles. Also grates, fenders and fire-irons. Hearths and surrounds made to measure. Restoration and repair service; also installation service.

Classic Furniture (Newport) Ltd

Audley Avenue
Newport, Shropshire
Tel: (0952) 813311
Manufacturers of reproduction Victorian ornamental cast-iron furniture including garden furniture, doorstops and footscrapers, fire-backs, fire-grates, stoves and lampposts.

Coalbrookdale

Glynwed Consumer & Building Products Ltd
P.O. Box 30, Ketley
Telford, Shropshire TF1 1BR
Tel: (0952) 51177
Produce quality castings including those for Aga and Rayburn cookers and Coalbrookdale multi-fuel stoves. Catalogue available.

Counterparts Demolition Ltd

Station Yard
Topsham
Exeter, Devon
Tel: (039 287) 5995
See EXTERIORS

T. Crowther & Son Ltd

282 North End Road
Fulham, London SW6 1NH
Tel: (01) 385 1375/6/7
Cable address: Antiquity
See EXTERIORS

C.S.L. Davey & Jordan

The Forge
3 Jennings Road
Kernick Industrial Estate
Penryn
Cornwall TR10 9DQ
Tel: (0326) 74762
See STAIRCASES

Dunedin Antiques Ltd

4 North West Circus Place
Edinburgh EH3 6ST
Tel: (031) 226 3074
A large stock of period chimneypieces and architectural items.

Eaton-Gaze Ltd

Office & Factory:
86 Teesdale Street, London E2 6P
Tel: (01) 739 7272
Showroom:
22 The Broadway, The Bourne
London N14
Tel: (01) 882 3132
See CEILINGS

Emsworth Fireplaces

Station Approach
North Street, Emsworth
Hampshire PO10 7AG
Tel: (02434) 3431
Trading name for a division of Reeves (Builders Supplies) Ltd.

Stephen English

English Fireplaces
16-18 East Street
Shoreham-by-Sea
Sussex BN4 2ZE
Tel: (079 17) 464808
Supplies and fits reproduction and renovated fireplaces of all periods. Renovates chimneys and supplies new ones using a quick clean modern method which only takes 2-3 days. Can fit a fireplace into a working chimney in one day if supplied with measurements of chimney opening. Also supplies authentic period fireplace furniture and supplies and fits gas coal- and log-effect fires to go with huge range of fireplaces. Works from the Sussex base all over the South-East, London, Oxford and the Midlands, and will happily undertake work anywhere in the British Isles. Transportation is no problem as Mr English has a pilot's licence and in emergencies will fly fireplaces and materials out.

The English Street Furniture Co

Somers House
Linkfield Corner
Redhill
Surrey RH1 1BB
Tel: (0737) 60986
Supply architectural metalware, cast-iron fireplace installations, balustrading and balcony metalwork, interior and exterior staircase supports, together with a range of cast gates, all of which are contemporary to the period 1800-1914. Most products are maintained on an ex-stock basis enabling rapid response to the requirements of architects and other specifiers engaged in conservation work. Agents in the United States, Australia and the majority of European countries.

An Englishman's Home

56 Stokescraft
Bristol 7, Avon
Tel: (0272) 424257
Savoy Showrooms:
New Road
South Moulton, N. Devon
Tel: (07695) 3342
Architectural salvage items including a range of marble fire surrounds, Victorian and Georgian grates, stained-glass light fittings and ironwork; also garden ornaments and railings, etc.

Feature Fires Ltd

32 High Street
Northwood, Middlesex
Tel: (092 74) 26699
Design fireplaces to customers' requirements, fit and D.I.Y. Also supply fireplace brassware, fire-guards, fenders, buckets, etc; gas, log/coal effect fires.

Fireplaces of Yesteryears

(incorporating Art Tile Distributors)
Showroom: Railway Station Platform
Station Road
Knaresborough, North Yorkshire
Tel: (0423) 863739
Office: 5 Albans Close
Bardsey, Leeds 17, West Yorkshire
Tel: (0937) 74288
Distributors of fine period mantelpieces and Victorian dado tiles plus hand-decorated tiles featuring floral, classical and bird designs, ideal for conservation work or in character properties as wall or fireplace tiles. Also border tiles in single, two and multi-colours. Catalogue available.

Fireworld (U.K.) Ltd

31 Welford Road
Leicester LE2 7AD
Tel: (0533) 546361
Fireplace builders merchants.

Galleon Claygate Ltd

216-230 Red Lion Road
Tolworth
Surbiton, Surrey KT6 7RB
Tel: (01) 397 3456-9
Supply period fireplaces in Georgian, Adam or Regency style. Also solid fuel appliances and accessories, i.e. dog grates, fire-guards, fire-screens, companion sets, coal scuttles, etc. Catalogue available.

Glover & Stacey Ltd

Oaklands House
Solartron Road
Farnborough
Hampshire GU14 7QL
Tel: (0252) 549334
Telex: 265871
See DOORS

Grahamston Iron Co

P.O. Box 5, Gowan Avenue
Falkirk
Stirlingshire FK2 7HH
Tel: (0324) 22661
Iron-founders, enamellers, founded 1868. Manufacturers of fires, stoves and cookers including a range of open fires and accessories. Catalogue available.

Grandisson Doors

Grandisson Court
The College
Ottery St Mary
Devon EX11 1DQ
Tel: (040 481) 2876
See DOORS

James Gray & Son Ltd
89 George Street
Edinburgh EH2 3EZ
Tel: (031) 225 7381
Specialists in the design and supply of period fireplaces, Georgian, Regency and Victorian reproduction and original fireplace mantelpieces, cast-iron Victorian fireplace interiors with hand-painted ceramic tile inserts, reproductions and originals, specially selected marble and fine rubbed slate hearths, jambs, lintels and interiors, wide selection of dog grates and basket grates, together with purpose-made chain mail screens. Supply on a mail order basis to U.S.A. and other countries.

Hallidays
The Old College
Dorchester-on-Thames
Oxfordshire OX9 8HL
Tel: (0865) 340028
Also: 28 Beauchamp Place
Knightsbridge
London SW3 1NJ
Tel: (01) 589 5534
Specialists in Georgian panelling and fireplaces, particularly carved pine mantelpieces. Catalogue available.

Havenplan's Architectural Emporium
1 The Old Station
Station Road
Killamarsh
Sheffield S31 8EN
Tel: *Day* (0742) 489972 *Evening* (0246) 433315
Full range of architectural items including staircases, old doors, in oak, pine or mahogany, fire inserts and surrounds, cast-iron grates, railings and panelling.

Samuel Heath & Sons plc
Cobden Works
Leopold Street
Birmingham B12 0UJ
Tel: (021) 772 2303
Specialists in the handcrafting of hearthside furniture in brass and copper, including companion sets, fire screens, fenders, hods and log holders, etc. Catalogue available.

H.G.A. Fireplaces
(Dept of Hampton Garden Accessories Ltd)
Cirencester Road
Chalford
Stroud, Gloucestershire GL6 8PE
Manufacturers of Cotswold cast-stone fireplaces in classic, country classic and modular ranges. Suppliers, retail and trade, of Adam-style fireplace surrounds with marble, slate and cast-stone inserts, solid fuel and gas fuel effect appliances, chimney components, paving and blocks of cast-stone, garden containers in cast-stone.

Simply Elegant, Hodkin & Jones Ltd
515 Queens Road
Sheffield S2 4DS
Tel: (0742) 556121
Telex: 547113
See CEILINGS

The House Hospital
68 Battersea High Street
London SW11
Tel: (01) 223 3179
See DOORS

House of Steel Antiques
400 Caledonian Road
Islington, London N1
Tel: (01) 607 5889
Also: 28 Camden Passage
Islington, London N1
Stockists of antique architectural and ornamental metalwork, 300-400 Victorian and Edwardian cast-iron fireplaces, original garden furniture, urns and statuary, spiral staircases, railings, balconies and gates. Restoration and polishing of metalware and fireplaces. Sand-blasting. Castings in iron, brass and aluminium.

Hunter & Son (Mells) Ltd
Frome
Somerset
Tel: (0373) 812545
Telex: 444785
Manufacturers of domestic heating appliances; also antique reproduction stoves. Catalogue available.

Ideal Fireplaces
300 Upper Richmond Road West
East Sheen
London SW14
Tel: (01) 878 7887
Supply antique marble, pine and cast-iron tiled surrounds as well as mahogany and ornate new pine fireplaces. Modern designs, wood-burning stoves and fireside accessories also stocked. Installation service.

Interoven Ltd
70-72 Fearnley Street
Watford
Hertfordshire WD1 7DE
Tel: (0923) 4676 1/2
Manufacturers and purveyors of solid fuel heating appliances and equipment. Main products Goodwood wood-burning stoves, Homerette back boilers, with Virgil and Cokeglo all-night-burning fires.

J. & J. Manufacturing
Burrows Lane Farm House
Burrows Lane
Eccleston
Prescot, Merseyside L34 6JQ
Tel: (051) 426 0534
See STAIRCASES

Knight's of London
The Antique Fireplace Consultants
2A Belsize Park Mews
London NW3 5BL
Tel: (01) 431 2490
A unique and professional service dealing with every aspect of period fireplace design, planning, search, supply, installation, advice and information for both private and commercial clients.

Langham Architectural Materials
Langham Farm
East Nynehead
Wellington
Somerset TA21 0DD
Tel: (082 346) 297
A wide range of period fixtures and fittings including beams, hobs, grates, fire surrounds, in stone, marble, cast iron and pine; also doors, stained glass, railings and metalwork.

London Stove Centre
49 Chiltern Street
London W1M 1HQ
Tel: (01) 486 5168
Suppliers of cast-iron solid fuel and wood-burning and gas stoves; central heating cookers. Full range of accessories and flue systems. Installation service.

M. & A. Main
The Old Smithy
Cerrig-y-Drudion
Corwen, Clwyd LL21 9SW
Tel: (049 082) 491
Also: 44 Argyle Street, Birkenhead
Tel: (051) 647 8000
See DOORS

Marble Hill Fireplaces Ltd
72 Richmond Road
Twickenham
Middlesex TW1 3BE
Tel: (01) 892 1488/8460
Manufacturers of fireplaces, fire grates and electric fires. Leading manufacturers of Adam-style mantels and baskets. A full range of fireplace accessories including fire irons, fenders, fire screens and gas, log and coal effect fires. Installation service. Catalogue available.

Bertram Noller (Reigate)
14A London Road
Reigate, Surrey RH2 9HY
Tel: (07372) 42548
Adam-style pine and marble mantelpieces, antique and modern marble-work. Restoration and supply of decorative metalwork.

Nostalgia
61B Shaw Heath
Stockport
Cheshire SK3 8BH
Tel: (061) 477 7706
Architectural antiques retailers. Specialists in fully restored Victorian, Georgian and Edwardian fireplaces, in cast iron, mahogany, oak, pine, marble and stone. Over 1,000 items in stock. Also a range of Edwardian bathroom fittings, baths, basins, W.C.s, brass taps, shower fittings, towel rails, etc, all original and fully restored. Fitting services available.

The Original Architectural Heritage of Cheltenham
Boddington Manor, Boddington near Cheltenham
Gloucestershire GL51 0TJ
Tel: (024268) 741
See WALLS

The Original Choice
1340 Stratford Road
Hall Green
Birmingham B28 9EH
Tel: (021) 778 382
Specialists in antique fireplaces, expertly restored and installed. Victorian, Georgian and Edwardian; marble, pine, mahogany, oak and cast iron. Also exclusive reproduction tiles; marble insets cut and supplied. Stockists of doors and antique fixtures and fittings. Over 500 Victorian and Edwardian stained-glass and leaded windows in stock. Restoration service available.

Pageant Antiques
122 Dawes Road
London SW6
Tel: (01) 385 7739
See EXTERIORS

Patrick Fireplaces
Guildford Road
Farnham
Surrey GU9 9QA
Tel: (0252) 722345
Specialist manufacturers of custom-built individual fireplaces. Installation service available.

Period Reclamation & Restoration Services
205 Salisbury Road
Burton
Christchurch
Dorset BH23 7JT
Tel: (0202) 473300/(0836) 246263
See EXTERIORS

Petit Roque Ltd
5a New Road
Croxley Green
Hertfordshire WD3 3EJ
Tel: (0923) 779291/720968
See FLOORS

Stan Pike, Traditional Blacksmith
Blacksmiths Shop
Bearsbridge
Whitfield, Hexham
Northumberland
Tel: (049 85) 210
High-quality ornamental ironwork including fire grates, fire dogs, wind vanes, gates, railings, etc. Leaf work and restoration work. Repousse in copper and sheet steel.

M. A. Pope (Fireplaces) Ltd
Rear of 62-64 High Street
Barnet, Hertfordshire
Tel: (01) 449 5863
Manufacture marble fireplaces. Installation service available.

Posterity Architectural Effects
Baldwins Farm
Dymock Road, Newent, Gloucestershire
Tel: (0531) 85597
See EXTERIORS

H. W. Poulter & Son
Showroom:
279 Fulham Road
London SW10 9PZ
Tel: (01) 352 7268
Workshop: 1A Adelaide Grove
off Uxbridge Road
London W12
Tel: (01) 749 4557
Specialists in English and French antique marble chimneypieces, grates, fender, fire-irons, etc, also chandeliers. Restoration and repair service.

D. A. & A. G. Prigmore
Mill Cottage
Mill Road
Colmworth
Bedford
Tel: (023 062) 264
See EXTERIORS

Quebb Stoves
Alton Road
Ross-on-Wye
Herefordshire HR9 5NF
Tel: (0989) 63656
Manufacturers of a range of multi-fuel stoves.

A. L. Rattray
Craighall
Blairgowrie
Perthshire
Scotland
Tel: (0250) 4749
See BATHROOMS

Reclaimed Materials
Northgate
White Lund Industrial Estate
Morecambe, Lancashire
Tel: (0524) 69094
See EXTERIORS

Smith & Wellstood Est (1984) Ltd
Bonnybridge
Stirlingshire FK4 2AP
Tel: (0324) 81217
Manufacturers of domestic heating appliances for use with solid fuel, oil and gas. Specialists in vitreous enamelled castings. Dragon and Dolphin heaters based on original Victorian designs, and feature fires for solid fuel, gas and electric, based on original Adam-period designs.

Stelrad Group Ltd
P.O. Box 103
National Avenue
Hull HU5 4JN
North Humberside
Manufacturers of central heating boilers and radiators.

Stuart Interiors
Barrington Court, Barrington ,Ilminster
Somerset TA19 0NQ
Tel: (0460) 42003
See DOORS

Studio Two (Interior Design) Ltd
3A Town Street
Thaxted
Essex CM6 2LD
Tel: (0371) 830234
See KITCHENS

Surroundings Ltd
136 Fortress Road
London NW5
Tel: (01) 485 2445
Supply and fit antique French marble chimneypieces, Victorian cast-iron and marble fireplaces. Installation service available.

Ti Creda Ltd
Creda Works
P.O. Box 5
Blythe Bridge
Stoke-on-Trent ST11 9LJ
Tel: (0782) 392281
Telex: 36243
Manufacturers of electrical appliances.

"Townsends" (London) Ltd
Shops: 1 Church Street, London NW8
Tel: (01) 724 3746
81 Abbey Road, London NW8
Tel: (01) 624 4756
Workshop & Showroom:
36 New End Square
Hampstead, London NW3
Tel: (01) 794 5706/7
See WINDOWS

Trianco Redfyre Ltd
Thorncliffe
Chapeltown
Sheffield S30 4PZ
South Yorkshire
Tel: (0742) 461221
Manufacturers of central heating boilers, domestic and industrial.

Verine Products & Co
Folly Faunts House
Goldhanger
Maldon, Essex CM9 8AP
Tel: (0621) 88611
Manufacturers of reproductions of original classical fireplaces, mantelpieces and architectural mouldings. Suppliers of door surrounds, porticos and canopies, columns and pilasters, window pediments, corbels and cornices. Catalogue available.

Walcot Reclamation
108 Walcot Street
Bath, Avon BA1 5BG
Tel: (0225) 66291
Architectural antiques with a wide range of fireplaces and accessories from all periods; also stained glass, panelled doors, flooring, roofing, beams, architectural joinery and bathrooms stocked.

A. J. Wells & Sons
Westminster Lane
Newport
Isle of Wight PO30 5DP
Tel: (0983) 527552
Telex: 869466
Manufacturers of multi-fuel, coal and wood-burning, stoves.

Whiteway & Waldron Ltd
305 Munster Road
London SW6
Tel: (01) 381 3195
See WINDOWS

W. J. Wilson & Son
Elm Tree Street
Mansfield
Nottinghamshire NG18 2HD
Tel: (0623) 23113
See CEILINGS

Woodstock (Totnes) Ltd
Station Road
Totnes
Devon PQ9 5JG
Tel: (0803) 864610
See DOORS

W. Woolaway & Sons Builders Ltd
(Joinery Division)
Junction Yard
Barnstaple
North Devon EX31 2AE
Tel: (0271) 74191
See DOORS

BATHROOMS

Adamez Bathrooms Ltd
Dukesway
Gateshead
Tyne & Wear NE11 0SW
Tel: (091 487) 4511/2
Showroom: 13-21 Percy Street
Newcastle-upon-Tyne
Produce modern and reproduction style sanitaryware including a wide range of taps and fittings.

W. Adams & Sons Ltd
Westfield Works
Spon Lane
West Bromwich
West Midlands B70 6BM
Tel: (021) 553 2161/3
Export Distributors:
Spring Ram International plc
P.O. Box 30
Spring Bank Industrial Estate
Sowerby Bridge
West Yorkshire MX6 3DG
Tel: (0422) 835062
Manufacturers of bathroom taps and mixers, antique and Georgian patterns, with accessories to match.

A. & H. Brass
201-203 Edgware Road
London W2 1ES
Tel: (01) 402 3981/1854
See DOORS

Allia (U.K.) Ltd
Whieldon Road
Stoke-on-Trent ST4 4HN
Tel: (0782) 49191
Company Head Office in Paris. Allia is a subsidiary of La Forge Coppee, Paris
Manufacturers of bathroom products: acrylic baths, washbasins, W.C. suites and bidets in vitreous china, shower trays and kitchen sinks.

Architectural Antiques Ltd
133 Upper Street
Islington
London N1
Tel: (01) 226 5565
See FIREPLACES AND STOVES

Architectural Components Ltd
(Locks and Handles)
4-10 Exhibition Road
London SW7 2HF
Tel: (01) 581 2401/(01) 584 6800
See DOORS

Architectural & Industrial G.R.P.
400 Ewell Road
Tolworth, Surrey KT6 7HF
Manufacturers of baths, basins and shower bases. One-off specialized baths to order. Also manufacturers of replacement building cornices and exterior stonework, in liaison with district surveyors and architects.

Armitage Shanks Group Ltd
Armitage Rugeley
Staffordshire WS15 4BT
Tel: (0543) 490253
London Showroom:
The Better Bathroom
303-306 High Holborn
London WC1V 7LB
Tel: (01) 405 9663
Sanitaryware manufacturers producing baths, bidets, washbasins and W.C.s, vanity units, plumbing products, showers and brassware. Catalogue available.

Arnull of London
13-14 Queen Street
Mayfair
London W1
Tel: (01) 499 3231
Importers and distributors of bathroom fittings and sanitaryware, also ceramic floor and wall tiles.

Bailey's Architectural Antiques
The Engine Shed
Ashburton Industrial Estate
Ross-on-Wye, Herefordshire HE9 7BW
Tel: (0989) 63015
See DOORS

Balterley Bathrooms Ltd
P.O. Box 154
Stoke-on-Trent ST1 2PT
Tel: (0782) 633118
Suppliers of sanitaryware, baths, bidets, W.C.s and washbasins. Also, Edwardian-style bathrooms with tub-style baths. Catalogue available.

The Bathroom People
10 Aldermans Hill
London N13 4PJ
Tel: (01) 882 6863
Bathrooms designed by Luigi Colani; leading suppliers such as Jameson, Jacuzzi, Nordic, Acqualise, Villeroy & Boch.

B. & E. Marketing Ltd
61 Whitecross Road
Weston-super-Mare
Avon BS23 1SJ
Tel: (0934) 25095
Bathroom accessories in vitreous china and ceramic.

Birds Baths of Hainault, Builders Merchants
13 Hainault Street
Ilford, Essex IG1 4EN
Tel: (01) 478 8213
Sanitaryware manufacturers specializing in reproduction bathrooms, e.g. Vernon Tutbury, Architectural Heritage, Sanitan. Brassware includes the Leonardo Rudge, Adams Antique, Sanitan, Adams Georgian, Holdmark, Barber Wilson, Maurice Herbeau. Also sell tiles from Worlds End, Period Tiles. Catalogue available.

Bonsack Baths (London) Ltd
14 Mount Street
Mayfair
London W1Y 5RA
Tel: (01) 629 9981
Telex: 88 14034
Suppliers of sanitaryware, taps, tiles, marbles and wallcoverings. Classical, Art Deco and high-tech styles. Catalogue available.

British Bathroom Centre
Unit 2 Amhurst Park Works
Eade Road
London N4 1DN
Tel: (01) 802 6696
Suppliers of bathroom products including baths, showers, whirlpools, tiles, sanitaryware, accessories, etc. Design service available.

Bridgwater Reclamation Ltd
Monmouth Street
Bridgwater
Somerset
Tel: (0278) 424636
See FIREPLACES AND STOVES

Cantabrian Antiques
16 Park Street
Lynton, North Devon
Tel: (0598) 53282
See FIREPLACES AND STOVES

Celmac Heatherley Ltd
Unit 3 Ferry Lane
Brentford
Middlesex TW8 0BG
Tel: (01) 568 7963
See DOORS

Peter Chapman Antiques
10 Therberton Street
Islington
London N1 0QX
Tel: (01) 226 5565
See FIREPLACES AND STOVES

Chilternhurst Designs Ltd
48 Coldharbour Lane
Harpenden, Hertfordshire AL5 4UR
Tel: (05827) 60281
Manufacturers of wooden bathroom furniture including toilet seats, reproduction washstands, bath panels, towel rails, cistern handles, chain pulls, wall lights. Matt or gloss lacquers.

The Complete Bathroom
16 Roundtree Close
Roundtree Way
Norwich, Norfolk NR7 8SX
Tel: (0603) 486298
Designers, suppliers and restorers of solid wood bathrooms; bathroom furniture made to customers' requirements.

Czech & Speake Ltd
Head Office:
244-254 Cambridge Heath Road
London E2 9DA
Tel: (01) 980 4567
Telex: 83147
Showroom:
39c Jermyn Street
London SW1
Tel: (01) 980 4567
Manufacturers of bathroom fittings, Edwardian range including sink mixers and accessories, in solid brass with porcelain fittings, available in polished brass, lacquered brass, nickel and chrome. Complementary range of accessories including towel rings, grab rails, robe hooks, soap dishes, etc. Catalogue available.

Hathaway Pine Furniture Ltd
Clifford Mill
Clifford Chambers
Near Stratford-upon-Avon
Warwickshire CV37 8HW
Tel: (0789) 205517
Fitted kitchens, in English hardwoods and pine, painted finishes, based on elegant 18th-century classical designs; also fitted bathrooms and full interior design services available.

Heaton's Bathrooms Ltd
Denby Way
Hellaby, Rotherham S66 8HR
Tel: (0709) 549551
Manufacturers of acrylic baths, panels, shower trays and vanity basins. Catalogue available.

The House Hospital
68 Battersea High Street
London SW11
Tel: (01) 223 3179
See DOORS

Jamesons
North Tyne Industrial Estate
Whitley Road
Longbenton
Newcastle-upon-Tyne NE12 9SZ
Tel: (091) 266 3474
Telex: 538252
Manufacture bathrooms and accessories including a Victorian-style bathroom with fittings to complement. Catalogue available.

The London Architectural Salvage & Supply Co
St Michael's Church
Mark Street off Paul Street
Shoreditch
London EC2A 4ER
Tel: (01) 739 0448
See DOORS

M. & A. Main
The Old Smithy
Cerrig-y-Drudion
Corwen, Clwyd LL21 9SW
Tel: (049 082) 491
Also: 44 Argyle Street, Birkenhead
Tel: (051) 647 8000
See DOORS

M.G.S. Distributors Ltd
33 Monkspath Business Park
Highlands Road
Shirley, Solihull
West Midlands B90 4NZ
Tel: (021) 745 9441
Bathroom and kitchen specialists. Sole distributors of Villeroy & Boch kitchen sinks and sanitaryware.

Modern Living
27-31 London Road
Kingston-upon-Thames, Surrey
Tel: (01) 549 6579 (Bathroom showroom)
(01) 541 1851 (Kitchen showroom)
One of London's largest showrooms for bathrooms and kitchens. Installation service available for kitchens.

Nostalgia
61B Shaw Heath
Stockport
Cheshire SK3 8BH
Tel: (061) 477 7706
See FIREPLACES AND STOVES

Original Bathrooms
143-145 Kew Road
Richmond, Surrey TW9 2PN
Tel: (01) 940 7554

S. Polliack Ltd
Head Office & Works:
Norton Industrial Estate
Norton, Malton
North Yorkshire YO17 9HQ
Tel: (0653) 5331
London Depot:
Goldhawk Industrial Estate
Brackenbury Road
Shepherds Bush
London W6 0BA
Tel: (01) 743 2461
Manufacturers of bathrooms, including Victorian and Edwardian styles with complementary accessories. Catalogue available.

Porcelain Newglaze Ltd
91 Godolphin Road
London W12 8JN
Tel: (01) 749 0720
Suppliers of Newglaze Epoxy coating for re-surfacing baths, tiles, washbasins, etc.

Posterity Architectural Effects
Baldwins Farm
Dymock Road
Newent, Gloucestershire
Tel: (0531) 85597
See EXTERIORS

A. L. Rattray
Craighall
Blairgowrie
Perthshire, Scotland
Tel: (0250) 4749
Architectural re-cyclers of Victorian bathroom fittings, doors, mantelpieces, panelling, iron and wood staircases, balconies, balustrades and stained, etched and cut-glass doors; also building materials such as flagstones, stone balustrading and garden statuary.

Riva Design Ltd
"The Ryecroft"
Fanavon Buildings
Warrington Street
Stalybridge
Cheshire SK15 2LB
Tel: (061) 303 0868
See KITCHENS

B.C. Sanitan
12 Nimrod Way
Reading RG2 0EB
Tel: (0734) 876161
Period bathroomware, including baths, W.C.s, in plain white or patterned in traditional Victorian designs. Range includes cast-iron rolled-top bath, mahogany panels and a range of traditional taps and accessories. Catalogue available.

Shires Bathrooms
Park Road
Guiseley, Leeds, West Yorkshire LS20 8AP
Tel: (0943) 73232
Manufacturers of ceramic sanitaryware, W.C. suites, basins, bidets and accessories; also acrylic baths, shower trays and bath panels. Catalogue available

Jayne Simcock Design Ltd
49 St Margaret's Grove
Twickenham, Middlesex TW1 1JF
Tel: (01) 892 9238
See WALLS

Tiles of Newport and London
Head Office:
Dumfries Place Estate
Lower Dock Street
Newport, Gwent
Tel: (0633) 50383
Also: The Talina Centre
Unit 9 23a Bagleys Lane
off New King's Road
London SW6
Tel: (01) 731 7338
Importers, distributors and retailers of ceramic tiles, bathroom equipment, baths, showers, shower doors, gold, silver and brass taps and accessories, shower curtains and wallpaper. Designers of hand-painted tiles. Importers of marble and designers of marble floors.

Traditional Bathrooms
(at Pipe Dreams)
105 Regents Park Road
London NW1 8UR
Tel: (01) 722 0094/5
Deal exclusively in period bathroomware, tiles, taps, accessories as well as bathroom suites.

Steven Tubb
Craigmore Farm
Stockiemuir Road
Blanefield
Glasgow G63 9AU
Tel: (0360) 70010
Manufacturers of oak toilet seats and other bathroom accessories.

Twyfords Bathrooms
P.O. Box 23
Stoke-on-Trent ST4 7AL
Manufacturers and exporters of a full range of bathroom products including complete suites, washbasins, cloakroom basins, W.C.s, and bidets made from vitreous china; acrylic and steel baths; taps, fittings and accessories, shower screens and shower trays.

Victoriana Bathrooms Ltd
439 Cleethorpe Road
Grimsby DN31 3BU
Tel: (0472) 55584
Specialize in the design and manufacture of reproduction Victorian bathroom furniture. Made in either solid mahogany or pine, a special technique is incorporated into the French-polished finish to ensure the furniture is both steam and water resistant, with complementary tiles, hand-painted in Victorian-based designs. The range includes panelled bath, corner bath, wall mounts and corner washstands, lavatory seats and dado rails. White sanitaryware and period reproduction brass taps optional. Catalogue available.

David Woods Antiques
The Chimneys, Swindon Road, Dauntsey Lock, Near Chippenham, Wiltshire
Tel: (0249) 891234
Deal only in genuine Victorian and Edwardian bathroom fittings. Stock includes cast-iron baths on feet, ceramic baths, showers, plain and coloured pattern W.C.s, wooden W.C. seats, washbasins, brass fittings (taps, bath-mixers, cistern handles, heated towel rails, etc).

Woodstock (Totnes) Ltd
Station Road, Totnes, Devon PQ9 5JG
Tel: (0803) 864610
See DOORS

B. & P. Wynn & Co
18 Boston Parade, Boston Road, London W7 2DG
Tel: (01) 567 8758
Sole U.K. importer and distributor for the Maurice Herbeau hand-made hand-basins which are individually decorated for the cloakroom by Maurice Herbeau of Lille. The range includes many accessories. Additionally importers and distributors for the Julia/Eloise range of luxury kitchen and bathroom mixers, showers, etc.

KITCHENS

A.B.C. Cuisines
Broomgrove, Croft Road, Goring,
Reading RG8 9ES   Tel: (0491) 872912
London Showroom:
A.B.C. Cuisines (London) Ltd, 715 Fulham Road
London SW6 5UN   Tel: (01) 736 9581
Manufacture solid wood kitchens with traditional rustic look, with antique finish.

Aga-Rayburn
(Coalbrookdale)
Glynwed Consumer & Building Products Ltd
P.O. Box 30, Ketley, Telford
Shropshire TF1 1BR
Tel: (0952) 51177 Telex: 35196
Kitchen ranges.

Allmilmö Ltd
Station Road, Thatcham
Near Newbury, Berkshire, RG13 4RD
Tel: (0635) 68181 Telex: 847884
Traditional and modern kitchen ranges. Catalogue available.

Alno (U.K.) Ltd
Unit 10 Hampton Farm Industrial Estate
Hampton Road West
Hanworth, Middlesex TW13 6DB
Tel: (01) 898 4781
Manufacturers of built-in kitchens, 33 ranges including traditional rustic, period and classical styles in red-brown oak with solid oak fronts, natural oak, light oak and brown oak; also in grey-white pigmented effect with pewter knobs.

Artisan Design
13 Palace Road
London N8
Tel: (01) 348 9159
Specializing in custom designing, anything from moulding to a panelled room, character shop fronts to Victorian kitchens, in a vast range of finishes – French polish, lacquer, gilding, rag-rolling.

Garry Blanch
Mounts Farm
Benenden, Kent
Tel: (0580) 240622
Individually cabinet-made kitchens in all types of solid wood.

Alfred Briggs (Lurgan) Ltd
P.O. Box No. 6
Alwood Cabinet Works
Lurgan
N. Ireland BT66 8DG
Tel: (076 22) 3296
Custom-built kitchens supplied in different colours of melamine laminates, truwood, texon or solid wood fronts, oak, ash, chestnut, etc. Catalogue available.

Geoff Brown (Woodgoods) Ltd
High Street, Odiham
Hampshire RG25 1LN
Tel: (04203) 7182
Individually designed and custom-built kitchens made from antique pine in Victorian style, all hand-made to order.

Bowater Joinery Ltd
Clare Kitchens
Castle Hedingham
Halstead, Essex CO9 3EP
Sales Office: Tel: (0787) 60676
Kitchens individually designed, ranging from the authentic farmhouse kitchen to more modern styles. Catalogue available.

Bulthaup Kitchens
474 Larkshall Road
Highams Park
London E4 9HH
Tel: (01) 523 2101
Suppliers of German kitchens, custom-built with a choice of 130 colours.

H. Burbidge & Son Ltd
Burnsall Road
Canley, Coventry CU5 6BS
Tel: (0203) 78721
Telex: 311493
Supply a wide selection of kitchens in fashionable ranges and traditional ranges, in maple, mahogany, ash, pine and several oaks, with smooth paint finishes and antique finishes. Catalogue available.

Chefco Products Ltd
9 Grove Market Place
London SE9 5PU
Tel: (01) 859 2735
Telex: 898168
Agents for Bauformat fitted kitchens.

Commodore Kitchens
Acorn Trading Centre
Grays, Essex RM16 1XP
Tel: (0375) 383733
Telex: 995934 G
A selection of modern and antique kitchens including a comprehensive selection of kitchen appliances. Catalogue available.

Crosby Kitchens Ltd
Orgreave Drive
Handsworth, Sheffield S13 9NS
Tel: (0742) 697371
Manufacturers of traditional-style ranges of self-assembly kitchen furniture – Caprice and Castagno – supplied throughout the U.K.

Cuisines Bonnet U.K. Ltd
10-12 Bromley Road
Beckenham
Kent BR3 2GE
Tel: (01) 658 0271
Supplier of French fitted kitchens. Catalogue available.

Dennis and Robinson Ltd
Blenheim Road
Churchill Industrial Estate
Lancing
West Sussex, BN15 8UH
Tel: (0903) 755321
Manufacture and supply of kitchens to the building industry.

Exactum Ltd
Acorn Trading Centre
Gumley Road
Grays, Essex
Tel: (0375) 382789/372027
Telex: 995934
Telefax: 0375 381311
Kitchen appliance and worktop distributors.

Foreson Partners Ltd
Longbridge Way
Cowley Mill Road
Uxbridge, Middlesex
Tel: (0895) 34866
Kitchen manufacturers; Panama Kitchens. General woodworkers and fabricators. The units range from melamine laminates, veneered oak, solid oak, mahogany and acacia.

Gallery Interiors Ltd
Kitchen Gallery
12 East Cross
Tenterden Kent
Tel: (0580) 64130
Designers and installers for leading manufacturers of kitchen and bathroom furniture. Specialists in antique pine, oak, hand-painted kitchens and personalized design and styling. Appointed by leading kitchen equipment and accessory manufacturers: Neff, Miele, Gaggenau, Kenwood. Suppliers of the more unusual ceramic quarry and terracotta tiles. Design and fixing service available.

Geba U.K. Ltd (Kitchens)
Abbey House
Wellington Road
London Colney
Hertfordshire AL2 1EY
Tel: (0727) 25147
Supply fitted kitchens, over 80 dealers in Britain. 60 high-quality ranges, from solid oak to high-tech laminates. Also bathroom furniture.

Goldreif Kitchens U.K. Ltd
Thames House
63 Kingston Road
New Malden, Surrey KT3 3PB
Tel: (01) 942 9347
Telex: 928184
Manufacturers of modern and traditional-style kitchens. Represented all over the world. Catalogue available.

Hathaway Pine Furniture Ltd
Clifford Mill
Clifford Chambers
Near Stratford-upon-Avon
Warwickshire CV37 8HW
Tel: (0789) 205517
See BATHROOMS

Jamesway Kitchen Centre
9 Masons Avenue
Wealdstone
Harrow HA3 5AH
Tel: (01) 863 2638
Modern and period kitchens.

John Lewis of Hungerford
13 High Street
Hungerford, Berkshire
Tel: (0488) 82066

Kingswood Kitchen Systems
Allied Manufacturing Co Ltd
Serena House
Grove Park, Colindale
London NW9 0EB
Tel: (01) 205 8844/(01) 205 5566 (24 hr)
Manufacturers, suppliers and installers of kitchens in countryside oak, solid mahogany and several "designer" colourways. Also components and accessories. Catalogue available.

The Kitchen People
348-354 Kensington High Street
London W14 8NS
Tel: (01) 602 4255/6
Also: 92 Heath Street
Hampstead, London NW3
Tel: (01) 431 0469
10 Aldermans Hill
London N13 4PJ
Tel: (01) 882 5701
Specialists in fitted kitchens, solid granite worktops. A range of 5,000 tiles in stock. Design and installation of bathrooms. Export and fixing services.

Lanzet (U.K.) Ltd
Unit 20 Headley Park – 10
Headley Road East
Woodley, Reading, Berkshire
Tel: (0734) 695707
Manufacturers of individually tailored kitchens with over 70 door styles, from modern to classical. Catalogue available.

Leicht Furniture Ltd
Leicht House
Lagoon Road
Orpington, Kent BR5 3QG
Tel: (0689) 36413/4

Lockhurst Kitchen Design
8-12 Lockhurst Lane
Coventry CV6 5PB
Tel: (0203) 668141
Manufacturers of kitchen furniture. Full installation service available.

The London Architectural Salvage & Supply Co
St Michael's Church
Mark Street off Paul Street
Shoreditch
London EC2A 4ER
Tel: (01) 739 0448
See DOORS

Malvern Studios
56 Cowleigh Road
Malvern
Worcestershire WR14 1QD
Tel: (06845) 4913
See LIGHTING

John Mead Country Kitchens
Roadside Farm
Little Salisbury
Pewsey, Wiltshire
Tel: (0672) 62365
Manufacturers of solid wood kitchens in sawn English oak, old pine, oak, ash, cherry or lacquered hardwood. Also individual items such as charcoal grills, wooden cornices and bookshelves. Catalogue available.

Mobens Kitchens Ltd
100 Washway Road
Sale, Cheshire M33 1RE
Tel: (061) 976 3136
Period-style kitchens.

Peal Furniture (Durham) Ltd
Littleburn Industrial Estate
Langley Moor
Durham DH7 8HE
Tel: (0385) 780232
Also: Radlett Kitchen Centre
359 Watling Street
Radlett, Hertfordshire WD7 7GB
Tel: (092 76) 5466

Pine Unlimited Country Kitchens
13A Greenwich South Street
London SE10
Tel: (01) 858 0506
Manufacturers of bespoke fitted kitchens using traditional methods of construction and genuine antique pine. Catalogue available.

Pine Village
42-43 Peascod Street
Windsor, Berkshire
Tel: (0753) 855730
Kitchen furniture.

Pinewood Custombuilt Kitchens
4 Harcourt Road
Redland, Bristol BS6 7RG
Tel: (0272) 49654
Traditional kitchens, with a variety of finishes – antique pine, hand-painted surfaces and a choice of coloured stains. Fitting service available. A full range of appliances and accessories. Catalogue available.

Prior Unit Design
Woodbury
Exeter EX5 1LP
Tel: (0395) 32237
Kitchen planners, cabinet makers and joinery specialists. In-house design and drawing office.

Qualcast (Fleetway) Ltd
Charlton Road
Edmonton
London N9 8HR
Tel: (01) 804 5051
Telex: 267922
Manufacturers of the Qualcast and Grovewood range of rigid and self-assembly kitchens. Designs range from traditional solid wood kitchens to hi-tech. Stockists throughout the country.

W. F. Rational
18 Queen Square
Bristol BS1 1NH
Tel: (0272) 277188
24 ranges of fully fitted kitchens in lacquers, laminate, wood and laminate combinations, veneers and solid oak or pine are available, offering over 170 front finish options. An extensive range of units, interior fitments, accessories and worktops. Planning and installation service. Brochures available.

Riva Design Ltd
"The Ryecroft"
Fanavon Buildings
Warrington Street
Stalybridge
Cheshire SK15 2LB
Tel: (061) 303 0868
Projects range from complete kitchens and bathrooms to room panelling and architectural joinery. Interior design and installation service also available.

Siematic U.K. Ltd
11-17 Fowler Road
Hainault Industrial Estate
Ilford, Essex IG6 3UU
Tel: (01) 500 1944
Kitchen interior designers providing an extensive range from the ultra-modern to the more traditional styles of Baroque Flemish and solid oak kitchens.

Smallbone of Devizes
Head Office: Unit 10-11
Nimrod Way, Elgar Road
Reading, Berkshire
Tel: (0734) 868044
Hand-crafted fitted kitchens in old pine and English oak. Also a range of hand-painted kitchens which are finished with different paint techniques such as dragging, rag-rolling, stippling and sponging. London showrooms in Wimpole Street, W1, and Harrods, Gloucester Road, SW7. Others in Bristol, Tunbridge Wells, St Albans, Edinburgh, Leamington Spa, Knutsford and Reading. Catalogue available.

Solent Furniture Ltd
Pymore Mills, Bridport
Dorset DT6 5PJ
Tel: (0308) 22305
Telex: 417243
Specialists in rigid ready-made kitchens in pine, mahogany and oak. Catalogue available.

Stately Home Kitchens Ltd
Coronation Parade
54 Cannon Lane
Pinner, Middlesex HA5 1HW
Tel: (01) 866 0973
Manufacture solid oak kitchens. Supply carcases alone, doors alone or complete kitchens, together with kitchen appliances.

Strand Furniture Ltd
Birchwood Way, Somercotes
Derbyshire DE55 4NP
Tel: (0773) 607411
Telex: 377310
Manufacture worktops, laminated door elements, blanks, solid wood doors for kitchen units, door trims and other solid wood accessories.

Studio Two (Interior Design) Ltd
3A Town Street
Thaxted, Essex CM6 2LD
Tel: (0371) 830234
Interior designers specializing in the restoration and recreation of English period kitchens and other "backstairs" areas and the restoration of ingle nooks and roasting hearths to complete working condition. All projects completely individual but most involve recreating or restoring traditional joinery and other furniture and the surrounding structure, brickwork, floors, etc. A network of specialist craftsmen from many parts of the country are used to recreate furniture, fitments and finishes, though antique furnishings, metalwork and equipment are used whenever practical. Also undertake the design and co-ordination of other interior joinery, such as staircases, panelling, library furniture, etc.

Styles Kitchens Ltd
2 Rowhedge Close
Wollaston Industrial Centre
Basildon, Essex SS13 1QQ
Tel: (0268) 727615
Fully fitted kitchens; the country colour range painted in any colour or shade, with two other similarly styled ranges – Country Pine and Country Oak, both in natural solid wood. A stippled, sponged, rolled or dragged effect can be added if required.

Sutton Kitchens
30 Beacon Grove, High Street
Carshalton, Surrey SM5 3BA
Tel: (01) 669 5281
Kitchen manufacturers who design and refurbish kitchens in period houses dating back to the 16th century. Doors are hand-crafted in genuine 200- or 400-year reclaimed oak. Pine, cherry and mahogany finishes are available. Design and installation service, advice on tiling and supply and fixing of tiles.

Tielsa Kitchens
Wakefield Road
Gildersome, Leeds LS27 0QW
Tel: (0532) 524131
Telex: 55260
Manufacture hand-crafted kitchens, exported world wide. Catalogue available.

Truelove of Bungay
2 Southend Road
Trading Estate off St John's Road
Bungay, Suffolk NR35 1DP
Tel: (0986) 2288
Manufacture classically styled kitchens recreated the traditional way, using reclaimed pine. Also specialize in decorative paint finishes such as dragging, stippling, rag-rolling and sponging. A wide range of English, Mexican and French hand-painted worktop and wall tiles and terracotta floor tiles stocked. Catalogue available.

M. Tuckey Joinery
20 Cherry Street
Warwick, CV34 4LR
Tel: (0926) 493679
Specialists in hand-made fitted kitchens and hand-made windows as copies of originals.

Victorian Showcase
Units 1-3 Burnham Street
Kingston, Surrey
Tel: (01) 546 4842
Hand-made quality kitchens constructed out of solid seasoned timber. Also specialize in decorative paint finishes such as rag-rolling, marbling and dragging. Catalogue available.

Wellman Ltd
Dartstone Industrial Estate
Wakefield Road
Gildersome, Leeds LS27 0QW
Tel: (0532) 524131
Telex: 55260
Kitchen manufacturers with over 39 programmes with 92 different front designs, including a range of accessories. Catalogue available.

Winchmore Furniture Ltd
Mildenhall, Suffolk IP28 7BE
Tel: (0638) 712082
Manufacture fitted traditional wood kitchens, in a range of nine styles. Brochures available.

Woodgoods
Office & Workshops:
Unit 40 Woolmer Trading Estate
Bordon, Hampshire GU35 9QZ
Tel: (04203) 7183
Showrooms: Woodgoods
High Street, Odiham, Hampshire RG25 1LN

Tel: (025 671) 2676
Hand-made traditional kitchens in seasoned timber; also supply a range of sinks, taps, tiles and appliances. Catalogue available.

Woodstock Furniture Ltd
23 Pakenham Street, London WC1X 0LB
Tel: (01) 837 1818
Design custom-built kitchens in solid hardwoods such as maple and cherry. Catalogue available.

LIGHTING

A. & H. Brass
201-203 Edgware Road
London W2 1ES
Tel: (01) 402 3981/(01) 402 1854
See DOORS

Bella Figura
154 Fulham Road, London SW10
Tel: (01) 373 1250
Specialists in distressed Florentine chandeliers and sconces in painted metal. Designs range from fairly simple to extravagantly floral, and can either hold candles or be adapted to electricity.

Best & Lloyd Ltd
William Street West
Smethwick, Warley
West Midlands B66 2NX
Tel: (021) 558 1191
Produces brass light fittings including traditional candlestick wall sconces after Adam and Hepplewhite, and Victorian pendants.

Beta Lighting Ltd
383-387 Leeds Road
Bradford BD3 9LZ
Tel: (0274) 721129
Commercial and architectural lighting manufacturers specializing in energy saving and low-voltage lighting.

The Birmingham Glass Studios Ltd
Unit 5 102 Edward Road
Balsall Heath, Birmingham B11 3SA
Tel: (021) 440 0909
Suppliers of all stained-glass materials, coloured and antique glass, manufacturers of leaded lights, Tiffany lampshades, terrariums.

Brighton Architectural Salvage
33 Gloucester Road
Brighton, East Sussex
Tel: (0273) 681656
See FIREPLACES AND STOVES

R. J. Chelsom & Co Ltd
Squires Gate Industrial Estate
Blackpool
Lancashire FY4 3RN
Tel: (0253) 46324
Specialize in period reproduction lighting and market Flemish, Georgian, Regency, Adam, Louis XV and XVI light fittings in polished brass. Fittings range from single-light wall brackets to a 42-light chandelier from the standard range. Additional ranges include classical English, Victorian, period American, as well as exterior lighting. Available from stockists nationwide. Catalogue available.

Classic Reproductions
404 The Highway
London E14 8DZ
Tel: (01) 790 5203
Manufacturers of replica antique exterior and interior decorative lighting, in copper and brass, covering period from 1780-1900. Catalogue available.

Clare House Ltd
35 Elizabeth Street
London SW1
Tel: (01) 730 8480
Specialists in making fine lampshades in silk, also repair and rewire light fittings. A range of antique lamps stocked.

Mrs M. E. Crick Ltd
166 Kensington Church Street
London W8 4BN
Tel: (01) 229 1338
Specializes in 18th- to 20th-century lighting, chandeliers, wall lights, candelabra, in cut glass and ormolu.

T. Crowther & Son Ltd
282 North End Road
Fulham, London SW6 1NH
Tel: (01) 385 1375/6/7
Cables: Antiquity
See EXTERIORS

Delomosne & Son Ltd
4 Campden Hill Road
London W8 7DU
Tel: (01) 937 1804
Antique dealers specializing in 18th- and 19th-century English glass chandeliers and candelabra.

Dernier & Hamlyn Ltd
17 Lydden Road
Wandsworth, London SW18 4LT
Tel: (01) 870 0011/2
Manufacturers of decorative light fittings of the 18th and 19th centuries. More than 200 different fittings, all available in eight different finishes. Also specialize in the restoration of light fittings. Catalogue available.

Emess Lighting (U.K.) Ltd
6 Anderson Road
Roding Lane South
Woodford Green
Essex IG8 8ET
Tel: (01) 551 4156
Manufacturers of outdoor lanterns, garden lights, downlighters, flush fittings, crystal chandeliers and single pendants.

End of Day Lighting Co Ltd
51 Mill Lane, London NW6
Tel: (01) 435 8091
Specializes in Victorian, Edwardian and Deco lighting; over 40 designs available, including ceiling pendants, wall brackets, table and desk lamps. Most are made of solid brass from original castings and vary in style from the simple to the ornate. Catalogue available.

An Englishman's Home
56 Stokescraft
Bristol 7, Avon
Tel: (0272) 424257
Savoy Showrooms:
New Road, South Moulton, North Devon
Tel: (07695) 3342
See FIREPLACES AND STOVES

The Facade
G. Owen, 196 Westbourne Grove
London W11 2RM
Tel: (01) 727 2159
Supply lighting 1880-1920.

David Fileman Antiques
Squirrels, Bayards
Horsham Road, Steyning
West Sussex BN4 3AA
Tel: (0903) 813229
Period lighting, chandeliers, candelabra and wall lights bought and sold. Restoration undertaken.

Fritz Fryer Decorative Antique Lighting
12 Brook End Street, Ross-on-Wye
Herefordshire HR9 7EG
Tel: (0989) 67416
Specialists in all forms of decorative antique lighting from Georgian to Art Deco. Main period 1850-1920. Advisory, planning and fitting services available.

H.L.C. Lighting
Unit 44A Moor End
Eaton Bray, Near Dunstable
Bedfordshire LU6 2HN
Tel: (0525) 220068
Lighting manufacturers to customers' requirements.

Hoffmeister Lighting Ltd
Unit 4 Preston Road
Reading, Berkshire RG2 0BE
Tel: (0734) 866941
Telex: 847625
Manufacturers of a wide range of lighting. Catalogue available.

Hooper & Purchase
303 and 305 King's Road
London SW3 5EP
Tel: (01) 351 3985
Selling 18th- and early 19th-century English and Continental antique chandeliers and wall lights.

David Hunt Lighting Ltd
Tilemans Lane
Shipston-on-Stour
Warwickshire CV36 4HP
Tel: (0608) 61590/62836
Manufacture light fittings for domestic and contractual use. Also restoration and conversion of period lighting and manufacture of one-off projects.

Illumin Glass Studio
82 Bond Street
Macclesfield
Cheshire SK11 6QS
Tel: (0625) 613600
Makers of stained-glass lighting and windows. Renovation of antique light fittings including a selection of original fittings in stock. Catalogue available.

Jardine Leisure Fur
Rosemount Tower
Wallington Square
Wallington, Surrey SM6 8RR
Tel: (01) 669 8265
Telex: 886870
Manufacturers and distributors of Italian marble, cut to any size, architectural fittings, friezes and panels, cast aluminium garden lighting, including lampposts, also ceiling fittings.

Jones (Lighting)
194 Westbourne Grove
London W11
Tel: (01) 229 6866
The largest selection of individual original lighting in Europe, c.1860-1960.

Kalmar Lighting (U.K.) Ltd
19 Dacre Street
London SW1H 0DJ
Tel: (01) 222 0161
Telex: 946600
Specialize in a wide range of products including traditional chandeliers. Catalogue available.

The Last Detail
341 Kings Road
Chelsea, London SW3 5ES
Tel: (01) 351 6294
Specialists in lighting.

Lighting Design Ltd
1 Woodfall Court
Smith Street, Chelsea
London SW3 4EJ
Tel: (01) 730 8585
Lighting designers and suppliers of light fittings, etc.

Maclamp Co Ltd
Beaumont Road, Banbury
Oxfordshire OX16 7RA
Tel: (0295) 50881
Manufacturers of domestic lighting specializing in spotlights, ceiling fittings, wall brackets, floor lamps, uplighters and downlighters.

Malvern Studios
56 Cowleigh Road, Malvern
Worcestershire WR14 1QD
Tel: (068 45) 4913
Designers and manufacturers of fitted kitchens, leading stockists of period-style lighting, plaster mouldings, alcoves, niches, etc. Brass and china door furniture.

Arnold Montrose Ltd
47-48 Berners Street
London W1P 3AD
Tel: (01) 580 5316/8
Designers and manufacturers of light fittings and architectural metalwork. Catalogue available.

Moorlite Electrical Ltd
Burlington Street
Ashton-under-Lyne
Lancashire OL7 0AX
Tel: (061) 330 6811
Telex: 668284
Designers and manufacturers of both standard and special luminaires for all types of domestic, commercial and industrial environments.

N.M. Lighting (U.K.) Ltd
(Homelight)
110 Goodmayes Road
Ilford, Essex
Tel: (01) 597 7509
Stockists of a large range of light fittings.

Planet Shades Ltd
P.O. Box 118
Lampard Grove
London N16 6XB
Tel: (01) 806 1013
Manufacturers of silk and fabric lampshades, hand-polished and antique brass, chandeliers and wall brackets, glass shades and single pendants, Strass chandeliers and wall brackets.

Poole Lighting Ltd
Cabot Lane, Creekmoore
Poole, Dorset BH17 7BY
Tel: (0202) 697344
Telex: 418352
Designers and manufacturers of a comprehensive range of traditional based and modern light fittings. Catalogue available.

R. & S. Robertson Ltd
Unit 13 36 Bankhead Drive
Sighthill Industrial Estate
Edinburgh EH11 4EQ
Tel: (031) 442 1700
Manufacturers of an extensive range of period lighting; also custom-made fitting to customers' specific requirements. Catalogue available.

Scan'Decor
13 Smith Street, Watford
Hertfordshire WD1 8AA
Tel: (0923) 27649
Telex: 918044
Manufacturers of quality domestic and commercial light fittings, specializing in brass and glass. Leading manufacturers of brass and chrome picture lights, brass spotlights, glass pendants and wall lights.

W. Sitch & Co Ltd
48 Berwick Street
London W1 4JD
Tel: (01) 437 3776
Dealers in 19th-century chandeliers, wall brackets, floor standards and other lighting fixtures. Repairers, bronzers, gilders and lacquerers to the trade. Also art metal workers and manufacturers.

Stair & Co Ltd
120 Mount Street, London W1Y 5HB
Tel: (01) 499 1784
Antique glass chandeliers, restoration, advice on decoration.

Starlite Chandeliers Ltd
127 Harris Way
Windmill Road
Sunbury-on-Thames TW16 7EL
Tel: (09327) 88686
Manufacture crystal light fittings, including chandeliers and wall brackets in Empire, Louis XV, Regency, Edwardian, Middle Eastern and contemporary styles. Fittings are available in a choice of Austrian Swarovski Strass crystal or Czechoslovakian Strass crystal. Frame finishes include 24ct gold plating.

Sugg Lighting Ltd
65 Gatwick Road
Crawley, Sussex RH10 2YU
Tel: (0293) 540111
Telex: 87323
Manufacturers of gas and electric lighting for exterior and interior application in traditional Victorian and Edwardian styles. Manufacturers of replica lamp columns and specialist lighting fittings. Refurbishment of light fittings and mountings.

Sussex Brassware Ltd
Napier Road
Castleham Industrial Estate
St Leonards-on-Sea
East Sussex TN38 9NY
Tel: (0424) 440734
Full range of brass electrical accessories in four traditional designs: Georgian, Victorian, Regency and Adam gilt. Finishes available are wrought-iron, satin brass, polished chrome, gold-plated and silver-plated.

Wilchester County
Stable Cottage, Vicarage Lane
Steeple Ashton
Trowbridge, Wiltshire
Tel: (0380) 870764
Manufacturers of primitive lighting copied from original American designs, available in candle or electrified form.

D. W. Windsor Ltd
Pindar Road, Hoddesdon
Hertfordshire EN11 0EZ
Tel: (0992) 445666
Telex: 263311
Specialists in Victorian and period street lighting equipment including lanterns in copper and brass, globe lanterns. Lampposts manufactured in cast iron and steel. Also pedestals, pillars and traditional wall brackets. Restoration and design services. Catalogue available.

Christopher Wray's Lighting Emporium
600 Kings Road
London SW6 2DX
Tel: (01) 736 8434
Telex: 946240
Branch tel. nos: Birmingham (021) 233 3364; Bournemouth (0202) 22660; Bristol (0272) 279537; Leeds (0532) 782653; Manchester (061) 832 5221; Nottingham (0602) 475494
Lighting specialists. Catalogue available.

CONSERVATORIES

Amdega – Victorian Elegance
Faverdale, Darlington
Co Durham DL3 0PW
Tel: (0325) 468522
Supply period-style conservatories direct to clients. World-wide exporters. Catalogue available.

Chelsea Conservatories
39 Smith Terrace
Chelsea, London SW3 5DH
Tel: (01) 352 6253
Design, manufacture and install a range of Victorian-style conservatories. Double-glazed doors and windows with all timber treated with microporous paint.

Grosvenor Products Ltd
Dollar Street House
Cirencester
Gloucestershire GL7 2AP
Tel: (0285) 67325
Conservatory importers and distributors.

Marston & Langinger Ltd
Main office & workshops:
Hall Staithe
Fakenham
Norfolk NR21 9BW
Tel: (0328) 4933
Shop & office:
20 Bristol Gardens
Little Venice
London W9 2JQ
Tel: (01) 286 7643
Supply both standard designs and one-offs, including conservatories enclosing swimming pools. Also sell conservatory furniture, ornamental garden urns, etc. Catalogue available.

Room Outside Ltd
Goodwood Gardens
Goodwood, Chichester
West Sussex PO18 0QB
Tel: *Daytime* (0243) 773593 *Evening* (0243)
776563
Specialists in design and supply of conservatories and garden accessories.

Jayne Simcock Design Ltd
49 St Margaret's Grove
Twickenham
Middlesex TW1 1JF
Tel: (01) 892 9238
See WALLS

SW82 Designs
104 Valetta Road
London SW3 7TW
Tel: (01) 740 0707
See WINDOWS

EXTERIORS

Architectural Antiques Ltd
133 Upper Street
Islington, London N1
Tel: (01) 226 5565
See FIREPLACES AND STOVES

Architectural Ceramics Ltd
Unit 120 Building A
Raleigh Wharf, 8-12 Creekside
London SE8 3DX
Tel: (01) 692 7287
Specialists in individual ceramic decoration for interior and exterior locations, designing, producing and installing work for restaurants, gardens and private homes, as well as limited editions for specialist shops.

Architectural and Industrial G.R.P.
400 Ewell Road
Tolworth, Surrey KT6 7HF
See BATHROOMS

Artistic Ironworkers Supplies Ltd
Wrought Iron Works
Unit 1 Whitehouse Road
Kidderminster, Worcestershire DY10 1HT
Tel: (0562) 753483
Suppliers of pre-made decorative forged metal scrolls, rosettes, finials, etc, which enable metal fabricators to produce finished units such as gates, balustrades, fencing, etc. Maintains a list of Registered Users, who, as skilled metal craftsmen, will make any item to suit individual design requirements utilizing the accurate pre-made modules.

Attracta Products Ltd
2nd Floor Hyde House
The Hyde, London NW9 6LH
Tel: (01) 200 7551
Manufacturers and distributors of garden equipment and D.I.Y. materials.

Baileys Architectural Antiques
The Engine Shed
Ashburton Industrial Estate
Ross-on-Wye
Herefordshire HE9 7BW
Tel: (0989) 63015
See DOORS

Don Bateman
Home Farm Pulham St Mary
Norfolk
Tel: (037 976) 784
See FLOORS

Bridgwater Reclamation Ltd
Monmouth Street
Bridgwater, Somerset
Tel: (0278) 424636
See FIREPLACES AND STOVES

Brighton Architectural Salvage
33 Gloucester Road
Brighton, East Sussex
Tel: (0273) 681656
See FIREPLACES AND STOVES

Britannia Architectural Metalwork & Restoration
5 Normandy Street
Alton, Hampshire GU34 1DD
Tel: (0420) 84427
Stockists of a wide range of standard traditional railings, balusters, brackets, gratings, etc, including Victorian and Georgian patterns. Restoration and repair work, pattern making and design services. Deliveries in the U.K. and abroad. Catalogue available.

Bromley Demolition Co Ltd
75 Siward Road
Bromley, Kent
Tel: (01) 464 3610
See DOORS

Capps & Capps Ltd
Llowes Court, Llowes
Hay-on-Wye, Herefordshire
Tel: (0497) 4602
Engaged in the repair of old buildings; masonry repairs a speciality.

Chilstone Garden Ornaments
Sprivers Estate
Horsmonden, Kent TN12 8DR
Tel: (089 272) 3553
Specialists in reproducing antique ornaments and architectural items including Doric and Ionic columns, architraves, cornicing, balustrades, mullions, temples, etc, as well as a standard range of over 250 classical garden ornaments. Catalogue available.

Classic Furniture (Newport) Ltd
Audley Avenue,
Newport, Shropshire
Tel: (0952) 813311
See FIREPLACES AND STOVES

Conservation Building Products Ltd
Forge Works
Forge Lane, Cradley Heath
Warley, West Midlands B64 5AL
Tel: (0384) 64219/(0527) 84497
Stockists of period roofing tiles, fittings, finials, bricks, oak beams, joists, quarry floor tiles, paving, pine doors, panelling and architectural ironwork.

Harry Cooper
The Studio, 1 Harbour Road
Seaton, Devon EX12 2LX
Tel: (0297) 21153
Sculptor of commissioned works of art in copper, wood, cold castings, etc, for use as garden ornaments, weather vanes or statuary. Range of hand-made weather vanes available from stock.

Counterparts Demolition Ltd
Station Yard, Topsham Exeter, Devon
Tel: (039 287) 5995
Stock timbers, slates, doors and occasionally fire surrounds.

T. Crowther & Son Ltd
282 North End Road
Fulham, London SW6 1NH
Tel: (01) 385 1375/6/7
Cables: Antiquity
A world-renowned, family-run antiques business, established over one hundred years ago, which operates from a very large late Georgian period building. Specializes in, among other things, Georgian architectural features, such as oak and pinewood panelling, carved wood and marble chimneypieces and metalware accoutrements (grates, fenders and fire-irons). The stocks of antique garden ornaments and statuary are probably the largest to be seen in the U.K., and cover such pieces as sundials, fountains, classical statues and animal figures, temples, urns and vases, seats and benches, wrought-iron gates, columns and doorways. Inside the large galleries are 18th-century English wall lights and chandeliers, and interior doorways. They offer a complete room panelling service, which starts with drawings, and advice where required, through manufacture and adaptation, which is handled by their own joinery works, and finally on to fixing on site, if required.

Crowther of Syon Lodge Ltd
Busch Corner, London Road
Isleworth, Middlesex TW7 5BH
Tel: (01) 560 7978/7985
Telex: 8951308
Major firm of architectural antiques and period garden ornament dealers, buying and selling period panelled rooms, antique chimneypieces, wrought-iron entrance gates, classical statuary and a wide range of period garden ornaments, including temples, vases, seats and fountains. Catalogue available.

C.S.L. Davey & Jordan
The Forge 3 Jennings Road
Kernick Industrial Estate
Penryn, Cornwall TR10 9DQ
Tel: (0326) 74762
See STAIRCASES

H.R. (Demolition) Sales Ltd
Fairwater Yard
Staplegrove Road
Taunton, Somerset
Tel: (0823) 337035
Suppliers of secondhand building materials, including slates, roof tiles, timber, basins, W.C.s.

The English Street Furniture Co
Somers House
Linkfield Corner
Redhill, Surrey RH1 1BB
Tel: (0737) 60986
See FIREPLACES AND STOVES

An Englishman's Home
56 Stokescraft
Bristol 7, Avon
Tel: (0272) 424257
Also: Savoy Showrooms
New Road
South Moulton
North Devon
Tel: (07695) 3342
See FIREPLACES AND STOVES

Glover & Stacey Ltd
Oaklands House
Solartron Road
Farnborough Hampshire GU14 7QL
Tel: (0252) 549334
Telex: 265871
See DOORS

Haddonstone Ltd
The Forge House
East Haddon
Northampton NN6 8DB
Tel: (0604) 770711
Design and supply reconstructed stoneware for garden, interior and architectural decoration, including balustrades, temples and pavilions, porticos, columns and pilasters, pier caps and finials, as well as an extensive range of garden urns and ornaments. Services include contract work, interiors, restoration and special commissions. Catalogue available.

Havenplan's Architectural Emporium
1 The Old Station
Station Road
Killamarsh, Sheffield S31 8EN
Tel: *Daytime* (0742) 489972 *Evening* (0246)
433315
See FIREPLACES AND STOVES

James Horrobin, Ironworker
The Forge, Park Lane
Carhampton
Minehead, Somerset
Tel: (0643) 821092
Architectural, ecclesiastical and domestic ironwork.

The House Hospital
68 Battersea High Street
London SW11
Tel: (01) 223 3179
See DOORS

House of Steel Antiques
400 Caledonian Road
Islington London N1
Tel: (01) 607 5889
Also: 28 Camden Passage
Islington London N1
See FIREPLACES AND STOVES

Kentish Ironcraft Ltd
Ashford Road
Bethersden
Ashford, Kent TN26 3AT
Tel: (023 382) 465/455
Manufacturers of wrought-iron gates. Specialists in the restoration and reproduction of period ironwork. Catalogue available.

Kestner Building Products Ltd
Station Road, Greenhithe
Kent DA9 9NG
Tel: (0322) 843281
Reproduction period rainwater fittings in glass reinforced plastic. Catalogue available.

Kibblewhite & Blackmur Ltd
Long Reach Road
Barking, Essex IG11 0JN
Tel: (01) 594 5591
Telex: 896409
Suppliers of sawn timber, hardwood and softwood, also hardwood and softwood mouldings, specialist milling services, fencing materials, plywood. chipboard and blockboard importers.

Langham Architectural Materials
Langham Farm
East Nynehead
Wellington, Somerset TA21 0DD
Tel: (082346) 297
See FIREPLACES AND STOVES

The London Architectural Salvage & Supply Co
St Michael's Church
Mark Street, off Paul Street
Shoreditch, London EC2A 4ER
Tel: (01) 739 0448
See DOORS

J. & W. Lowry Ltd
64 Bath Lane
Newcastle-upon-Tyne, Tyne & Wear NE4 5TT
Tel: (091) 232 3586
General builders and contractors, special stonemasonry contractors, stonework restoration and repair. Also specialist joinery makers.

Terry Martin, R.S.S. Blacksmith & Farrier
Old Mission Forge
Main Street
Newthorpe, Nottinghamshire
Tel: (077 37) 713868
All wrought-iron work undertaken, fire baskets and accessories. Restoration work, forge work, security bars, grilles and gates. On-site welding. Park gates and fencing restored and made.

McCurdy & Co Ltd
Manor Farm
Stanford Dingley
Reading, Berkshire RG7 6LS
Tel: (0734) 744866
Consultants and craftsmen specializing in the repair and restoration of historic timber-framed buildings. Services include surveys and advice on the repair of timber-framed buildings, the moving and facsimile reconstruction of timber-framed buildings.

Mounts Hill Woodcraft Ltd
The Depot, Mounts Hill
Cranbrook Road, Benenden
Cranbrook, Kent
Tel: (0580) 240270
See DOORS

The Original Architectural Heritage of Cheltenham
Boddington Manor
Boddington
near Cheltenham
Gloucestershire GL51 0TJ
Tel: (024 268) 741
See WALLS

Pageant Antiques
122 Dawes Road
London SW6
Tel: (01) 385 7739
Dealers in 18th- and 19th-century garden furniture and fine chimneypieces, in marble and wood.

B.L. Pattern & Foundry Co
37 Church Street
London SW1V 2LT
Tel: (01) 834 1073/824 7486
Designers, manufacturers and restorers of cast- and wrought-iron works.

Period Reclamation & Restoration Services
205 Salisbury Road
Burton, Christchurch, Dorset BH23 7JT
Tel: (0202) 473300/(0836) 246263
Suppliers of restoration materials such as peg tiles, slates, bricks, oak beams and marble and pine fireplace surrounds; also oven ranges.

T. & O. Plaster Castings
7 Collier Row Road
Collier Row
Romford, Essex
Tel: (0708) 45619/46742/24633
See CEILINGS

Posterity Architectural Effects
Baldwins Farm
Dymock Road
Newent, Gloucestershire
Tel: (0531) 85597
Stockists of architectural salvage items, specializing in columns in stone, marble and cast iron. Also stock of fire surrounds, doors, windows, bar fittings, bathroom fittings, flooring, etc.

D. S. & A. G. Prigmore
Mill Cottage, Mill Road
Colmworth, Bedford
Tel: (023 062) 264
A wide range of bricks, slates, ridge tiles, timber, panelling, fireplaces and wood blocks.

Richard Quinnell Ltd
Rowhurst Forge
Oxshott Road
Leatherhead, Surrey KT22 0EN
Tel: (0372) 375148
Architectural metalworkers and wrought-ironworkers, working in all types of metal. Specialist restorers of antique wrought and cast ironwork.

Rattee & Kett Ltd
Purbeck Road
Cambridge CB2 2PG
Tel: (0223) 248061
Specialists in stonemasonry and joinery, hand-carving in wood and stone, heraldic work and lettering, leadwork, casting in stone finish with Codestone, to reproduce or repair architectural features and ornaments.

Reclaimed Materials
Northgate
White Lund Industrial Estate
Morecambe, Lancashire
Tel: (0524) 69094
A good selection of slates, flagstones, yellow pine timber, timber flooring and fire surrounds.

Relic Antiques
Brillscote Farm, Lea
near Malmesbury, Wiltshire
See DOORS

Renaissance
Norwood Industrial Estate
Killamarsh
Sheffield S31 8HB
Tel: (0742) 488025
Manufacture period entranceways, interior and exterior mouldings, including fascias, door surrounds, pilasters, porticos, bow window units and columns. Catalogue available.

Renzland Forge
London Road, Copford
Colchester, Essex CO6 1LG
Tel: (0206) 210212
Craftsmen in metal, manufacturing gates, railings, street lamps, lanterns, posts, arches, corner tops, nameplates, weather vanes, door grilles and bootscrapers. Catalogue available.

Rogers Demolition & Dismantling Service Ltd
Belgrave Road
Portswood, Southampton
Tel. (0703) 449173
Salvage material including bricks, panelling, flagstones, skirting boards, coloured glass, peg tiles, pan tiles, door handles, strip parquet flooring and even complete period rooms.

Solopark Ltd
The Old Railway Station
Station Road
near Pampisford
Cambridgeshire CB2 4HB
Tel: (0223) 834663
See DOORS

Southwell (Stockwell) Ltd
26A Rye Road
London SE15
Tel: (01) 635 0950
Specialize in the casting, fabrication, restoration and site fixing of cast-iron work, with a vast range of pattern equipment and original mouldings of street railings, balustrades, window guards, boot scrapers, spiral and straight staircases, balconies, gates, etc, from which cast-iron reproductions are cast. Catalogue available.

Stuart Interiors
Barrington Court
Barrington
Ilminster
Somerset, TA19 0NQ
Tel: (0460) 42003
See DOORS

R.G. Trade Supplies and Engineering Ltd
Taurus Ornamental Design
Foley Street, Fenton
Stoke-on-Trent ST4 3DR
Tel: (0782) 599125
Ornamental gate and railing specialists.

Paul Temple Ltd
Temple Gardens
Holloway Lane
Harmondsworth
West Drayton, Middlesex UB7 0AD
Tel: (01) 759 1437
Water features and fountains, garden design and landscape gardening.

Walcot Reclamation
108 Walcot Street
Bath, Avon BA1 5BG
Tel: (0225) 66291
See FIREPLACES AND STOVES

Weller Patents Development
1-8 Grand Parade Mews
Putney, London SW15 2SP
Tel: (01) 788 6684
See STAIRCASES

Wing & Staples
The Forge, Motcombe
near Shaftesbury, Dorset SP7 9PE
Tel: (0747) 3104
Period pieces reproduced from drawings or photographs. Restoration, traditional or contemporary ironwork undertaken. A choice of finishes available, antique appearance, armour bright, matt or gloss paints. Catalogue available.

OTHER USEFUL ADDRESSES

Acanthus
Associated Architectural Practices Ltd
Vosey House, Chiswick, London W4 4PN
Tel: (01) 995 1232
Specialist knowledge available in the following disciplines:
Consultancy on listed buildings and conservation areas; historic building surveys and analysis; feasibility studies on uses for old buildings; garden and landscape design; quinquennial reports and programmes of maintenance and repair; special consultancy in building defects; conservation of sculpture and murals, among many others.

Architectural Association
34-36 Bedford Square
London WC1
Tel: (01) 636 0974

Architectural Salvage
Netley House
Gomshall, Surrey GU5 9QA
Tel: (048 641) 3221
Maintains an index of all kinds of architectural items, and for a £10 registration fee will put buyers in touch with appropriate seller. No items directly for sale or on display.

Art Workers Guild
6 Queen Square
London WC1N 3AR
Tel: (01) 837 3474
Guild of artists, architects, craftsmen and others engaged in the design and practice of the arts.

B.R.E. Scottish Laboratory
Kelvin Road
East Kilbride, Glasgow G75 0RZ
Advisory service Tel: (03552) 33941
Information on the durability of walls and roofs, etc.

British Ceramic Tile Council
Federation House
Station Road
Stoke-on-Trent ST4 2RU
Tel: (0782) 45147

British Decorators Association
6 Haywra Street, Harrogate
North Yorkshire HG1 5BL
Tel: (0423) 67292/3
Over 1,000 members who specialize in the decoration of period homes.

British Institute of Interior Design
1c Devonshire Avenue
Beeston, Nottingham NG9 1BS
Tel: (0602) 221255
Established in 1899 and now a leading organization in the interior design industry. Its objectives are to encourage a better understanding, care and improvement of interior design. Has over 223 registered practices and about 1,500 members. A recommended shortlist is available.

British Wood Preserving Association
Premier House
150 Southampton Row
London WC1B 5AL
Tel: (01) 837 8217
A free and impartial advisory service on all problems connected with timber preservation and flame retardant. Publishes a number of free leaflets and priced publications, available from the secretary.

The Brooking Collection
C. B. Brooking
Woodhay, White Lane
Guildford, Surrey GU4 8PU
Tel: (0483) 504555/68686
A collection of architectural elements rescued from demolition. Comprises up to 20,000 building components and provides a unique record of the development of architectural details, with particular reference to features such as windows, doors, fireplaces, decorative ironwork, etc. Information service available.

Building Conservation Trust
Apartment 39
Hampton Court Palace
East Molesey, Surrey KT8 9BS
Tel: (01) 943 2277
An independent educational charity established to promote the better care of buildings of all types and ages, with a permanent exhibition on house maintenance and home improvement.

Cadu – Welsh Historic Monuments
9th Floor, Brunnel House
Fitzalan Road, Cardiff CF2 1UY
Tel: (022) 465511
Awards grants for repairing historic buildings throughout Wales.

Chartered Institution of Building Services Engineers (C.I.B.S.E.)
Delta House, 222 Balham High Road
London SW12 9BS
Tel: (01) 675 5211
Advice on plumbing, heating, ventilation, etc.

Church Farm House Museum
Greyhound Hill
London NW4 4JR
Tel: (01) 203 0130
A collection consisting mainly of 19th-century domestic material, with two period furnished rooms, the kitchen set at c.1820 and the dining room at c.1850.

Civic Trust
17 Charlton House Terrace
London SW1Y 5AW
Tel: (01) 930 0914
Encourages the protection and improvement of the environment.

Design Council
28 Haymarket
London SW1
Tel: (01) 839 8000

English Heritage
25 Savile Row
London W1X 2BT
Tel: (01) 734 6010 Ext: 501
Provides specialist and technical advice on repair, maintenance and preservation; also gives grants for repairing historic buildings throughout England.

The Georgian Group
37 Spital Square
London E1 6DY
Tel: (01) 377 1722
Gives advice on repair and restoration to owners of Georgian buildings.

The Guild of Master Craftsmen
166 High Street, Lewes, East Sussex
Tel: (0273) 477374
Trade association helping to put prospective clients in touch with experienced craftsmen able to carry out restoration work. Also publishes Guide to Restoration Experts.

C. M. Hemming
Thrashers Barn
Norchard, Crossway Green
Stourport, Worcestershire
Tel: (0299) 250223
Timber-framed barn and house restoration.

The Historic Buildings Company
P.O. Box 150
Chobham, Surrey GU24 8JD
Publishers of the Period Property Register, *a publication devoted solely to the marketing, maintenance and improvement of period properties.*

Historic Homes of Britain
21 Pembroke Square, London W8
Tel: (01) 937 2402

Historic Houses Association
38 Ebury Street, London SW1
Tel: (01) 730 9419

National Federation of Building Trades Employers
82 New Cavendish Street London W1M 8AD
Tel: (01) 580 5588
Recommends stonemasons, painters and decorators, plasterers, etc.

The National Fireplace Council
P.O. Box 35, Stoke-on-Trent ST4 7NU
Tel: (0782) 44311
Trade association.

The National Trust
36 Queen Anne's Gate London SW1
Tel: (01) 222 7391

The National Trust for Scotland
5 Charlotte Square, Edinburgh EH2 4DU
Tel: (031) 226 5922
London office:
15 Queen Anne's Gate, London SW1
Tel: (01) 222 4856

Paint Research Association
Waldegrave Road
Teddington, Middlesex TW11 8LD
Publishers of the Paint and Pretreatment Products Directory *and the* Evaluation of Biocidal Masonry Coatings and Guide to Paint Film Biocides.

Royal Commission on Ancient and Historic Monuments in Wales
Edleston House, Queens Road
Aberystwyth, Dyfed, Wales
Tel: (0970) 4381
Answers queries from the general public concerning the age, type and function of buildings.

Royal Commission on Historical Monuments
Fortress House
23 Savile Row, London W1X 1AB
Tel: (01) 734 6010

Royal Incorporation of Architects in Scotland
15 Rutland Square
Edinburgh EH1 2BE
Tel: (031) 229 7205

Royal Institute of British Architects (R.I.B.A.)
66 Portland Place
London W1N 4AD
Tel: (01) 580 5533

Royal Institute of Chartered Surveyors (R.I.C.S.)
12 Great George Street
Parliament Square
London SW1P 3AD
Tel: (01) 222 7000

The Scottish Civic Trust
24 George Square, Glasgow G2 1EF
Tel: (041) 221 1466

Scottish Development Department of Historic Buildings and Ancient Monuments
3-11 Melville Street, Edinburgh EH3 7QD
Awards grants for repairing historic buildings throughout Scotland.

The Society for the Protection of Ancient Buildings
37 Spital Square
London E1 6DY
Tel: (01) 377 1644
Can supply names of specialist architects and other professionals. Issues technical publications on historic buildings repairs. Advises against conjectural restoration of period details.

The Victorian Society
1 Priory Gardens, Bedford Park
London W4 1TT
Tel: (01) 994 1019
A conservation amenity group dedicated to the preservation of Victorian and Edwardian buildings.

Martin Miller, Geoff Dann, John Helfrick and Caroline Brown were specially commissioned to take photographs for this book. Thanks are also due to the *The World of Interiors* for Clive Frost's photograph on page 69, no. 9, and to David C. Golby for the photographs on page 73, nos. 10 and 11.

The following people allowed photography in specific houses or gave generously of their time or expertise: Jacqui and Colin Small, Alan and Smokey Parsons, Jeremy and Annie Parker, Christopher and Frances Everill, Ian and Jill Pooley, Doug and Pam Stewart, Paul and Angie Marsh, Gaby Tubbs, Liz and John Denning.
In America: Dr and Mrs Roger Gerry (Roslyn Landmark Society), Dr Stanley Fischer, Joe and Carolyn Roberto, Mrs Jean Bartlett.

For individual photographs and access to interiors the authors are also grateful to the sources named in the credits list below. The code letters are those used in picture captions throughout the book.

PICTURE CREDITS: ABBREVIATIONS

A — Amdega, Faverdale, Darlington, County Durham.

AB — A. Bell, Kingsthorpe Road, Kingsthorpe, Northampton.

AF — Acquisitions (Fireplaces) Ltd, 269 Camden High Street, London NW1.

AH — Architectural Heritage, Boddington Manor, Boddington, Nr Cheltenham, Gloucestershire.

AR — Aga-Rayburn (Coalbrookdale) Glynwed Consumer & Building Products Ltd, PO Box 30, Ketley, Telford, Shropshire TF1 1BR

AS — Armitage Shanks, Armitage, Rugeley, Staffordshire.

AS&S — Architectural Salvage and Supply Co., St Michael's Church, Mark St off Paul St, London EC2

B — Bisque, The Radiator Shop, 244 Belsize Road, London NW6.

Be — Beardmore Ltd, 3-5 Percy St, London W1P 0EJ.

BCS — B.C. Sanitan, 12 Nimrod Way, Reading, Berks.

BH — Bowne House, 37-01 Bowne Street, Flushing, New York, NY 11354.

BP — Bartow Pell Mansion, Shore Road, Pelham Bay Park, Bronx, NY 10464.

Br — Brass Art Craft Birmingham Ltd (Brassart) 76 Atwood St, Lye, Stourbridge, West Midlands.

C — Crown Decorative Products Ltd, PO Box 22, Queen's Mill, Hollins Rd, Darwen, Lancashire BB3 0BD.

CB — Christopher Boulter, 43 Goodrich Rd, London SE22.

CF — Classic Furniture Group, Audley Avenue, Newport, Shropshire.

C&F — Colefax and Fowler, 39 Brook St, London W1.

CG — County Group, 102 High St, Tenterden, Kent CN30 6HU.

CP — Chilston Park, Sandway, Nr Maidstone, Kent.

CPH — C.P. Hart, Newham Terrace, Hercules Road, London SE1.

CS — Czech and Speake, 39c Jermyn Street, London SW1.

C of SL — Crowther of Syon Lodge, London Road, Isleworth, Middlesex.

EDL — End of Day Lighting, 44 Parkway, London NW1.

EW — Erme Wood Forge, Woodlands, Ivybridge, Devon PL21 9HF.

FE — Fired Earth Country Floors, Middle Aston, Oxfordshire.

G&G — Goddard & Gibbs Studios, 41-49 Kingsland Road, London E2.

GH — The Georgian House, 7 Great George Street, Bristol, Avon.

GJ — G. Jackson & Sons Ltd, Rathbone Works, Rainville Road, London W6.

H — Hallidays, 28 Beauchamp Place, Knightsbridge, London SW3.

Ha — Hathaway Country Kitchens, Clifford Mill, Clifford Chambers, Stratford-upon-Avon.

HH — Headquarters House, 215 East 71st Street, NYC 10021

H&H — Herschel House, 19 New King's Street, Bath.

HJ — Hodkin & Jones (Sheffield) Ltd, 515 Queen's Road, Sheffield S2 4DS.

HPS — Hand Painted Stencils, 6 Polstead Rd, Oxford OX2 6TW.

HW — Hamilton-Weston Wallpapers, 11 Townsend Rd, Richmond, Surrey TW9 1YH.

H&S — Hunter & Son (Mells) Ltd, Frome, Somerset BA11 3PA.

JBF — The James Buchanan Foundation for the Preservation of Wheatland, 1120 Marietta Ave, Lancaster, Pennsylvania 17603.

JL — John Lewis of Hungerford, 13 High Street, Hungerford, Berkshire.

JO — John S. Oliver Ltd, 33 Pembridge Rd, London W11 3HG.

LAS — London Architectural Salvage and Supply Co. Ltd, Mark Street, London EC2 4ER.

LG — Lyn Le Grice, Alsia Mill Street, Buryon, Cornwall TR19 6HG.

LH — Leighton House, 12 Holland Park Road, London W14.

LSH — Linley Sambourne House, 18 Stafford Terrace, London W8.

MA — Marthe Armitage, 1 Strand-on-the-Green, Chiswick, London W4 3PQ.

M — Moben Kitchens Ltd, 100 Washway Road, Sale, Cheshire M33 1RE.

MH — Marble Hill Fireplaces Ltd, 72 Richmond Road, Twickenham, Middlesex.

MJ — Morris Jumel Mansion, West 160th and Edgecombe Avenue, New York, NY 10032.

ML — Marston and Langinger, Hall Staithe, Fakenham, Norfolk.

MR — Maria Rosenthal, Kingsgate Workshops, 110-116 Kingsgate Road, London NW6 2J6.

OB — Original Bathrooms, 143-145 Kew Road, Richmond, Surrey TW9 2PN.

O&L — Osborne & Little, 304 King's Road, London SW3.

OMH — Old Merchants House, 29 East 4th Street, New York, NY 10003.

PC — Paris Ceramics, 543 Battersea Park Road, London SW11.

PCA — Peter Chapman Antiques, 10 Theberton Street, Islington, London, N1.

PF — Patrick Fireplaces, Guildford Road, Farnham, Surrey GU9 9QA.

PH — Phillip Henderson Co., 27 John Adam Street, London WC2.

PV — Pine Village, 42-43 Peascod Street, Windsor, Berks.

RC — No. 1 Royal Crescent, Bath, Avon.

S — Smallbone of Devizes, Unit 10-11, Nimrod Way, Elgar Road, Reading, Berks.

SG — Sekon Glassworks Ltd, Essian Street, London E1 4QE.

SI — Stuart Interiors, Barrington Court, Barrington, Nr Ilminster, Somerset TA19 0NQ.

S of D — Shaws of Darwen, Waterside, Darwen, Lancashire BB3 3NX.

S&P — Strutt & Parker 13 Hill St, London SW1.

SP — S. Polliack, Norton Industrial Estate, Norton, Malton, North Yorkshire YO17 9HQ.

SR — Sylvia Robinson, Clarence House, Winchester Hill, Romsey, Hampshire SO51 7NJ.

ST — Studio Two, 3d Town Street, Thaxted, Essex CM6 2LD.

S&W — Smith & Wellstood Esse (1984) Ltd, Bonnybridge, Stirlingshire FK4 2AP.

SWH — Sands Willet House, The Cow Neck Peninsula Historical Society, 336 Port Washington Boulevard, Port Washington, New York, NY 11050.

T — Tissunique, 10 Princes St, Hanover Sq, London W1.

TB — Traditional Bathrooms, 105 Regents Park Road, London NW1 8UR

TP — Tim Plant, 7 Bramham Gardens, London SW5.

TC — Toynbee-Clarke Interiors Ltd., 95 Mount Street, London W1.

V — Verdigris, Clerkenwell, Unit B.18, 31 Clerkenwell Close, London EC1.

VB — Victoriana Bathrooms Ltd, 439 Leethorpe Road, Grimsby DN31 3BU.

VC — Van Cortlandt Mansion, W.242nd Street and Broadway, Bronx, NY 10471.

VNS — Van Nostrand Strakins House, 221 Main Street, Roslyn, New York.

W — Woodstock Furniture, Pakenham Street, Mount Pleasant, London WC1.

Wa — Watts & Co, 7 Tufton Street, Westminster, London SW1.

WA — W. Adams & Sons Ltd, Westfield Works, Spon Lane, West Bromwich, West Midlands B70 6RH.

WB — Winther Brown & Co. Ltd, Nobel Road, Eley's Estate, Edmonton, London N18 3DX.

WW — Warren Wilkey, 741 Main St, Roslyn, New York.

W&W — Whiteway & Waldron Ltd, 305 Munster Road, London SW6.

Z — Zoffany Ltd, 27a Motcomb St, London SW1.

Adam brothers 20, 21, 38, 42, 74, 80, 83, 98, 99, 120, 121
Robert 9, 20, 167
Aga cooker 152
Aitchison, George 73, 113
American Empire style 38, 63
Anaglypta wallpaper 104
Andiron (endiron) 114, 127
Architrave 12, 31, 34, 47, 74, 76
moulded
plaster 83
Art Deco 24, 153
lamps 154, 158
stoves 149
Art Nouveau 24, 48, 49, 51, 88
lighting 158, 159
marquetry panels 81
Arts and Crafts Movement 24, 48, 57, 112, 128, 135
houses 135

"Bacon flake", Yorkshire 147
Balconies 22, 60, 160-64
Balusters 106, 107, 108, 110
cast-iron 110, 112
flat 106
fluted 108
wrought-iron 108
Balustrades 18, 106, 107, 161, 162
iron 15, 107, 108
Barleysugar twist 108
Baroque 18
Basements 46, 66, 165
semi- 165
Bathrooms 22, 138-144
Baths 138, 139, 140
marble 139
plumbed-in 139, 141
portable metal 139, 141
roll-top 138, 139, 141
Bay windows 10, 22, 23, 25, 59, 60, 62, 165
Beams 96, 97, 114
Bedrooms 22, 101
Bells 51, 59
Belton House 15
Bidets 138, 142, 143
Blinds, window 61
Boot-scrapers 30
Bow windows 59
Bricks 10, 24, 160, 162
Elizabethan herringbone 160
"Bull's eye" glass 26, 55, 56
Burghley House 12
Burlington, Lord 18
Butler sinks 146

Cabinets 142
Cames 54, 55, 56, 57
Campbell, Colen 18
Candelabra 155, 156
Candle sconces 155, 156
Candlesticks 154, 156, 157

Canopies 22
Carpets and rugs 67, 68
Casement windows 55, 56, 58, 61, 67
Ceiling roses 100, 102, 103
cleaning 100, 102
Ceilings 17, 66, 96-105
plaster 83, 97, 98, 99, 106
wooden 96
Chair rail see DADO RAIL
Chamber pots 142
Chandeliers 154, 155, 156, 157
Chimney crane 147
Chimney pieces 9, 31, 121
Chimney cloth 130
Chimneys 10, 12, 58, 78, 114, 115, 116, 120, 124, 131, 150
Chinoiserie 22, 41
Clapboard 23
Cleaning:
cornices 99
floors 71
marble 71
old windows 56
tiles 71
Colonial architecture 19, 38
Colour 94
for doors 26, 37, 44
for tiles 91
for walls 85, 94
Columns 12, 15, 20, 76, 83, 101
Conservatories 166-7
Cooking ranges 117, 146, 150, 151, 152
Cornices 25, 42, 74, 78, 79, 80, 83, 95, 98, 100, 101, 104
cleaning 99
Cottage ornée 22
Coving 96
Craquelure process 119
Cupboards 80-1

Dado rail 17, 31, 38, 74, 85, 88, 94, 95, 107
Damask 94
Damp 66, 71
Dana, Richard Henry 38, 39
Dating a house 9
Distemper paints 84, 85, 109
removing 104
Door cases 9, 17, 26, 31, 33, 42, 44, 46, 164
Door furniture 26, 34, 37, 47, 48, 50-3
finger plates 47
knockers 26, 37
letterboxes 37
Doors 17, 18, 26-53, 75, 160
oak studded 27
sliding 80
Dormer windows 15, 60
Double-pile plan 15
Doulton lavatory ware 144
"Down hearth" 146, 147
Dressers, kitchen 146, 147, 151

Edison lamps 158
Egyptian Revival 42, 155
Electric light 154, 158
Endiron see ANDIRON
Entablatures 12, 42-43, 60, 120
Exteriors 160-165
Fanlights 9, 22, 26, 34, 36, 38, 44, 46
Federal period 44, 63, 99
Fences 160, 162
Fenestrals 54, 55
Fielded (raised) panels 28, 31, 32
Firebacks 9
Fire baskets 118
Fire-dogs 114, 125
Fire grates 117-18, 128, 129, 131
Fireplace furniture 118, 130, 147
Fireplaces 10, 17, 21, 114-137, 150
Flaxman, John 121
Floor boards 66, 67, 68, 96
Floors 10, 66-73
carpets and rugs 67, 68
linoleum 68
stone flags 70, 71
Franklin stove 127
Friezes 10, 12, 76, 82, 83, 94, 97, 98, 99, 100, 104, 121

Gardens 22, 161
Gas fires 128
Gas light 154, 157
Gates 160, 162
Gibbons, Grinling 18, 120
Glass 10, 55, 56, 57
Colonial 38
etched 46, 49, 142
plate 60
stained 48, 49, 55, 57
Glazing bars 38, 54, 58, 59, 60, 61
Gothick style 21
Gothic Revival 23, 50
Great Exhibition (1851) 167
Great Fire of London 10
Greek Revival 19, 21, 23, 31, 35, 38, 44, 45, 64, 127, 142

Halls
entrance 10, 15, 38, 46, 73, 92, 107, 108, 113
lighting for 156, 158
Handrails 107, 108, 110, 112
Hearths 10, 146, 147, 151
Hedges 160, 162
Hinges 26, 27, 28, 29, 32, 34, 50, 51
Hoods 40-41, 162

Inglenook fireplaces 114, 146, 147, 150
Ironwork 22, 30, 107, 160-65

Jones, Inigo 9, 12, 13, 14, 18, 59, 98, 107, 116, 118

Kent, William 18, 79, 121
Kitchens 22, 66, 72, 117, 146-153

Landings 107, 112
Lanterns 156, 157, 158, 160
Larders 146, 147, 151
Lavatories 144, 145
Leighton House 24, 73, 113
Letterboxes 37, 51, 52
Lighting 154-159
Lincrusta wallpaper 85, 88, 104
Linenfold panelling 10, 26, 28, 32, 75, 76, 96
Linoleum 68
Locks 34, 50, 51, 52, 67

Mantelpieces 9, 31, 121
Marble 70
baths 138, 140
cleaning 71
mosaic floors 73
polishing 71
Marquetry 87
Middle rail see DADO RAIL
Minton 73
tiles 132
Mirrors 118, 128, 138
Morris, William 24, 61
Mouldings 10, 27, 28, 31, 32, 75, 85, 94, 147
drip 40
Mullions 23, 54, 55, 56

Nash, John 22
Newel posts 106, 107, 108, 110, 112, 163

Oil lamps 154, 155, 157
Orangeries 166, 167
"Oriel" windows 10, 59
Overmantels 82, 115, 120, 128, 130

Paints 84-5, 109
for doors 33, 34, 37, 42
for panelling 77, 78
stripping 40
Palladian style 14, 18, 19, 40, 59, 82, 83, 84, 98, 108, 161, 165, 167
Palladio, Andrea 12, 13
Panelling 17, 18, 24, 31, 38, 62, 66, 74, 75-9, 80, 83, 84, 94, 95, 107, 113
doors 26-34, 44
linenfold 10, 26, 28, 32, 75, 76, 96
on stairs 106, 107, 108, 110, 113
terracotta 161
wall 17, 74, 107
waxed pine 78, 79
Pantiles 96
Pantries 147
Parget work 74, 82, 161

Parquetage 67
Paxton, Joseph 167
Pediments 17, 19, 25, 31, 42, 43, 79, 83, 120, 160, 161
Piano nobile 14, 46, 60, 128
Picket fences 162
Picturesque movement 21, 22
Pilasters 12, 15, 17, 25, 42, 43, 46, 75, 76, 120, 121, 160, 161
Pine
doors 33
floor boards 67
kitchens 152, 153
panelling 78, 79, 107
stripped 84, 129, 132
tables 148
"Pineapples" (pine cones) 160, 162
Plasterwork 9, 10, 18, 74, 80, 82-3, 100
ceilings 97, 98, 106
exterior 160
Porches 22, 36, 40, 41, 48, 162, 164, 165
Porte-cochère 46
Pratt, Sir Roger 13, 14
Pugin, A. W. N. 23

Quarries 54, 55, 56, 57
Quarry tiles 70, 71, 72
Queen Anne style 18
Quoins 160

Radiators 137
Railings 15, 160, 162, 164, 165
Ranges, kitchen see COOKING RANGES
Roasting hearth 147
Roofs 161
hipped tile 25
mansard 22
Rot 66, 97
dry 68

Samborne, Linley 92
San Francisco 23
Sash windows 23, 58, 59, 60
Sculleries 147, 150
Shaving tables 142
Shaw, Richard Norman 24
Shutters 55, 59, 61, 62-3
Sill, panelling 95
Sinks, kitchen 146, 147
Skirting boards 17, 74, 94, 95
Skylights 110
Slate
cleaning 71
floors 70
roof 166
Spice cupboard 80, 117
Spun (Crown) glass 55, 56
Stairs/staircases 10, 15, 18, 92, 106-113, 165
lighting for 156
Statues 161

Stencilwork 85
on floors 68
on wallpapers 84
Steps (see also STAIRS) 160, 164, 165
marble 108
stone 46, 106, 110, 165
Still rooms 147
Stoves 126, 136
Stripping paint 40
Stucco 22, 42, 43, 74, 82, 161

Tabernacle frame 42
Taps 142, 143
Tiffany lamps 158
Tiles 24, 71, 72, 117, 134
bathroom 140
ceramic 70, 74
cleaning 71
Delft 91, 117, 132
early 19thC 129
"encaustic" 73
hand-painted 90
Minton 132
Trompe l'œil 91, 108

"Universal plan" 15
Urns 17, 161

Wainscoting 10, 75, 80, 84, 95, 138
Wall coverings 10, 74-81, 82, 83, 84, 92, 94
Wall lights 158
Wallpaper 74, 82, 84-5, 94, 104, 139, 141
Walls 74-95
Wash basins 138, 140, 142, 143, 144
Washstands 138, 142
Water closets (see also LAVATORIES) 143, 144
Wattle and daub 10
Weatherboarding 14
Webb, John 116
Webb, Philip 24
Wedgwood, Josiah 121
Window frames 46, 54, 58, 59, 160
Windows 13, 15, 18, 24, 54-65, 160, 164
accessories 64
bars 20
bay 59, 60
bow 59, 60
cleaning 56
dormer 15, 60
sash 23, 58
Woodcarving 18
Wood family 20
Woodworm 67, 68, 97
Wren Christopher 13
Wyatt, James 21